ROMAN
SPAIN

ROMAN SPAIN

S.J. Keay

University of California Press/British Museum

© 1988 Simon Keay

Published by the University of California Press
in the United States 1988

Library of Congress Cataloging-in-Publication Data

Keay, S. J.
Roman Spain.
(Exploring the Roman world; 2)
Bibliography: p.
Includes index.
1. Spain – History – Roman period, 218 B.C.–414 A.D.
2. Spain – Antiquities, Roman. 3. Romans – Spain.
4. Portugal – History – To 1385. 5. Portugal – Antiquities,
Roman. 6. Romans – Portugal. I. Title. II. Series.
DP94.K4 1988   936.6′03   87–35722
ISBN 0–520–06380–5

Designed by Harry Green

Set in Palatino by
Butler & Tanner Ltd
and printed in Great Britain by
Butler & Tanner Ltd
Frome and London

Half-title page Reverse of Iberian coin from the mint at Carmo
(modern Carmona).

Title page The Roman theatre at Saguntum
(modern Sagunto).

CONTENTS

INTRODUCTION

While I was writing this book a friend was astonished to learn of its contents and exclaimed, 'I didn't even know that the Romans reached Spain!' Others were aware that they had conquered Iberia at some stage and recalled memories of the magnificent Roman aqueduct at Segovia. Such ignorance is not surprising. The virtual absence of any comprehensive and up-to-date work on the archaeology of Roman Spain and Portugal has led to the omission of the Spanish provinces from many works on the Roman Empire.

This is a lamentable state of affairs. The Spanish provinces were amongst the very first to be acquired by Rome in her relentless expansion through the Mediterranean during the second and first centuries BC. As a result, they are a touchstone for our understanding of the development of other provinces like Gaul, Africa and Britain. Spain and Portugal have as fine a heritage of Roman buildings, mosaics and artistic treasures as any other western province. They also produced Trajan and Hadrian, two of Rome's greatest pagan emperors, as well as Theodosius I, the last great Christian emperor in the west. Moreover, many distinguished poets, dramatists, writers, generals, clerics and saints are ample witness to the cultural achievement of Roman Spain. To remain in ignorance of this, and much more, is surely to impoverish our common European cultural heritage.

Spanish, Portuguese and French scholars have been quick to realise this and enjoy a long tradition of important archaeological field-work stretching back to the turn of the century. However, the last ten years have witnessed a data explosion in Iberia. In 1982, for instance, some 133 Roman sites were being excavated in Spain alone, and in 1984 there were at least forty-eight major journals in Spain and fourteen in Portugal, many of which were reporting on new sites and finds of the Roman period. However, the absence of any sustained British interest in the archaeology of Roman Spain has meant that no English synthesis has appeared since the books by Bouchier (1914), Sutherland (1939), Wiseman (1956) and MacKendrick (1967). A few dedicated archaeologists and ancient historians, such as J. Richardson (1986), have shed light on aspects of the military, fiscal and economic life of the Spanish provinces. In addition, interest in the subject is growing in British universities.

Clearly, therefore, there is need of a reassessment of the archaeology of Roman Spain in English, and it is hoped that this book will go some way towards satisfying it. The complexity of the subject, however, and the absence of syntheses on many topics make the task difficult. Moreover, the breadth of the subject and the sheer volume of recent discoveries have enforced a subjective approach. Nine different themes in the development of Roman Spain and Portugal between 218 BC and AD 580 have been carefully chosen in an attempt to appeal both to the general reader and students of the archaeology of the Roman Empire. At this point it should be stressed that the rich evidence from the Balearic Islands has been excluded from the narrative, although in administrative terms they formed part of the Spanish provinces.

It would be impossible to acknowledge all the help and encouragement that I have received in the daunting task of writing this book; but I must mention my many friends and colleagues at Barcelona, Gerona, Empúries and Tarragona who for many years have come to tolerate my persistent curiosity about the Roman archaeology of Spain. Particularly, I should like to thank Sr Don Francesc Tarrats, Director of the Museu Arqueologic Nacional de Tarragona; Sr Don Xavier Dupré of the Taller-Escola d'Arqueolgia del Ajuntament de Tarragona; Prof. Dr José Remesal of the Departamento de Historia Antigua of the Universidad Complutense de Madrid for the loan of photographs and plans; and Stefanie Martin-Kilcher of the Kaiseraugst Museum in Switzerland for providing me with copy of a *titulus pictus* from Augst. In England I owe thanks to Drs David Peacock Tom Blagg, Tony King, Martin Millett, Richard Reece, Margaret Roxan, Roger Wilson and Professor Michael Crawford for commenting upon earlier drafts of individual chapters. My debt is even greater to Dr Tim Potter, who patiently read and corrected various drafts of all the chapters. However, I claim all responsibility for the views expressed in the book. I should also like to thank Chris Unwin for doing the line drawings and maps, the staff at British Museum Publications, especially Deborah Wakeling and Celia Clear for all their co-operation and persistence. Above all, my greatest debt is to my wife Nina, to whom this book is dedicated.

SIMON KEAY
University of Southampton, January 1988

SPAIN
BEFORE
THE ROMANS

Anyone who visits Spain or Portugal and explores the National Archaeological Museums at Madrid and Lisbon will not be disappointed. The sheer range and brilliance of the cultures and civilisations of ancient Iberia are reflected in a dazzling display of jewellery, sculpture and metalwork. They can also be experienced at first hand at such well-preserved sites as the Greek town of Emporion, near Gerona, the Roman town of Italica, near Seville, or the great medieval castle at Gormaz, near Soria. These, and many others, are eloquent testimony to a long historical process, which has seen Phoenicians, Celts, Greeks, Carthaginians, Romans, Goths, Arabs and Franks jostling with the native peoples for control of the peninsula.

There is little doubt that the Roman episode, which forms the subject of this book, is one of the most exciting and important in the development of Spain and Portugal. Nearly 700 years of continuous Roman involvement have left their mark on many aspects of contemporary life. However, before we can even start to appreciate Rome's impact on Iberia we must be aware of the range of highly sophisticated peoples living in the peninsula on the eve of the Roman conquest; for the emergent Hispano-Roman civilisation was a unique blend of these and culture imposed from authority centred at Rome.

Iberia is the largest peninsula (580,160 square kilometres) in Europe and comprises many geographically distinct areas; it also occupies a unique position separating the Atlantic from the Mediterranean and Europe from Africa. This explains why Iberia has always been a country of passage, contact and confrontation between invaders and native peoples. However, the peninsula has prominent regional characteristics which help us to understand the archaeology of prehistoric and Roman Iberia. There are six

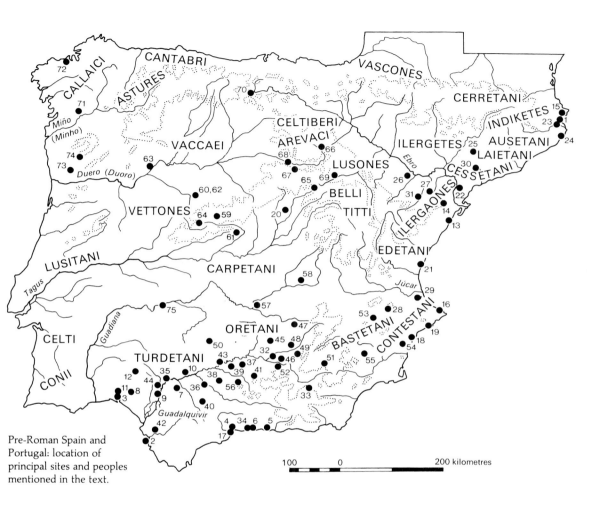

Pre-Roman Spain and
Portugal: location of
principal sites and peoples
mentioned in the text.

100   0   200 kilometres

1 Emporion	* 24 Castell de la Fosca	* 47 Torre de Juan Abad	69 Arcobriga
2 Gadir	* 25 Moli de l'Espigol	* 48 Santistebán del Puerto	* 70 Monte Bernorio
3 Onoba	* 26 Cabezo de Alcalá (Azaila)	* 49 Mogón	* 71 Cameixa
4 Malaka	* 27 Sant Antoniode Calaceite	* 50 Los Almadenes de	* 72 Elvinia
5 Sexi	* 28 La Bastida Mogente	Pozoblanco	* 73 Sabroso
* 6 Toscanos	* 29 Cova de les Meravelles	* 51 Galera	* 74 Citania de Britieros
7 Carmo	* 30 L'Espluga de Francolí	* 52 Tugia	* 75 Medellín
8 Niebla	* 31 El Palao	* 53 Cerro de los Santos	
9 El Carámbolo	32 Castulo	54 Illici	*modern name
10 Setefilla	33 Basti	* 55 El Cigarrelejo	
* 11 Cabezo de la Joya	* 34 Cerro del Mar	* 56 Baena	
12 Cerro Salamón	35 Ilipa	* 57 Alarcos	
* 13 Puig de Benicarló	36 Astigi	* 58 Pedro Muñóz	
* 14 Coll de Moro	37 Obulco	* 59 Las Cogotas de Cardeños	
15 Rhode	38 Munda	* 60 Osera	
16 Hemeroskopeion	39 Ategua	* 61 Guisando	
17 Mainake	40 Urso	* 62 Mesa de Miranda	
18 Akra Leuke	41 Tucci	* 63 Picote	
19 Alonis	42 Hasta Regia	* 64 Ulaca	
* 20 Yeles	* 43 Colina de los Quemados	65 Segeda	
21 Saguntum	* 44 Pajar del Artillo	66 Numantia	
* 22 Castellet de Banyoles	* 45 Despeñaperros	67 Termes	
* 23 Puig de Sant Andreu	* 46 Cortijo del Ahorcado	68 Uxama	

main geographical regions — the Mediterranean coast, the Ebro valley, Andalusia, the north and south *meseta*, the Atlantic coast, and the north-west.

The Mediterranean coastline, alternately rugged and gentle, is Spain's 'window' on the Mediterranean. It is dissected by great winding rivers like the Llobregat, the Júcar, the Guadalhorce and, especially, the Ebro, and is shut off from the rest of the country to the west by great hills and mountain systems which rarely rise above 1,500 metres. However, in the north-east, where the uplands blend into the Pyrenees, and in the south-east, some mountains soar over 3,500 metres above sea-level. The landscape harbours a patchwork of well-irrigated areas suitable for a wide range of crops. The climate is typically Mediterranean, with long hot summers and wet winters, although the Catalan provinces (Barcelona, Gerona, Tarragona) are marginally greener than the arid southern provinces of Alicante, Almería and Málaga. Wine is the most famous produce, while citrus and other fruits and legumes are the pride of small farms and co-operatives in the provinces of Valencia, Alicante and Murcia. The other major natural resource is, of course, the abundant marine life.

Turning away from the Mediterranean and leaving the coastal strip, the visitor will be aware of a rapid change in the landscape and climate. Nowhere is this more apparent than in the winding course of the river Ebro from the flat alluvial delta to the south of Tortosa into the harsh table-lands of the Ebro valley. This is one of the great river systems of Europe, running from its source in the Cantabrian mountains 355 kilometres to the coast. It is therefore the main route of communication between the Mediterranean and north-western Spain, while its tributaries — especially the river Jalón — provide rapid access to central Spain and the foothills of the Pyrenees. Towns like Lleida, Zaragoza and Alfaro sit in the midst of glaring, arid plains divided into plateaux and dissected by ravines. In summer the climate is much drier and hotter than that on the Mediterranean coast and in winter much colder. Nevertheless, the lower part of the Ebro does support all the classic Mediterranean staples.

To the south the visitor crossing the Sierra Nevada mountains from the coast into south-eastern Spain finds himself in the peninsula's prime agricultural area — the Guadalquivir valley — which roughly corresponds to northern Andalusia. Dominated by the river Guadalquivir, it is closed off to the north by the Sierra Morena mountains. The river rises in the Sierra de Cazorla, near modern Linares, and flows for over 320 kilometres down into the undulating plains of the lower Guadalquivir valley and the Atlantic ocean north of Cádiz. This is the major route of communication between the Atlantic and the innermost recesses of south-eastern, south-western and central Spain and has been one of the area's main attractions since remotest antiquity. Another is its very fertile soils, well suited to the large-scale production of wheat and other cereals in the plains. More significant, however, are the olive trees which crowd the river terraces in kilometre after kilometre of neatly planted rows. Horse-breeding and the raising of cattle, sheep, pigs and goats are also important, with major transhumance routes criss-crossing the valley. The third great attraction of the area is its very rich sources of iron, lead, copper and silver in the Sierra Morena mountains, and in the hilly uplands of the Río Tinto.

These three different zones – the Mediterranean coastline and the Ebro and Guadalquivir valleys – embrace another distinct area, the *meseta*. This is a vast table-land dominating central Spain. Its northern edge is defined by the Cantabrian mountains and the Ebro valley, while the coastal mountains and the Sierra Morena contain its east and south sides. The northern *meseta* is a sweeping plain (225 by 177 kilometres) 760 metres above sea-level and is typified by undulating arid plains divided into steep-sided plateaux. This topography and the harsh dry climate are well suited to wheat production, making the area one of the greatest sources in the peninsula, although sheep and other livestock are also important. The southern edge of the northern *meseta* is bordered by the snow-capped Guadarramas, which tower some 2,500 metres over the surrounding plains and are easily visible from Madrid. The southern *meseta* (480 by 240 kilometres) varies from hills and sharp escarpments in the north-east to rolling plains in the south-west. It is well suited to the cultivation of wheat and other cereals, while vineyards are predominant in the uplands of Ciudad Real province. To the west the quality of the sheep, pigs and goats bred in the province of Badajoz has achieved a special renown.

The *meseta* is drained by three great rivers – the Duero (Portuguese Douro), Tagus (Tajo) and Guadiana – which flow into the Atlantic and provide important routes of entry into central Spain. The mouths of these rivers and the adjacent coastline form another geographical region – the Atlantic coast. This face of Iberia is a narrow coastal strip which runs for 442 kilometres from the river Minho (Spanish Miño) in northern Portugal down to the flatlands of the Tagus estuary. Here the climate is much gentler and supports a wide range of crops. Vines are common on the hillsides of the upper Douro (behind Porto) and in the Tagus estuary. Olives and wheat are other important products, while precious metals are found occasionally in central Portugal. Like the Mediterranean, the seas off the south-west coast offer a very rich assortment of marine life.

The Atlantic coast blends imperceptibly into the other major region of Iberia – the rocky nub of Galicia and the majestic Cantabrian coastline. Galicia is a large rolling plateau (160 by 320 kilometres), some 455 metres above sea-level, broken up by such picturesque rivers as the Miño and the Tambre. The coast has been carved into a myriad of spectacular rocky bays and inlets. This broken landscape precludes many crops and lends itself instead to the raising of sheep, cattle and other livestock. At the same time the coastal waters are extremely rich in marine life which is prey to the large fishing fleets based at La Coruña and Vigo. The other main natural resource is gold, which is found in great quantity both in rivers like the

Tormos and Genil and in rich veins in the hills. The Cantabrian mountains to the east are another great source of gold, as well as iron ore. These huge peaks soar up almost 2,500 metres, running the length of the northern Spanish coast and shutting off the Cantabrian coast from the rest of Spain. The coast itself is quite narrow (approximately 25 kilometres wide) and rugged, with few natural harbours.

By the eve of the Roman conquest in 218 BC this rich and varied country had given rise to a mosaic of peoples with contrasting origins and cultural traditions. Recent archaeological research has begun to trace their development from the isolated family groupings of the Lower Palaeolithic 300,000 years ago, through to the more complex communities of the Argaric culture of south-eastern Spain (c. 1500 BC) and the later Bronze Age settlements of north-eastern Spain and the Ebro valley. In every case the early peoples of Iberia impress the archaeologist with the scope and originality of their artefacts.[1]

In the first half of the first millennium BC the communities of south and eastern Spain were confronted by alien peoples, the Phoenicians and the Greeks. Literary sources tell us that Gadir (modern Cádiz) was the earliest Phoenician settlement in Iberia and claim that it was founded by colonists from Tyre in modern Lebanon, around 1100 BC. Archaeology, however, is beginning to show that the settlement was established in the eighth century BC and lies in the vicinity of the modern cathedral.[2] It was followed by a chain of later offshore trading communities, like Onoba (modern Huelva) at the mouth of the Río Tinto, Malaca (modern Málaga), Sexi (modern Almuñécar) and Toscanos, founded by colonists from the Phoenician homeland, or from their near-by colony at Carthage, in modern Tunisia.[3] They were attracted by the great agricultural and mineral wealth of southern Spain, and their settlements rapidly developed into major centres of Phoenician-Carthaginian culture, presided over by such fearsome deities as Melkaart, Baal-Hammon and Tanit. One of the most important achievements was to introduce the technology of iron-working to south-eastern Spain.

The Phoenicians' trading partners were the legendary kings of Tartessos (Biblical Tarshish), whose heartland seems to have covered the lower Guadalquivir and Guadiana rivers, although their wider influence, however, probably extended as far north as the upper Guadiana (province of Badajoz) and the Júcar (province of Albacete).[4] Major fortified settlements uncovered at Carmo (modern Carmona), Niebla (Huelva) and El Carámbolo (Seville)[5] were regularly planned, dignified with imposing stone buildings and were no doubt inhabited by a mixed population of Turdetanians, Phoenician merchants and Celts. Society was sharply stratified, with its wealthiest members distinguished by fine clothes and exquisite gold jewellery. One of the finest collections of jewellery was discovered at El Carámbolo in 1958 and is now on display in the Museo Arqueológico Provincial de Sevilla. Similarly, wealthy graves are prominent at cemeteries like Setefilla

(Seville), and are evident from the great stone mausolea, like that at Cabezo de la Joya (Huelva). Their owners' lives were ruled over by a great goddess of the underworld, a sanctuary to whom has been discovered at Concho Romo de Zalamea de la Serena (Badajoz).[6]

Tartessos' wealth lay in its monopoly of the very rich sources of copper, lead and silver in the Sierra Morena and the hilly uplands of the Río Tinto. Indeed, a mining settlement of the eighth to sixth centuries BC has been discovered at the Cerro Salomón in the Río Tinto (Huelva).[7] The rich soils of the Guadalquivir valley were another major resource. Successive kings, like Arganthonios,[8] took advantage of all this, exchanging metals and foodstuffs with the Phoenicians and receiving in return a splendid array of Phoenician goods. These included fine red-slipped ceramic plates, alabaster jars, carved ivory, bronze cauldrons and brooches. A complex series of exchange networks dominated by Tartessos ensured that many of these prestigious imports filtered into important sites throughout Iberia. They followed the course of the Guadalquivir and Segura rivers to south-eastern Spain, trickled northwards across the Guadiana, Tagus and Duero to north-central Spain, and by sea to the Atlantic coast of Portugal. Tin, for the making of bronze, was one of the goods exchanged in return. This traffic had peaked by the seventh century BC, exercising a profound influence upon developing communities in western Iberia, while Phoenician influence upon Tartessos gave rise to a new degree of originality in her own culture.[9] This so-called 'orientalising' influence is visible in her jewellery and sculpture.

The temple of Asklepios at the Greek colony of Emporion (modern Empúries).

Tartessos also had a wider commercial role, acting as middleman in exchanges between the distant communities of Ireland, western France and Sardinia.[10]

The native communities of coastal Spain between the Pyrenees and the modern province of Alicante had been largely unaffected by these developments, although a few sites like Puig de Benicarló (Castellón) and Coll de Moro (Tarragona) did import some luxury goods from the Carthaginian colony of Ebusus (modern Ibiza).[11] After the mid-sixth century Greek colonists from the Ionian port of Phocaea (modern Foca), on the west coast of Turkey, founded colonies at Rhode (modern Roses), Emporion (modern Empúries), Hemeroskopeion (modern Denia) and Mainake (near Málaga), using the primary colony of Massalia (modern Marseilles) as their base.[12] They introduced iron technology to the peoples of north-east and eastern Spain. The colonists exchanged a rich array of luxury goods culled from sources throughout the Mediterranean, for agricultural produce and, to a lesser extent, iron ore from local communities. In this way fine grey pottery from the Ionian coast, Phoenician amphorae, Etruscan ceramics and, of course, fine pottery from mainland Greece made its way to a few of the larger local settlements.[13] These items were highly prized and are symptomatic of the important cultural influence of the Greeks on the peoples of the east coast.

Towards the middle of the sixth century BC south and eastern Spain experienced profound cultural change. In 535 BC the combined fleets of the Etruscans and Carthaginians defeated the Phocaeans at the battle of Alalia, off the coast of Corsica, definitively breaking their power in the western Mediterranean. An early casualty of this was the destruction of Mainake as a commercial centre. However, Greek commercial interests in the western Mediterranean were soon resumed. New colonies were founded at Akra Leuke (modern La Albufereta) and Alonis (modern Benidorm). Emporion and Hemeroskopeion were the main commercial centres during the fifth and fourth centuries BC.[14] The former funnelled exotic ceramics, amphorae and other goods into native sites along the Catalan coast and up the Ebro valley about as far as modern Zaragoza. The southern colonies exported similar goods to a large number of native sites in the modern provinces of Albacete and Cuenca – in the eastern *meseta* – occasionally reaching as far west as Yeles (Toledo).[15] Despite a clash of commercial interests with the Carthaginians, their goods also reached native communities in south-eastern Spain.

In this way the Greeks profited from the agricultural resources of the Catalan coast, the Ebro valley and La Mancha, as well as metal resources – like the iron in Jaén province. Moreover, their presence had a profound effect on the native Iberian communities with whom they traded. Greek influence spread extensively and is evident in many aspects of their culture.

A number of ancient writers (Strabo, Avienus and others) describe how

The foundations of houses and workshops at the Iberian hillfort of Sant Antoni de Calaceite.

the major Iberian peoples were dispersed on the eve of the Roman conquest in the late third century BC. The Contestani lived between the Segura and Júcar rivers (the modern province of Alicante); the Ilercaones occupied the hilly hinterland between modern Sagunto and the lower Ebro valley near Gandesa (Tarragona); to the east lay the Edetani, in the uplands of Castellón and Teruel provinces; while further north the great tribal confederation of the Ilergetes and the Sedetani respectively occupied the modern provinces of Lleida and Zaragoza. The more temperate lands to the north of the Ebro were inhabited by the Cessetani (the province of Tarragona), Laietani (the coastal area of Barcelona province), Ausetani (in the vicinity of the Vic plateau), the Indiketes (province of Gerona), the Bergistani and Cerretani (foothills of the Pyrenees), the Sordones (the French Catalan province of Roussillon) and the Elisyces (the French Catalan province of Languedoc); towards the interior the Lacetani lived in the mountainous hinterland of Catalonia near Berga and Solsona.[16]

Prior to the second century BC the control of local communities may well have been in the hands of oligarchies living in semi-urban settlements. They master-minded local alliances with whichever power intruded into the confines of their narrow worlds. Saguntum (modern Sagunto), one of the largest Iberian settlements, seems to have been run along similar lines to a Greek town, having its own executive ruling body composed of wealthy aristocrats.[17] The communities of the Catalan coastal peoples may have been organised in the same way. By contrast peoples like the Ilergetes and the Ausetani were led by military leaders such as Amusicus and Mandonius, whose sympathies lay in temporary alliances with neighbouring tribes – or invaders – for short-term objectives. Nevertheless, there are strong Greek-inspired similarities between all these Iberian peoples. This is most readily appreciated in their settlement sites, which lie mainly in spectacular and easily defensible positions on high ground and are surrounded by walls and bastions which are clearly influenced by Greek military architecture. At Saguntum, traces of a monumental defensive wall can still be seen on the craggy eastern side of the plateau which dominates the coastal plains to the north of Valencia.[18] Further north the settlement of Castellet de Banyoles (Tivissa, Tarragona) covers 40,000 square metres at the end of a long plateau overlooking the Ebro valley.[19] The visitor can still appreciate the foundations of the great diamond-shaped bastions flanking its narrow entrance. They were built from large stone blocks while the towers themselves were composed of sun-baked brick. The most spectacular example, however, is without doubt the great *oppidum* at Puig de Sant Andreu (Ullastret), a few kilometres to the south-west of Emporion. Here the great stone walls on the west side of the site still run for 460 metres, clinging to the sinuous contours of the hillside.[20] At least one square and six round bastions survive, together with a well-recessed gateway.

In fact many years of excavation here have given us a clear impression of how the interior of an Iberian settlement was laid out. Upon entering the west gate one follows a broad street winding up to the summit of the hill and reaches the small citadel (acropolis). A small Greek-style temple has been discovered here and enjoys commanding views over the surrounding countryside. Elsewhere the street has been intersected by paths and alleys which lead to many small rectangular houses of stone and mudbrick. These jostle for space within the crowded settlement and follow a regular plan, with huge cisterns for their water supplies and cavities for the storage of grain and other perishable foods. Although the houses were simple inside, with little trace of any embellishment, this site is so large, sophisticated and rich in imported Greek and Carthaginian luxuries that many scholars have suggested that it may actually have been a Greek town – possibly the much-sought town of Cypsela. However, it is only fair to point out that a similar layout has been discovered at many other Iberian sites, even though these are often on a smaller scale: Castell de la Fosca (modern Palamós), Moli de l'Espigol (modern Tornabous), Cabezo de Alcalá (modern Azaila), San Antonio de Calaceite (Teruel) and La Bastida Mogente (Valencia), to mention but a few examples.[21] Another characteristic of Iberian sites is that apart from the occasional temple and open space (agora) for commercial transactions, large public buildings are absent.

The larger hillforts were important centres of craft specialisation. Terracotta loom-weights and iron-slag are frequently found in excavations, pointing to weaving and the manufacture of iron tools and weapons. It is not yet clear, however, whether these were exclusively for the use of the inhabitants of individual hillforts, or whether they were traded with their neighbours. There seems little doubt, though, that the fine plain wheel-turned ceramics produced near the larger settlements were exchanged

Stone foundations of mudbrick towers flanking the entrance to the Iberian hillfort of Castellet de Banyoles (Tivisa).

extensively with neighbouring hillforts and peoples. Indeed, some fragments have been found as far afield as southern France (Provence).[22] Little stone sculpture or decorative metalwork was produced by the Iberians living to the north of the river Júcar. One exception, however, was the magnificent hoard of gold-plated silver bowls and jugs discovered at the Castellet de Banyoles.[23]

Little is known about Iberian religion, as Classical writers are largely silent and the few texts to have survived are uninformative. Caves, like the Cova de les Meravelles (Valencia) and that at the Font de l'Espluga de Francolí (Tarragona), acted as small, personal sanctuaries to gods of the winds, trees and streams. At most sites there is little to suggest that any formal provision was made for communal worship. We know virtually nothing about the gods themselves, and our principal sources of evidence are the jugs, plates, kalathoi, pithoi and oenochoi, from sites along the coast, which were adorned with delightful human figures, birds and flowers in brown and ochre paint.[24] Some of the female figures have been interpreted as the Phoenician fertility goddess Astarte, while group scenes are often seen to symbolise ritual ceremonies. How far Phoenician or Greek deities really penetrated amongst the Iberians is still open to dispute.[25] We do know, however, that animal-inspired cults were quite important. A small sanctuary to a bull was discovered at the hillfort of Cabezo de Alcalá, and a stylised stone bull has been recovered from Saguntum. Similarly, two stone horses were discovered at the hillfort of El Palao (Alcañiz, Teruel).[26]

By the later third century BC, therefore, a mixture of native tradition and Greek influence gave rise to a sophisticated semi-urban Iberian society. A similar development took place amongst contemporary communities in south and south-eastern Spain. Towards the end of the sixth century BC there seems to have been a collapse of the social and economic basis of many sites in the Tartessos area, marked by the abandonment of such important settlements as El Carámbolo and Cabezo de Esperanza and the deliberate destruction of religious sanctuaries. The cause of this is not known, although some scholars have suggested that it was indirectly due to the pressure of Celtic population movements in northern Spain and Portugal, or an attack upon the capital of Tartessos by Carthage. The effect of the collapse was the disintegration of Tartessos' cultural area into a number of small warring kingdoms. Technically, these peoples were Iberians and related to the peoples of the east coast of Spain, but at the same time they differed by sharing the common cultural heritage of Tartessos and centuries of Phoenician and Carthaginian influence.[27]

Turdetania was the most important of these regional groups to emerge and encompassed the whole of the Guadalquivir valley. The Greek geographer Strabo, writing in the first century AD, remarked that the 'Turdetanians are ranked as the wisest of the Iberians; and they make use of an alphabet, and possess records of their ancient history, poems and laws written in verse that are 6,000 years old'.[28] To the north of Turdetania were the Oretani, who dominated the mineral-rich lands of Jaén and had a major settlement at Castulo (Cazlona). The Bastetani lay to the east, with an important centre at Basti (modern Baza), while the Mastieni lived along the south-eastern coast of Spain. There were also Iberian Celts, known as 'Celti', in southern Portugal (Alemtejo). After a period of cultural stagnation which lasted until the middle of the fifth century BC, Carthaginian and Greek influences combined with local traditions to produce a brilliant regional culture that survived until the Roman conquest and formed the cultural basis of the Roman province of Baetica.

The intensification of Carthaginian influence in southern Spain occurred at the expense of the Phoenicians, whose loose, individualistic enterprise in the western Mediterranean collapsed towards the middle of the fifth century BC. Carthage then undertook a much more aggressive and methodical exploitation of southern Spain's agricultural and mineral resources. She used the Phoenician colonies to promote her own interests throughout the western Mediterranean. Recently excavated sites like Villaricos (Almería)[29] have shown that these colonies were importing a broad range of Carthaginian pottery, Greek pottery and foodstuffs in amphorae, to be exchanged for metals and agricultural products from Oretania and Bastetania.

The social structure of these southern Spanish peoples was different from those of the Iberian communities on the east coast. Turdetania, for example, was essentially a loose federation that included the Cilibiceni, Kelkiani, Etemaei, Olbisii and Igleti, held together by such leaders as Luxinius and Corribilus. Culchas, about whom rather more is known, ruled over twenty-eight towns at the time of the Roman conquest in the late third century BC. There is every reason to believe that the 200 towns in Turdetania mentioned by Strabo resembled small city-states with their own agricultural hinterlands.[30] During the conquest Roman military commanders recognised these Turdetanian kings, signing treaties with them in an attempt to sever their allegiance to the Carthaginians, and then playing them off against one another to Rome's advantage. The Romans also came to use many Turdetanian settlements as the basis of their own urban network.

Ilipa (modern Alcalá del Río), Astigi (modern Écija), Obulco (modern Porcuna), Urso (modern Osuna), Tucci (modern Martos) and Asta (Mesa de Asta) are but a few of the many which became major Roman towns. Indeed, excavations at the Colina de los Quemados (Córdoba) and the Pajar del Artillo (modern Santiponce) have uncovered traces of the Turdetanian predecessors of Roman Corduba and Italica.[31] Sadly, however, excavation has yet to provide us with a plan as complete as any of those from the Iberian hillforts along the east coast. Very often the settlements crowned the summit of rocky plateaux, like the great *oppidum* of Urso.[32] The same is true of the Oretanian settlement at Despeñaperros. The layout of streets and private houses was probably similar to that of Iberian *oppida*, like Puig de Sant Andreu. However, settlements in southern Spain seem to have differed in having public buildings. A beautiful carved stone capital from Cástulo adorned an imposing building as early as the fourth century BC and clearly reflects the influence of the Greek Corinthian style. By contrast a capital discovered at Cortijo del Ahorcado (Baeza, Jaén) is carved in a style which embodies native and Carthaginian influence.[33]

The mainstay of these kingdoms was still the mineral and agricultural wealth that had been so extensively exploited by Tartessos. Production of both was monopolised by an aristocracy, who lavished much of their opulence upon very fine-quality gold and silver jewellery and monumental tombs for themselves. Important treasures have been discovered at the Torre de Juan Abad (Ciudad Real), Santistebán del Puerto (Jaén), Mogón (Jaén) and Los Almadenes de Pozoblanco (Córdoba), often containing exquisite silver torques, bracelets and brooches.[34] Spectacular private mausolea, in the form of conical *tumuli*, have been found near settlements like Castulo and Galera and reveal elaborate arrangements for the ashes of the deceased, including a central square chamber, painted walls and gravegoods. Even more elaborate are the chambered tombs (hypogea) discovered at sites like Basti (modern Baza), El Almedinilla and Tugia (modern Toya, Jaén). They were built from freshly cut stone blocks by architects who often worked from Etruscan prototypes. The grave-goods from one hypogeum at Tugia included an impressive array of stone sculpture, painted boxes, personal gold jewellery, weapons and the remains of a chariot.

The religious beliefs of the Turdetanians, Bastetanians and others focused upon large open-air communal sanctuaries on hilltops, where individuals deposited votive offerings to placate divine forces. These were often small bronze statuettes of armed warriors and priestesses. A flourishing centre for the manufacture of these bronzes grew up by the side of the great settlement and sanctuary of Despeñaperros, in the region of Oretania.

Elsewhere votive offerings were made in the form of near life-size statues of seated and standing women, like the famous example of a priestess offering a cup ('Gran dama ofreciente'), which adorned the great sanctuary at Cerro de los Santos (Albacete), in the fourth century BC, and the famous 'Lady of Elche' (Dama de Elche), from Illici. Both women wear elaborate head-dresses and extremely rich jewellery. The artists who carved these were clearly influenced by the coastal Greek and Carthaginian colonies, and some scholars have identified them with the Carthaginian goddess Tanit or the Greek goddess Athena. Similarly, the painters of fine pottery in south-eastern Spain, especially at Illici, produced vessels decorated with motifs resembling those of the Iberians on the east coast. Even though native communities may have adapted some of the symbols and iconography of these foreign deities, there is nothing to suggest that they actually assimilated the divinities themselves. The life-size sculptures of fantastic bulls, horses, lions and stags from sanctuaries at Obulco, Baena (Córdoba) and El

The 'Dama de Elche', an important example of Iberian sculpture of the late 5th century BC.

Cigarrelejo (Murcia), as guardians of the underworlds, point to the existence of animal-based cults.[35]

These sanctuaries, wealthy cemeteries and large settlements are the hallmarks of the notable cultural achievement of south and south-eastern Iberia during the fifth, fourth and third centuries BC. This was the sophisticated and affluent society that was to attract Carthage's cupidity and confront the Romans in the later third century BC. It was an exciting fusion between strong native tradition and east Mediterranean originality, differing from that which had taken place in the Iberian communities on the eastern coast. In turn the Oretanian, Bastetanian and Turdetanian peoples prevailed upon the communities of the south and eastern *meseta*, transmitting aspects of Mediterranean culture to major settlements like Alarcos (Valdepeñas) and Pedro Muñoz (La Mancha). For a large part of southern and eastern Spain the Mediterranean was therefore the main cultural stimulus during the pre-Roman Iron Age.

This was not the case with the peoples of north-western and western Iberia; they were heirs to very different traditions from the Celtic world to the north. As early as 1000 BC people characterised by a distinctive form of bronze-working had migrated from south-western France into northern Spain. They exploited the tin resources of the area, using it for their own bronze-work and trading it with Tartessos.[36] By about 700 BC this 'Atlantic Bronze Age' culture had established itself throughout Portugal north of the Tagus, the northern *meseta* and the Spanish north-west. It was followed by an important period of change during the sixth and fifth centuries BC. Archaeologists have suggested that northern Spain was invaded by Celtic peoples from south-eastern France and the Danube basin, bringing the technology of iron with them. During this 'First Iron Age' Celtic iron-using communities settled throughout Spain to the north of the Tagus.[37]

The 'Second Iron Age' followed between the fifth and late fourth centuries BC and was marked by the more widespread use of iron for weapons and the wheel for making pottery. This did not, however, completely displace earlier traditions of bronze-working and pottery manufacture. Archaeologists are now starting to identify different cultural areas in the north-west and northern *meseta*. Communities in what are now the provinces of León and Zamora, for instance, lived in round houses within small, unfortified settlements and had an economy split between exploiting the local metal resources and raising cattle. One of the most distinctive of all these regional cultures, however, developed in the provinces of Ávila and Salamanca, in the foothills of the central Sierra. It is named the Las Cogotas II culture, after the settlement of Las Cogotas de Cardeñosa (Ávila).[38] This was walled, with rectangular houses built around the inside of the defensive wall and opening on to planned streets. The use of iron was widespread, and metalworking techniques were sufficiently sophisticated to enable native craftsmen to produce fine-quality swords, daggers and brooches, inlaid with silver and copper, that were buried with important warriors at cemeteries like Oserá (Chamartín de la Sierra, Ávila) and Las Cogotas itself. Funerary sites were sometimes marked by life-size stone bulls and pigs found outside settlements such as Las Cogotas and Mesa de Miranda (Ávila), and as far west as Picote (Tras os Montes) in northern Portugal. Although they are not as fine as their fantastic counterparts in south-eastern Spain, they indicate the high status accorded to the dead. There were also bleak, open-air sanctuaries like that at the centre of the settlement at Ulaca (modern Solosancho, Ávila). Here rock-cut steps led up to a platform where human and animal sacrifices were offered up to nameless gods and powers.

The Romans first came into contact with the peoples of central and northern Spain during the second century BC. By this time curiosity about the fierce tribes continually confronting the Roman legions was strong enough for contemporary observers like Polybius to record important observations about them. These were compiled by later writers like Strabo and are an invaluable supplement to the archaeological evidence. It seems that by the third century BC the land between the Tagus and Douro – in what is now central Portugal – was occupied by the Lusitani. North-western Spain between the Douro and the Cantabrian sea was the territory of the Callaici (modern provinces of Braga, Orense, Coruña, Pontevedra), the Astures (provinces of León and Zamora) and the Cantabri (provinces of Palencia and Santander); to the south were the Vettones (provinces of Salamanca, northern Cáceres and Ávila), Vaccaei (province of Palencia) and the Carpetani. In addition there was an assortment of lesser peoples to the north of the Ebro (Autrigones, Caristii, Varduli and Vascones) and in the northern *meseta* (Lusones, Titti, Belli, Berones and Turmodigi).[39]

The most famous of all these peoples, however, were the Celtiberi, a people who comprised a number of tribes (such as the Arevaci), and who probably lived in the region of the modern provinces of Zaragoza, Guadalajara and Soria. Their notoriety in the Classical sources derives from their prolonged and bitter resistance to Rome during the second half of the second century BC rather than from any clearly defined cultural difference. In fact Celtiberia, as its name suggests, was a zone of growing cultural contact between the Iberian peoples to the east and the people of Celtic ancestry to the west.[40] The Celtiberi were clearly an enterprising people, borrowing certain hallmarks of the Iberian peoples and adapting them to their indigenous Celtic background. Thus Segeda (Belmonte de Perejil, Calatayud) and the Arevacian sites of Numantia (modern Garray, Soria) and Termes (modern Tiermes, Soria) echo earlier Iberian sites along the Ebro valley, such as San Antonio de Calaceite (Teruel). The settlements are large and in times of war acted as places of refuge for the surrounding population or smaller unfortified settlements. Similarly, the so-called Celtiberian pottery from sites like Numantia, Uxama (modern Osma, Soria) and Arcobriga (Monreal de Ariza, Zaragoza) recalls Iberian painted wares of the lower Ebro and the east coast.

Celtiberian metalwork was also distinctive, the most famous examples being the short swords which were to be adapted by the Roman army as the 'Hispanic sword' (*gladius hispanicus*). Between the later fourth and first centuries BC, this 'Celtiberisation' gradually spread through the peoples of the northern *meseta*. However, with the inexorable advance of the Roman conquest across central Spain and Portugal it was inevitably the fortification of settlements which most clearly reflected techniques and planning from further east. Some hilltop settlements, like Monte Bernorio (Palencia) in Vaccaeian territory, were surrounded with single or double rings of walls. Further to the west, in the territories of the Lusitani and Vettones where settlements like the Mesas de Miranda (Chamartín de la Sierra, Ávila) and Castillejos en Sanchorrega (Ávila) were already defended, the fortifications were extended to enclose large annexes.[41]

In social terms the peoples of the northern *meseta* and north-west were organised into different clans (*gentilitates*). These worked on a co-operative basis, so that in cultivating the land all members of the clan shared in the collective labour and its results. It follows that there was no system of monarchy, as in southern Spain. Indeed, in peaceful times the regulation of affairs in any one clan reposed in the hands of a group of elders who were answerable to the clan as a whole. However, there was a warrior aristocracy and in times of war leadership of the clan was conferred upon selected members. Clans of major peoples, like the Vaccaei, Arevaci, Pelendones, Astures, Cantabri and Vettones, would then combine into larger military groupings. This kind of solidarity, and the ease with which confederations could be built up, goes some way towards explaining why it took the Romans nearly 200 years to subdue the peoples of northern Spain. Unlike the centralised peoples of south and eastern Spain, centres of rebellion could never be isolated and most Roman commanders were too inexperienced to mount a comprehensive counter-strategy.

The peoples of northern Portugal and north-western Spain (modern Galicia), were of Celtic extraction and therefore shared a common cultural background with the peoples of the northern *meseta*. However, the very rugged country and the close proximity of the Callaici, Astures and Cantabri, as well as the Albiones, Lungones and Vadinienses meant that there were insufficient agricultural resources to support a stable society. As early as the fifth and fourth centuries BC continual warfare had given rise to a society characterised by a myriad of fortified settlements clinging to rocky hilltops and plateaux. Like their neighbours in the northern *meseta*, they too were comprised of clans who seem to have had long-standing ties. However, they were not conquered by the Romans until the end of the first century BC and were able to profit from the experience of neighbouring peoples to the south and east by fortifying their settlements (*castros*) with sophisticated defensive systems.[42] The north-western provinces are littered with *castros*, characterised by a random arrangement of round houses surrounded by drystone defensive walls. Fine examples have been excavated at Cameixa (Orense), Elvinia (Coruña) and Sabroso (Guimarães). One of the most magnificent, however, is still to be found crowning a long rocky plateau at Citania de Britieros (Guimarães) in northern Portugal.[43] The settlement itself (256 by 155 metres) consists of about 150 stone huts haphazardly situated within large building plots defined by wide roads. Most of the huts are round with small ante-chambers and stone seats running around the insides; others, however, are square. No large public buildings have been discovered. The whole settlement was surrounded by an elaborate defensive work, consisting of four wall circuits following the contours of the plateau sides. The walls were built from irregular stone blocks and pierced by a few narrow gateways.

The *castros* of the north-west are the last chapter in the prehistory of Iberia. It will now be clear that the story of the peoples of Iberia before the Roman conquest is complicated, and that their sheer variety and sophistication were very much products of the regionalism of the peninsula itself. In essence the theme of the story is the way in which the native peoples of Iberia repeatedly absorbed cultural influences from the south, east and north, giving rise to distinctive, closely related peoples and kingdoms. All of these, however, were to be transformed beyond recognition by the Roman conquest between the late third and late first centuries BC. Iberia was to gain a new degree of cultural uniformity at the expense of strong regional differences.

FURTHER READING

The geography of Iberia is discussed in Strabo's *Geography*, Book 3, and by Pliny The Elder in his *Natural History*, Book 3. Both are available in English in the Loeb Classical Library. Among modern works the *Geografía de España y Portugal*, Tomo I (1952), Tomo II (1954), Tomo IV.1 (1958) and Tomo V (1955) provide much detail, while C. Delano Smith, *Western Mediterranean Europe. A Historical Geography of Italy, Spain and Southern France since the Neolithic* (1979), is also important. Among the early colonisers of Iberia, the Phoenicians and Carthaginians are now the subject of a collection of important studies collected in G. Del Olmo and M.-E. Aubet, *Los Fenicios en la Península Ibérica* (Sabadell, 1986), and in *Phönizier im Western*, Madrider Beitrage 8 (Mainz, 1982). For the Greek episode A. García y Bellido, *Hispania Graeca* I (History), II (Archaeology) and III (Plates) (Barcelona, 1947), is still of importance. A useful synthesis of the later Bronze and Iron Age cultures of Spain and Portugal is to be found in F. Jordá Cerdá, M. Pellicer Catalán, P. Acosta Martínez, M. Almagro Gorbea, *Historia de España I. Prehistoria* (Madrid, 1986), 341–532. Details about Tartessos and the genesis of the Iberians can be found in *Simposi Internacional: Els Origens del Mon Iberic. Ampurias 38–40* (Barcelona, 1977), *V Symposium Internacional de Prehistoria Peninsular. Tartessos y sus Problemas* (Barcelona, 1969), and in *Protohistoria Catalana. 6e Colloqui Internacional de Puigcerdà* (Puigcerdà, 1986). Their later development is well covered in Arribas 1963, Nicolini 1974 and *La Baja Época de la Cultura Ibérica* (Madrid, 1981). An introduction to the Celtic peoples of Iberia is provided by J. Maluquer and B. Taracena, in 'Los pueblos de la España céltica', *Historia de España* (ed. J. Maluquer *et al.*), Tomo I, Volumen III (Madrid, 1954), 5–299, and in Savory 1968. An analysis of the Iberian and Celtiberian languages is well beyond the scope of this book, but A. Tovar, *The Ancient Languages of Spain and Portugal* (1961), provides a readable starting-point.

— 2 —

THE
ROMAN
CONQUEST

The Roman conquest of Iberia is the compelling story of nearly 200 years of continuous military campaigns. These were often brilliant but frequently marred by incompetence and downright treachery. Nevertheless, Rome's eventual victory ensured that for the first time the peoples of Iberia were united under a single authority. Unlike other western Roman provinces, such as Britain or Germany, most of what we know about this immensely complicated conquest comes from the accounts of writers like Polybius, Livy and Appian.[1] This is because the military archaeology of Roman Spain and Portugal is still in its infancy: only a few discoveries have been made, mainly in the centre and north-west of the peninsula.[2] However, these are exceptionally important and shed precious light on the evolution of the Roman army as a fighting force. Indeed, the bitter lessons that Rome learnt in Iberia were successfully applied to her conquests elsewhere in the empire.

Rome's conquest of Iberia was the direct result of an epic power struggle with her old North African rival, Carthage, to control the western Mediterranean. The first stage of this had ended in the first Punic (Carthaginian) War (264–241 BC), in which Rome defeated her, deprived her of Sicily, Sardinia and Corsica as sources of wealth and manpower, and imposed a massive financial indemnity.[3] Carthage, therefore, focused her attention on south-eastern Spain as an alternative source. She had had a long history of involvement in the area, but this now assumed special importance. In 228–227 BC her aggressive and expansionist ambitions in Spain culminated in the foundation of an important strategic base at Carthago Nova (modern Cartagena), on the fringe of the silver-rich lands on the east coast. Carthaginian influence along the Mediterranean coast was soon strong enough to alarm Massalia (modern Marseilles) and its closely linked daughter-

ROMAN SPAIN

1 Carthago Nova
2 Saguntum
3 Emporion/Emporiae
4 Tarraco
5 Iliturgis
6 Castulo
7 Castrum Album
8 Gadir/Gades
9 Baecula
10 Ilipa
11 Italica

* 12 Almedinilla
13 Rhode
* 14 Puig de Sant Andreu
15 Segontia
16 Numantia
* 17 Alpanseque
* 18 Cerca (Angular de Anguita)
* 19 Tentellatge
20 Munda
21 Mons Chaunum
22 Complega

23 Gracchuris
24 Tribola
25 Urso
26 Erisana
27 Arsa
28 Brutobriga
29 Castra Servilia
30 Turris Caepionis
31 Castra Caepiana
32 Valentia
33 Olisippo

* 34 Alpiarca
35 Bracara Augusta
36 Talabriga
* 37 Mondego
38 Aritium Praetorium
39 Segeda
40 Uxama
41 Toletum
* 42 Mourão
43 Ocilis
44 Nertobriga

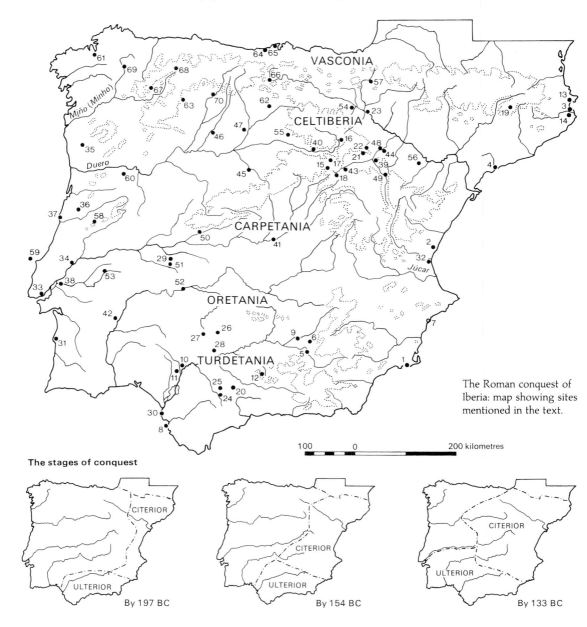

The Roman conquest of Iberia: map showing sites mentioned in the text.

100   0   200 kilometres

The stages of conquest

By 197 BC

By 154 BC

By 133 BC

colonies in the north-east, like Emporion (modern Empúries). Rome also was wary, as she had signed a treaty with Massalia in an attempt to ensure secure land and sea routes between Italy and Iberia. The detailed sequence of events is highly complex; but in 226 BC Rome signed a treaty with Carthage, limiting the latter's influence to the south of the river Ebro.

Rome against Carthage (218–206 BC)

Seven years later, however, in 219 BC, the great Carthaginian general Hannibal laid seige to and sacked Rome's ally in Iberia, the town of Saguntum (modern Sagunto). This provoked an immediate response. In 218 BC the Roman general Cnaeus Cornelius Scipio tried to block Carthaginian reinforcements moving towards Italy by disembarking at the Greek colony of Emporion, in north-eastern Spain, with two legions. He rapidly moved southwards and established a military bridgehead at Tarraco (modern Tarragona), which is to be identified by the stretches of magnificent stone walls still crowning the modern upper town.[4] In the late third century BC three stone defensive towers and adjoining walls were built on this rocky plateau, with large irregular limestone blocks at the foundations and regular squared masonry in the upper courses. This stronghold overlooked the Iberian settlement which lies beneath the lower town of Tarragona and which may be identified perhaps with Cissis (Kese). After the middle of the second century BC the walls were extended around three sides of the plateau and included the settlement of Cissis.[5]

In 217 BC Scipio defeated a Carthaginian fleet commanded by Hasdrubal, the brother of Hannibal, at the mouth of the Ebro. Reinforcements led by Scipio's brother then arrived, and in 215 BC the Romans managed to advance as far south as Iliturgis (modern Mengíbar), Castulo (Cazlona) and Castrum Album (near Alicante). This was crowned with the capture of Saguntum from the Carthaginians in 214. However, in the following year disaster struck: Hasdrubal mustered an army of 40,000 men together with many Iberian mercenaries drawn from the Ilergetes and the Suessetani and routed the Romans near Castulo. Both the Scipio brothers perished, and the Romans were nearly driven out of Iberia altogether.

Fortunately for the Romans, however, the command of Roman affairs in the peninsula was now entrusted to the young P. Cornelius Scipio. The son and namesake of the original Roman commander in Spain, he felt that he 'was marked out to be the avenger of his father, his uncle and his fatherland'.[6] In 209 BC he advanced upon Carthago Nova at the head of 20,000 infantry and 1,000 cavalry, while one of his lieutenants approached it by sea. Carthago Nova was the most important Carthaginian supply-base in Spain and was defended only by a small garrison. However, the town was built upon an isthmus within a lagoon opening into the Mediterranean, making it extremely difficult to capture. Scipio therefore blockaded its landward side, while a fleet of heavily armed ships surrounded its lagoon sides. The Greek historian Polybius describes how the 2,000 Carthaginian defenders first of all tried to break through the Roman forces stationed on the isthmus but were then forced back inside the town walls. In the end Scipio ingeniously launched simultaneous assaults from the north and east at low tide and successfully breached the walls. The most awful carnage ensued, as Scipio allowed his troops to sack the town, and many of its inhabitants were massacred. Amongst the prizes seized by the Romans were thirty-three warships, a large number of weapons, supplies of grain, ivory, gold and silver, and a large number of Roman and Iberian prisoners.[7]

The Carthaginians may have been astounded at the loss of their major strategic centre in Spain but they were not yet beaten. The following year

Defensive tower of the late 3rd-/early 2nd-century BC (Torre de Minerva), at the military bridgehead of Tarraco (modern Tarragona).

found Carthaginian forces divided between Mago at Gadir (modern Cádiz), Hasdrubal Gisgo on the Mediterranean coast, and Hasdrubal Barca near Castulo. Scipio exploited this situation by scoring a major strategic and psychological victory over Hasdrubal at Baecula (modern Bailén), on the edge of the Sierra Morena mountains, before the other Carthaginian generals could join forces. Hasdrubal Barca withdrew and in 207 left Spain for Italy. He was replaced by another general, Hanno, who brought reinforcements across from Africa. Hanno also tried to recoup losses in manpower by recruiting Celtiberian mercenaries in central Spain with Mago. This move was rapidly countered by Scipio, who dispatched his legate, Marcus Iunius Silanus, to central Spain where he defeated the Carthaginians. Mago managed to flee southwards to Turdetania. This part of the country was held by Hasdrubal Gisgo, who was based at Gadir and had 50,000 infantry, 4,500 cavalry and thirty-two elephants at his disposal. Nevertheless, the Carthaginian position here was being undermined rapidly by the defection of Turdetanian towns to the Roman cause. Culchas, for instance, the king of twenty-eight Turdetanian towns, had managed to raise 3,500 men for Scipio's army. The death-blow came in 206 BC when Scipio managed to lure a reluctant Hasdrubal Gisgo into battle at Ilipa (modern Alcalá del Río), on the banks of the Guadalquivir, and decisively defeated him. This victory was consolidated by the foundation of a stronghold of retired Roman soldiers at Italica (modern Santiponce). Shortly afterwards, through a mixture of Roman intrigue and Mago's incompetence, the Carthaginians lost control of Gadir, their last foothold in the peninsula.

By virtue of his three major victories at Carthago Nova, Baecula and Ilipa, Scipio had succeeded in winning for Rome the almost unlimited sources of precious metals around Carthago Nova and in Turdetania. This was to prove as valuable to Rome's long-term fortunes as it was disastrous to those of Hannibal. Scipio returned to Rome, where he was elected to carry the war against Hannibal to Africa. He eventually defeated him at Zama in 202 BC, earning the name of Scipio Africanus.

The early conquest (205–155 BC)

Late in 206 BC a rebellion broke out amongst the north-eastern tribes, led by the Ilergetan chieftains Indibilis and Mandonius. The Ilergetes had been co-operating closely with the Carthaginians and were clearly a serious threat to the Romans. Like other Iberian warriors, they were '. . . virtually all of them, peltasts [lightly armed], and wore light armour on account of their brigand life, using javelin, sling and dirk and intermingled with their forces of infantry was a force of Cavalry'.[8] Few Iberian weapons have actually survived; however, excavations at sites like Almedinilla (Córdoba) have uncovered examples of their graceful curved sword, known as the *falcatus*, knobbed daggers and the fearsome iron lance (*solliferreum*).[9] The Iberian revolt was compounded by a mutiny amongst Roman troops stationed on the river Sucro (modern Júcar), to the south of Saguntum.

Left Curved Iberian iron sword (*falcatus*); *right* Iberian iron javelin (*solliferreum*).

Scipio acted with his usual speed and successfully eliminated any threat posed to Roman interests in eastern Spain.

Scipio's work was undone in the following year when Indibilis and Mandonius fomented another revolt, abetted by the Lacetani and Ausetani tribes. Scipio's successors, Lentulus and Acidinus, managed to suppress this but at the same time imposed very harsh terms on the Iberians: these included the doubling of their occasional payments towards the upkeep of the Roman army.[10] Not surprisingly this added insult to injury, and resentment against Rome soon boiled over into a major rebellion.

The trouble began in Turdetania in 197 BC and rapidly spread to the tribes of central and north-eastern Spain. The Romans had little initial success in quelling this, and in 195 the situation was serious enough to merit the personal intervention of the consul Marcus Porcius Cato at the head of 70,000 men.[11] First of all he sacked the *castellum* at the Greek colony of Rhode (modern Roses): this may have been a small fortified redoubt on the hill now occupied by the Romanesque church of Santa María de Roses.[12] Cato then defeated a large tribe in the vicinity of Emporion. It is possible that this can be identified with the Indiketes and that the enormous hilltop settlement (*oppidum*) at Puig de Sant Andreu (modern Ullastret) was the focus of their resistance. Excavations have shown that part of the site was abandoned during this period,[13] perhaps as a consequence of the battle. Cato then reconquered much of the east coast and the lower Ebro valley.

In southern Spain, meanwhile, the two Roman governors were being harrassed by forces of Turdetanians and their Celtiberian mercenaries. Cato therefore marched southwards down the east coast and relieved the situation by skirmishing with the Turdetani and parleying with the Celtiberi. He then offered the latter free passage back to their homelands in the *meseta*. In this way peace was soon restored throughout Roman possessions. Cato, however, seems to have decided to make an example of the Celtiberi returning to the north-east by way of the *meseta*, laying seige to Segontia (modern Sigüenza) and marching past Numantia (modern Garray). Surviving traces of this campaign may be sought perhaps in the two Roman camps discovered at Alpanseque (near Medinaceli) and Cerca (Anguilar de Anguita).[14] The latter lies a short distance to the east of Segontia and consists of a stone wall enclosing a sub-rectangular area of 12.4 hectares.

Upon arrival in the north-east Cato had to repacify the Iacetani, Suessetani and Bergistani. A small, contemporary Roman fort has been discovered at Tentellatge (modern Navés), with upstanding walls built from large, irregular limestone blocks.[15] It is located in the magnificent foothills of the Pyrenees to the east of Solsona and defended the major natural route of communication between the territory of these tribes and the hinterland of Emporion.

Livy records that Cato then returned to Rome bearing a vast quantity of booty captured from the Iberians. He marched in triumphal procession through the city, with 25,000 Roman pounds of silver, 1,400 Roman pounds of gold bullion, 54,000 Oscan silver coins and 123,000 other silver issues. He also distributed 1,610 bronze coins to each of his cavalrymen and 270 to each infantryman.[16]

Although it can be argued that Rome was drawn into coming to Iberia as a result of her conflict with Carthage, the determination with which Cato put down the Iberian rebellion signalled that from 195 BC she was there to stay. Moreover, in 197 the Romans divided their Iberian territory into two separate provinces.[17] The province of Hispania Citerior comprised the east coast between Carthago Nova and the Pyrenees, and included the inland territory of the Ilergetes and the Ausetani. Tarraco was its principal military base, but there were additional garrisons at towns like Carthago Nova and Castulo. There was probably one at the supply-base at Emporion too. Here, on the low plateau behind the Greek port, part of what may have been its garrison building has been discovered. It was a long rectangular building (50 by 28 metres) with an outer wall built from large polygonal stone blocks. The interior of the eastern end was filled by three huge water cisterns open to the sky and surrounded by roofed service areas.[18]

Roman military and diplomatic action in Citerior between 194 and 178 BC aimed at pacifying the eastern *meseta* and thus guaranteeing the security of the subdued coastal areas. In the earlier years, for instance, governors of Hispania Citerior like Terentius Varro and Fulvius Flaccus tried to eliminate the threat posed by such tribes as the Carpetani, Vettones and Celtiberi.[19] The first decisive success did not come until 180 to 178 BC, during the governorships of Lucius Postumius Albinus and Tiberius Sempronius Gracchus. The latter advanced northwards from his base in the south of Ulterior province with two legions and a large complement of allies, sacking Munda (modern Montilla) and then breaking resistance to Rome in Carpetania and Oretania. Further to the north he defeated the Celtiberi in a major battle near the Mons Chaunus: the battlefield has not been located but probably lay near modern Complega.

Gracchus' victory broke the power of the Celtiberi for the time being, and they sued for peace. Gracchus accepted and, in the words of Appian, 'made carefully defined treaties with all the tribes [which included the Belli, Titti, Arevaci and Vaccaei], binding them to be the friends of Rome and giving and receiving oaths to that effect'.[20] The terms stipulated that the tribes pay tribute and furnish contingents for the Roman army and also prohibited the Celtiberi from building any new settlements. Indeed, it has been suggested that Gracchus may have promoted Roman influence by the foundation of new settlements: Gracchuris (modern Alfaro) was certainly one, and some scholars have suggested that Iliturgis (modern Mengíbar in the Guadalquivir valley) was another.[21]

Roman military action in Iberia at this time was not limited to Citerior. Between 195 and 180 the Romans campaigned extensively in Ulterior, probably in an attempt to establish the river Guadalquivir as the western edge of the province.[22] At this time Hispania Ulterior corresponded roughly to modern Andalusia and was under constant threat from the powerful Lusitanian people to the west. The Lusitani were, indeed, a formidable people, and stone statues of their warriors have been discovered at a number of different sites in Portugal.[23] The Lusitani raided Ulterior in 194, although it was left to the governor Lucius Aemilius Paullus to defeat them in battle (190 BC) and to establish a temporary peace. It was short-lived, however, and in 179 Lucius Postumius Albinus attempted a more radical solution. First he marched northwards, across the upper Guadiana and Tagus rivers, and severely punished the northern tribe of the Vaccaei, who had been assisting the Lusitani. Then he attacked the Lusitani themselves, and in the end may well have imposed a treaty similar to that of Gracchus in Celtiberia.[24]

The Lusitanian wars (155–139 BC)
and the expedition to Gallaicia (138–136 BC)

Albinus' settlement was only partially successful, and Lusitanian raids persisted into the 160s BC. However, from 155 BC their threat became more serious as the Lusitani came under unified leadership and their raids were better co-ordinated.[25] They achieved some notable successes between 155 and 151 BC, defeating successive Roman governors and raiding Hispania Ulterior extensively.[26] Finally, in 151, they managed to inflict a major defeat on the governor of Ulterior, Servius Sulpicius Galba, with the loss of up to 7,000 men. As a consequence Galba joined forces with the governor of Citerior, Licinius Lucullus, and tried to catch the Lusitani by means of a 'pincer strategy'. Galba took the sea-route to Lusitania and sailed along the Algarve coast, while Lucullus advanced overland through the area presently within the provinces of Badajoz and Cáceres. The strategy proved successful, and the Lusitani sought an end to the fighting and the renewal of an earlier peace treaty. In one of the more notorious episodes of the Roman conquest Galba appeared to comply but at the same time, on the pretext of offering them new and fertile land in which to settle, 'he surrounded them with a ditch and sent in soldiers who slew them all, lamenting and invoking the names of the gods and the pledges which they had received'.[27] In this and two subsequent cold-blooded massacres Galba shocked public opinion at Rome by treacherously slaughtering 9,000 Lusitani and selling off 20,000 as slaves.

Not surprisingly this outraged the Lusitani and indirectly led to the emergence of Viriathus as their resourceful and energetic new leader. This man had survived Galba's massacres and by virtue of impressive military successes against the Romans soon became the voice of anti-Roman sentiment throughout Iberia. His first success came in 147 BC. At the head of 10,000 Lusitani he ambushed the army of Caius Vettilius at Tribola, to the south of Urso (modern Osuna) in Ulterior, killing 10,000 Romans. Virtually the whole of the province was now at Viriathus' mercy, and he ranged as far west as the Guadiana and as far north as the Tagus, terrorising Carpetania and sacking Segobriga (Cabeza del Griego). In 142–141 Quintus Fabius Maximus Servilianus was initially successful against the Lusitani in Ulterior itself. He then turned westwards and advanced into the lands of the Conii (modern Algarve), and ventured northwards into Lusitania itself. Here his luck ran out and he was defeated by Viriathus at Erisana (Azuagia) in Baeturia, midway between the Guadiana and the Guadalquivir. Viriathus was rather more magnanimous than many Roman governors and drew up a treaty with Maximus, in which Rome was to respect as Lusitanian the territory which his followers then occupied and Viriathus himself was to be recognised as a 'friend of the Roman nation'.[28]

Predictably, the Romans soon broke this treaty. In 140 the governor of Ulterior, Quintus Servilius Caepio, took the offensive with a strategy to

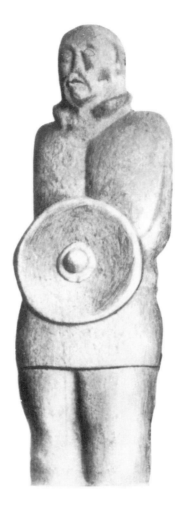

Stone statues of Lusitanian warriors.

contain Viriathus' forces within Lusitania. He began by seizing the town of Arsa, in Baeturia, and drove Viriathus and his followers into Lusitania. Moving rapidly, Caepio then sealed the Lusitani off from any contact with tribes to the east by building a military road between the headwaters of the Guadiana and the Tagus. This was fortified by a number of garrisons, one of which was the Castra Servilia (in the vicinity of modern Cáceres). Advancing along this road and laying waste large expanses of territory belonging to the Vettones and Callaici, he successfully isolated the Lusitani from any assistance to the north. Caepio also prepared for the arrival of Roman reinforcements by consolidating ports at Turris Caepionis (modern Chipiona) and Castra Caepiana. At the same time Marcus Popilius Laenas, the governor of Citerior, co-operated by attacking the Lusitani southwards from the Duero valley.

This joint strategy split the Lusitanian forces and isolated them from any allied peoples. As a result panic and confusion broke out, and in an attempt to salvage the situation Viriathus sued for peace. The Romans appeared to accept this, but shortly afterwards Caepio deviously bribed Viriathus' most trusted friends to murder him. One night Audax, Minurus and Ditalco waited until he was asleep and then stabbed him in the throat. Viriathus' death effectively spelt the end of co-ordinated Lusitanian resistance to Rome.[29]

The Romans now controlled all the territory of ancient Baeturia, which lay between the Guadalquivir and the Guadiana. This was now part of Hispania Ulterior, and the area between the Guadiana and the Douro became a 'buffer zone' against the northern tribes.[30] The Romans also scattered Viriathus' followers as widely as possible, in an attempt to prevent a resurgence of Lusitanian aggression. In 138 BC, for instance, Decimus Iunius Brutus settled some of them at Valentia (modern Valencia), to the south of Saguntum in eastern Spain.[31]

Decimus Iunius Brutus' governorship (138–133 BC) was important in witnessing the extension of Roman aggression to the coastal lands of the Callaici, which lay to the north of the Douro. In strategic terms this could be explained away as a means of punishing the Callaici for assisting Viriathus over the past decade. However, there is little doubt that this expedition was also aimed at seizing some of their rich metal resources. Brutus' first move was to fortify the coastal settlement at Olisippo (modern Lisbon) and then to set up his command centre at a place called Moron. This has been identified with a large earthwork at Alpiarca, in western Portugal. The site consists of a large earth rampart (3.5 metres high) which runs around three sides of a large plateau and has an entrance on its south-eastern side. It was further defended by a deep ditch with a V profile running around the outside.[32]

After carrying out limited military action in Lusitania, Brutus marched up the coast into Gallaicia, crossing the Limia and Miño rivers. He then returned inland, ravaging lands in the vicinity of Bracara (modern Braga) and terrorising the coastal town of Talabriga (near Flusses). By the close of his campaign Brutus had killed 50,000 tribesmen, taken 6,000 prisoners, and seized an enormous quantity of booty. He had also succeeded in extending Roman territory as far north as the river Mondego (central Portugal) and consolidated it with a Roman garrison at Aritium Praetorium (near Alvega) to the south.

The Celtiberian wars (155–133 BC)

The treaties signed between Tiberius Sempronius Gracchus and the Celtiberian tribes in 178 had ensured a long period of peace in north-central Spain, with only a few infringements.[33] However, a decisive break came in 153, when the Belli and Titti enlarged the walled perimeter of Segeda (Belmonte de Perejil, near Calatayud) and encouraged the inhabitants of smaller towns to settle there. This was a deliberate breach of one of the treaty clauses and sparked off nearly twenty years of continuous warfare. The Roman Senate was so alarmed at this uprising that it actually brought the date of the New Year forward from 15 March to 1 January.[34] This allowed the consul Fulvius Nobilior, the new governor of Citerior, to set out for Celtiberia as soon as possible. He marched from Tarraco to Segeda with some 30,000 men, taking full advantage of the campaign season. He destroyed the town, although its inhabitants had withdrawn to the Arevacian town of Numantia before he arrived.

At this point it is worth pausing to consider Numantia. It still crowns a long plateau rising dramatically some seventy metres above rolling plains to the north of Garray (near Soria). The site was discovered by the German archaeologist Adolf Schulten, who in 1905 undertook a remarkably thorough excavation of the site.[35] Most of the upstanding walls that greet today's visitor are the remains of the later, Roman town and have largely obliterated the Arevacian site. Sufficient remained, however, for Schulten to deduce that the site covered some twenty-four hectares. Moreover, his account of the excavations makes it clear that this pre-Roman town was divided up into regular building lots by two major metalled streets and at least eleven perpendicular minor streets. The houses were quite small, with stone and mortar foundations and mudbrick walls, and many were adjacent to small pits in which grain and other agricultural products were stored. No larger, public buildings have yet been discovered. The complex was surrounded by one major defensive wall (3.4 metres wide), built from large pebbles, and a lesser wall with small huts crowding along its inner side.

This, then, was the haven to which the refugees from Segeda fled. Nobilior pursued them, and despite being ambushed with heavy losses arrived at Numantia. He set up camp on the hill of La Gran Atalaya, five kilometres to the east of the town. The summit of this hill was excavated between 1908 and 1912 by Schulten, who revealed an extraordinary palimpsest of five Roman camps built between 195 and 75 BC but with the majority belonging to the Celtiberian wars.[36] These are, in fact, amongst the earliest-surviving Roman military camps from the western empire. Nobilior's winter camp of 153 BC was identified with a fifty-hectare fort, enclosed within a stone defensive wall which traced an irregular path over the rocky hillside. The interior was subdivided by two major roads (the *via principalis* and the *via quintana*) into rectangular lots, filled with stone-built barracks for the soldiers. Nobilior's headquarters building and the parade ground (forum) were situated at the centre of the camp, while the higher-ranking officers (tribunes and prefects) were lodged in quarters on either side of the *via principalis*. The camp accommodated two Roman legions, while Iberian auxiliary troops were billeted in their own quarters in an annexe at the south-eastern corner.

Nobilior first attempted a pitched battle against the Celtiberi in front of Numantia, assisted by elephants and cavalry sent by King Massinissa,

Rome's ally in Numidia, North Africa. However, the elephants ran amok amongst the Romans, and Nobilior was badly defeated. After attempting an attack on neighbouring Uxama (modern Burgo de Osma),[37] he retired to his camp at La Gran Atalaya. In the following year he was replaced by the consul Marcus Claudius Marcellus, a man who had gained valuable experience in Iberia during 169 BC. He was less impulsive than Nobilior, playing for time and recruiting more men for his army. He also tried to

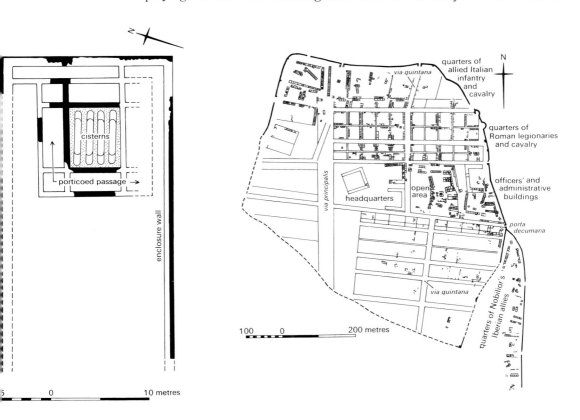

Above Military building beneath the later, Roman town of Emporiae, early 2nd century BC; *above right* Camp of the consul Fulvius Nobilior at La Gran Atalaya (Renieblas), near Numantia, 153 BC.

whittle away at the confederation of Celtiberian tribes by cajoling certain settlements like Ocilis (modern Medinaceli) and, with more difficulty, Nertobriga (modern Calatorao) into submission. Soon, peace negotiations with the Arevaci, Belli and Titti resulted in envoys being sent to Rome. Indeed, these tribes wanted a restoration of the old Gracchan treaties. If these agreements had been respected, then both Rome and Iberia would have been spared years of bloodshed. As it turned out, the Roman Senate had other ideas and insisted that the tribes be severely punished. Nevertheless, Marcellus worked hard at putting the treaty into effect and managed to persuade the tribes to comply before the arrival of his successor, Lucius Licinius Lucullus, in 151.

Rather than accept the restored peace Lucullus opted to recommence the war with little motive other than greed and personal ambition. As a pretext he accused the neighbouring Vaccaei of maltreating the Carpetani, who were allies of Rome, and then waged a pointless and bloody campaign against them. He attacked Cauca (modern Coca) and, after extracting hostages and tribute, treacherously massacred nearly all of its 20,000 adult males and sacked the town. After an abortive attempt to take Intercatia (modern Villalpando) and after abortive skirmishes near Pallantia (modern Palencia), Lucullus turned southwards. He then assisted Galba in an equally vindictive and bloody campaign against the Lusitani.

Surprisingly, Lucullus' behaviour did not spark off further trouble in Celtiberia. Instead, the tribes adhered closely to Marcellus' settlement and there was peace until 143 BC.[38] Appian records that the Lusitanian leader, Viriathus, then persuaded the Arevaci, Belli and Titti to break with Rome in an attempt, no doubt, to break up the concentration of Roman forces arrayed against him. As a response to this the consul Quintus Caecilius Metellus was quickly sent to Celtiberia with a force of 30,000 infantry and 2,000 cavalry. He took Nertobriga, Centobriga (modern Ricla) and Contrebia (modern Botorrita) but found that many of the Arevaci had taken refuge in Termes (modern Tiermes) and, of course, Numantia. In 141 he was succeeded by the consul Quintus Pompeius Aulus, who attempted launching a direct assault against Numantia but was badly defeated by its 8,000 defenders. After a similar attack against Termes, Pompeius was eventually obliged to seek a peace treaty with the Numantines. Despite their delicate situation the Romans still managed to coax favourable terms out of them. The treaty obliged the Numantines to deliver up hostages to the Romans, together with an assortment of Roman prisoners and deserters and an indemnity of thirty silver talents. After the Numantines had fulfilled their part of the bargain, Pompeius then totally betrayed their trust. He denied that the treaty had ever existed, and within a short time the Romans recommenced the war.

In 137 BC the consul Caius Hostilius Mancinus embarked on one of the more notorious episodes in Roman military history. He established his camp on the hill of Castillejos, to the north of Numantia, and then fielded some 20,000 men against the besieged inhabitants. After some unfavourable skirmishes he panicked and eventually surrendered his entire army to the Numantines. Recalling Gracchus' treaty of 178 BC, sufficient trust in Roman sincerity remained for them to propose a negotiated peace. This was to take the form of a 'treaty of equals' (*foedus aequum*) between Rome and the Arevaci. Predictably, however, the concept of equality implicit in the treaty was unacceptable to the Roman Senate, which indignantly refused to recognise it. Another chance for peaceful coexistence between Rome and the peoples of north-central Spain was lost, and the war continued.

After two further years of indecisive fighting the Roman Senate decided that Numantia had to be subjugated and the Celtiberian war concluded at all costs. Thus in 134 the governorship of Hispania Citerior was entrusted to the consul Publius Cornelius Scipio Aemilianus, the great general famed for his destruction of Carthage in 146 BC. He was accompanied by a group of friends, including the Greek historian Polybius, who is known to have written an account of the war. This has survived by being later incorporated into a narrative of Appian. What has come down to us verbatim, however, is Polybius' important account of the organisation of the Roman army.[39] Although he probably used sources of the earlier second century BC, his account gives us a clear idea of the efficient fighting force which confronted the Numantines in the 130s BC.

Polybius tells us that the Roman army was composed of Roman citizens drawn from Rome and other towns in Italy. They were grouped into large fighting units, called legions, of between 4,200 and 5,000 men. Each legion was composed of four different categories of soldier: the *velites*, *hastati*, *principes* and *triarii*. There were 1,200 *velites* in each legion, each man being lightly armed with a sword, a small circular shield (*parma*) and a javelin. The *velites* were the youngest and most inexperienced men in the legion and were often used to draw the enemy's fire at the start of an engagement. The *hastati* and *principes* were older and more experienced, and were grouped into ten units (maniples) of 120 men apiece. All of them were heavily armed, each wearing a bronze breastplate, helmet and leg-covers (greaves), as well as carrying a large convex oval shield (*scutum*), short Spanish sword (*gladius*) and two throwing spears (*pila*). The *triarii* were the most experienced men in each legion. They were organised into ten maniples of sixty men, each similarly heavily armed and carrying a large thrusting spear. Apart from foot-soldiers each legion had a complement of some 300 lightly armed cavalry, who were divided up into bands (*turmae*) commanded by *decuriones*.

Roman helmet of Republican date, now in the British Museum.

Sadly, few pieces of Roman armour of any date have been recovered from sites in Iberia, and it is only by examining contemporary finds from Italy and France that we can learn about the kind of armour worn by Scipio's soldiers. However, monuments like the great funerary sculptures from Urso (modern Osuna) and Ostipo (modern Estepa)[40] in Ulterior may give us an impression of Roman military dress in the first century BC.

One of the great strengths of this citizen army was its thorough training, discipline and professionalism, which ensured that the legions could be manoeuvred rapidly in battle. However, this depended on an efficient system of delegated command, although the governor was in overall charge of all the legions in any one province. Occasionally he was assisted by senators (*legati*), who were delegated to take charge of particular units or tasks by the Roman Senate. The most senior officers in the legion itself were the tribunes, career men from the order of knights or the senatorial order at Rome. Below these two centurions were appointed to take charge of each maniple within the legion, together with two seconds-in-command (*optiones*) and two standard-bearers (*signiferi*).

This, then, was the composition of the army that Scipio Aemilianus led against the Celtiberian tribes. He had recruited volunteers sent by kings and towns friendly to him and, together with the remnants of Mancinus' ill-fated force and local recruits, was able to field a force of some 60,000 men. Scipio's strategy was first to cut off Numantia and Termes from any assistance which might be offered by neighbouring towns like Pallantia. He then arrived at Numantia and proceeded to surround the settlement with an elaborate siege-work.

Much of this is still evident. Indeed, it is the earliest and one of the largest siege-works that has survived from the Roman world. Scipio's seven military camps are still visible on the crests of the hills – Raza, Dehesilla, Alto Real, Travesadas, Valdevorrón, Peña Redonda and Castillejos – surrounding Numantia. Castillejos, of course, was also the site of the earlier camps of Marcellus and Pompeius. However, the remains of the Scipionic camp were quite well preserved, with the headquarters building opening on to the *via principalis* at the western end and the various barrack blocks abutting the *via praetoria*. The camp at Peña Redonda was also excavated by Schulten, although the narrowness of the hilltop meant that the camp had an oblong plan with an unusual internal layout. A large number of Roman spears, javelins, ballista bolts (fired from powerful spring-loaded machines), arrowheads and swords were found here and, indeed, at other camps around Numantia. More dramatic was the discovery of large round stones which were catapulted by great stone-throwing machines against the walls of Numantia. All these camps were connected by a nine-kilometre perimeter wall, which ran no closer than 250 metres and no further than one kilometre away from Numantia. Schulten found stretches of this *vallum*, noting that it was built from stone, some 2.5 metres thick and 3 metres high. It ensured rapid communication between the Roman camps and also prevented the

Map of the Roman siege
works laid out by Scipio
Aemilianus at Numantia
(province of Soria).

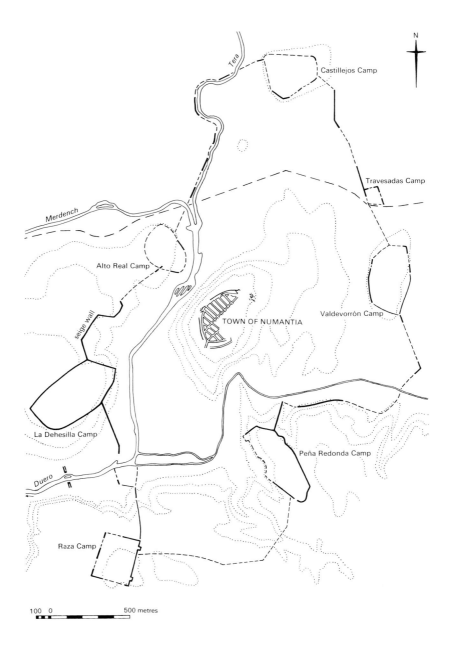

defenders of Numantia escaping the siege. Vigilance was further improved
by the installation of watch-towers every thirty-three metres and the
excavation of a defensive ditch and palisade in front of the *vallum.* The
only possible route of escape open to the Numantines would have been
along the river Duero, or its tributaries, which run close to the town. Yet
Appian describes how Scipio even blocked this exit, by building towers on

either side of the river and then, between them, suspending large logs bristling with very sharp knives and spears.

After several valiant attempts to break out of this cordon, the Numantines were slowly starved and towards the end succumbed to cannibalism. Schulten's excavation of the town revealed graphic evidence of the defenders' long struggle against the Romans. Arevacian baked-clay sling shots were found in the burnt debris of the settlement, together with prized Celtiberian iron daggers still in their bronze scabbards, spearheads, arrowheads and Roman ballista bolts. The defenders eventually surrendered to Scipio in 133 BC. He promptly razed Numantia to the ground and sold most of the inhabitants as slaves.

The destruction of the focal point of Celtiberian hostility to Rome spelt the end of serious resistance to Rome in this part of Iberia. It is true that peace was broken in 104 BC by the invasion of Germanic peoples (the Cimbri and Teutones) from Gaul,[41] and again between 99 and 82, when the Celtiberi, Arevaci and Vaccaei rebelled against Rome;[42] but none of these incidents rivalled the scale or bitterness of the Celtiberian wars. After 133 BC most of the northern *meseta* was absorbed into Hispania Citerior and the gradual Romanisation of its communities began.

The wars of Sertorius (82–72 BC)

Political life at Rome during the 80s BC was dominated by three men of great personal ambition – namely, Caius Marius, Lucius Cornelius Sulla and Lucius Cornelius Cinna. The source of their power lay in the command of armies in provinces that were vital to Rome's interests. Originally, the young Senator Quintus Sertorius had been a supporter of Marius' regime in Rome. However, after his death in 86 BC Sertorius rose to prominence as a follower of Cinna. In 83 he was appointed as governor of Hispania Citerior, and his first accomplishment was to expel the incumbent governor, a supporter of Sulla.[43]

For the next ten years Sertorius tried to gain control of both Spanish provinces, defeating in succession the armies of Caecilius Metellus, Cnaeus Domitius Calvinus and Pompey the Great, which had been sent against him from Rome.[44] These victories rapidly attracted the respect of dissatisfied Lusitani and Celtiberi who readily flocked to his standards. By 77 BC Sertorius had won over most of Citerior to his cause and established his capital at Osca (modern Huesca)[45] in northern Spain. The Arevaci, Vaccaei, Celtiberi, Vettones, Pelendones and factions of the Ilergetes were amongst his staunchest supporters. Although these campaigns were a personal crusade for Sertorius, they were also a great opportunity for these peoples to be rid of the impersonal and brutal military power which was often the most visible face of Roman interests in Iberia.

The fiercest fighting took place in western Ulterior (between the Guadalquivir and the Tagus) between 79 and 76 BC, the east coast of Citerior (between the mouth of the Ebro and the northern *meseta*) between 76 and

75 BC, and in the Ebro valley and northern *meseta* between 76 and 72 BC. As yet archaeology has yielded little evidence for any of these campaigns. One exception is the two-legion fort built by Caecilius Metellus at Castra Caecilia, two and a half kilometres to the north-west of modern Cáceres. It lay on the line of Caepio's military road between the Guadiana and the Tagus, which Metellus probably used in an attempt to contain Sertorius' forces in the south-west. Excavations have shown that it was rectangular in plan (twenty-four hectares), with stone walls and surrounded by two ditches. The interior revealed traces of the *via principalis* and *via quintana*, as well as the headquarters, quarters belonging to tribunes and a granary.

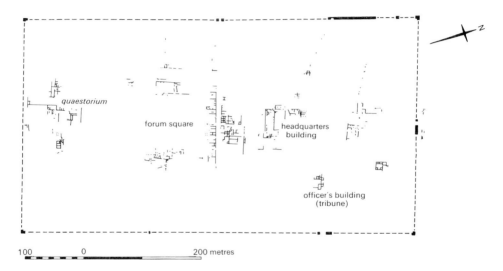

100   0   200 metres

Castra Caecilia to the north of Cáceres, early 1st century BC.

The layout of the fort was markedly different from those around Numantia and reflects some important organisational changes undergone by the Roman army under Marius at the end of the second century BC. Other bases along the road included the Vicus Caecilius (Baños) and the newly founded settlement of Caecilia Metellinum (modern Medellín). Metellus also built a coastal base at Caeciliana (Setúbal) in western Lusitania. A camp which roughly dates to this period has been identified at Almazán (Soria) in central Spain.[46]

The superior number of troops at the disposal of Pompey and Metellus gradually wore down Sertorius and his generals. Moveover, in the last years of the wars Sertorius was further weakened by the defection of many Celtiberian and Vaccaeian allies. Finally, in 72 BC, he was murdered by Perperna, one of his own generals. Peace had been restored in Citerior, although it was not considered complete until harsh revenge had been visited upon Sertorius' Celtiberian and Vaccaeian allies. Pompey thus rounded off the affair by sacking Calagurris, Uxama, Termes, Clunia (modern Coruña del Conde), Osca, and the magnificent settlement at Cabezo de

Alcalá (modern Azaila).[47] He also founded the town of Pompaelo (modern Pamplona) in Vasconia to the north, probably in an attempt to watch over the northern *meseta* communities.[48]

The later conquest (61–19 BC)

Between 72 and 62 BC the peace of Hispania Ulterior was periodically broken by a resurgence of Lusitanian raids. Indeed, in 61 BC the situation became so bad that the provincials called upon the new governor, Caius Julius Caesar, to restore order.[49] His strategy saw the dislodgement of the Lusitani from the security of their hilltop settlements and their forcible resettlement on new sites in the lowlands. In western Portugal, in the vicinity of the Mons Herminius, he then confronted the Lusitani again and sacked the settlement of Medubriga (modern Ranhados). Those inhabitants that escaped took refuge on an offshore island (the modern Ilhas Berlengas), which Caesar then assaulted with a squadron of ships supplied from Gades (modern Cádiz).[50]

Caesar's strategy proved successful in the short term, leaving him free to pursue other objectives. Following in the footsteps of Iunius Brutus, he marched northwards to Gallaicia with 15,000 men and succeeded in capturing the stronghold at Brigantium (modern Betanzos). He was then able to return to Rome with the kudos of impressive military victories and enough booty to assuage his creditors. Indeed, his expedition to the northwest is best understood as an attempt to profit from the rich metal resources in the area, even though it was also an important boost for his political career at Rome.

Rome does not seem to have taken any steps to consolidate Caesar's achievements in Gallaicia and Lusitania, and prior to 29 BC we hear only of Lusitanian revolts (54, 36 and 35 BC).[51] Indeed, the energies and attentions of the Roman authorities in the Spanish provinces between 49 and 44 BC were almost exclusively taken up by battles and clashes between the forces of Caesar and Pompey. These were essentially part of a struggle for the control of the Spanish provinces rather than an episode in the conquest of the Iberian peninsula itself. In fact, these conflicts were sequences in a prolonged civil war which stretched from one end of the Roman world to the other.[52] Caesar emerged as the victor, with momentous consequences for the future of the Roman Empire.

The completion of Rome's conquest of Iberia came with the Cantabrian wars of the emperor Augustus (29–19 BC).[53] Unlike any other stage of the conquest, these were part of a planned strategy with clearly defined aims. The principal peoples of the north-west, the Cantabri and Astures, had often acted as mercenaries for tribes like the Vaccaei, who were hostile to Rome. On other occasions they had upset tribal relationships by raiding the territory of the Vaccaei, Turmodigi and Autrigones. Thus, if Augustus had needed a pretext for the conquest of the north-west, he could have argued that the future overall stability of the area hinged upon the subjugation of the Astures and Cantabri. At the same time there is little doubt that the annexation of the gold and tin resources of Gallaicia was another powerful motive.

Preparations for the wars began in 29–27 BC, under the leadership of Augustus' military representatives (legates), Statilius Taurus, Caius Calvisius Sabinus and Sextus Appuleius. Taurus fought against the Astures and Cantabri in the mountainous areas now within the modern provinces of Asturias, León and Santander. Moreover, he denied them a source of potential assistance by subjugating the Vaccaei in the region of modern Palencia and northern Burgos.

In 27–26 BC Augustus himself took charge of the war and planned his strategy during a sojourn at Tarraco. At his disposal he had some 70,000 men, of which the legions I and II Augusta, IIII Macedonica, VI Victrix and IX Hispana were under the leadership of himself and Caius Antistius Vetus, the legate of Citerior. The V Alaudae and X Gemina legions were led by Publius Carisius, the legate of Ulterior. They were deployed along a front 400 kilometres wide, stretching from the modern Basque province of Guipuzcoa to northern Portugal. By contrast, the north-western tribes were able to muster about 100,000 mainly concentrated in their many hilltop settlements (*castros*) scattered across the rugged landscape. They were therefore more effective in conducting guerrilla warfare against the Romans than attempting pitched battles.

Augustus established his field headquarters at Segisama, in the lowlands to the south of Cantabrian territory. This site is traditionally identified with Sasamón,[54] in the province of Burgos, but the site (three and a half hectares) is far too small to have accommodated the legions under Augustus' personal command. There was another military base at Asturica (modern Astorga) and coastal bases at Portus Blendium (possibly modern Suances) and Portus Victoriae (possibly modern Santander). The war began in earnest in 26–25 BC, with the Romans campaigning in three different areas. Augustus advanced northwards from Segisama against the eastern Cantabrian strong- hold of Aracillum (modern Aradillos), assisted by sea-borne troops moving southwards from Portus Victoriae. Ill health, however, soon forced him to retire from the field, and Antistius Vetus assumed sole command and eventually captured Aracillum. He then advanced to the north-west and took the Cantabrian redoubt at Bergidum (modern Villafranca del Vierzo). The defenders fled and took refuge at the Mons Vindius (north of El Vierzo) but were finally worn down through privation. Antistius rounded off his work with the capture of Lucus (modern Lugo), on the river Miño. Elsewhere in the area Publius Carisius had also experienced success, managing to outmanoeuvre an attack by the Astures in the lowlands and eventually capturing the stronghold at Lancia (modern Villasbariego). As far as Augus- tus was concerned, the north-west was now pacified, and he left Hispania in 24 BC to celebrate a triumph at Rome.

In reality the situation was still unstable. In 24 BC Lucius Aemilius Lamia, the legate of Citerior, managed to suppress a serious revolt amongst the Cantabri and Astures. This involved the destruction of numerous *castros* and the resettlement of their inhabitants in the lowlands. Other complications developed in 22 BC. Publius Carisius was still in command of the army of Ulterior and succeeded in securing some of the main gold-mining areas by advancing northwards through the Pajares and Manzanal passes. The threat of continued Roman expansion in the north-west coupled with Carisius' reported brutality sparked off another revolt amongst the Cantabri. This was put down with the timely assistance of Caius Furnius, the legate of Citerior.[55] However, resentment against the Romans still ran high and in 19 BC it boiled over into a major rebellion.[56] This was, in fact, the last serious resistance to Roman authority in the north-west and was sufficiently grave to require the personal intervention of Marcus Vipsanius Agrippa. He had been the architect of Augustus' great victory over the forces of Antony and Cleopatra at Actium in 31 BC and soon brought the Cantabri firmly under Roman domination.

After nearly 200 years of continuous warfare the Iberian peninsula was finally subjugated. The Roman conquest had been haphazard, characterised by short campaigns and the lack of any consistent policy. This reflects the absence of any long-term Roman objectives and was partly conditioned by the character of the native peoples themselves. The peninsula was a mosaic of warring factions, shifting alliances and peoples of differing cultural traditions, which the Romans were obliged to conquer settlement by settlement and region by region. Rome eventually succeeded through a mixture of superior organisation, persistence and diplomacy, not unmixed with deceit. As Rome had conquered the whole of the Iberian peninsula, she was eventually able to reduce her garrison to one legion and a few auxiliary units.[57] This was very different from the situation in provinces like Britain, whose conquest was never finished and which always needed a large garrison.

FURTHER READING

A good introduction to the conflict which drew Rome into Iberia is provided by B. Caven, *The Punic Wars* (1980). The role of the much-disputed Ebro treaty as a catalyst in the war between Rome and Carthage in Iberia is discussed in Richardson 1986, 20–30. Most of our understanding of the sequence of conquest comes from the writers Polybius, Appian and Livy (available in English in the Loeb Classical Library and Penguin Classics), and is the basis of the work of Sutherland (1939). Knapp (1977) and Badian (1958) discuss Rome's use of diplomacy as a tool of conquest, while Richardson (1986) examines Rome's motives in conquest and the absence of any long-term strategy. The Augustan conquest of the north–west is studied in depth in Syme 1970. Apart from Schulten's excavations at the Numantine camps (1927, 1929), the archaeological evidence lags behind that of the written sources. García y Bellido 1974 is a useful summary of work, while Ulbert's study (1985) of Castra Caecilia is perhaps the most accessible and detailed analysis of a Roman Republican camp in Iberia. The organisation of the Roman army in Iberia under the Republic is studied by Roldán (1974). The significance of the completed conquest of Iberia in the wider strategic organisation of the Early Empire can be appreciated by reading J. Mann, 'The frontiers of the Principate', *Aufsteig und Niedergang der römischen Welt II.I* (1974), 508–33.

3

THE
MAKING OF
THE PROVINCES

After expelling the Carthaginians in 206 BC, Rome inherited a huge expanse of conquered territory in Iberia. She soon started to exploit its enormous mineral and agricultural resources. This was not an easy task, as the Iberian peninsula was a mosaic of different peoples and landscapes: there was no tradition of centralised authority amongst peoples whose energies were largely dissipated in bloody inter-tribal disputes. The Romans therefore gradually evolved a centralised framework of government which guaranteed the military peace, allowed newly conquered peoples to be assimilated, and ultimately made Iberia profitable to them. In achieving this end the Romans literally changed the face of the Iberian landscape. Her extensive network of roads, towns, forts and villas, together with her enormous gold- and silver-mines, are evidence of this and are an indelible feature of modern Spain and Portugal.

The first sign of Rome's long-term intentions towards Iberia came in 197 BC.[1] Iberia was formally divided into two provinces, the largest of which was Hispania Citerior. It comprised the Mediterranean coastal strip from the Pyrenees to, roughly, the modern town of Linares: its capital was perhaps at Carthago Nova. Hispania Ulterior comprised most of modern Andalusia to the east of the lower Guadalquivir, and Corduba was its capital. These provinces marked important cultural differences between the centralised Turdetanian settlements of Ulterior and the scattered Iberian communities within Citerior. Both provinces had a substantial army under the control of the governor, allowing them to contain and, eventually, to counter the threat posed by the Celtiberian and Lusitanian tribes.

The accumulation of conquered territory during the Republic meant that by 27 BC Hispania Ulterior encompassed the whole south and west of the Iberian peninsula. Moreover, all the legions in Iberia were now concentrated

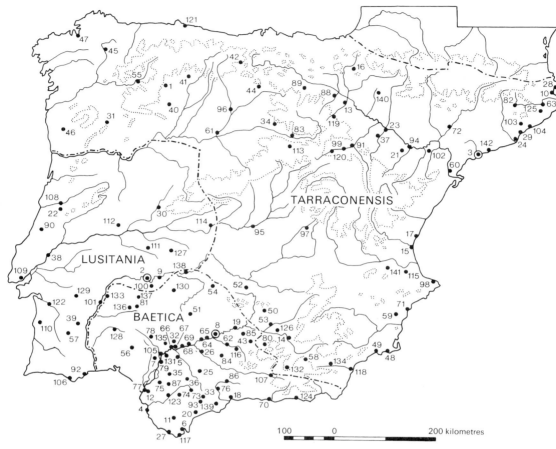

The Spanish provinces in the early empire: map showing the principal sites mentioned in the text.

in the north-west, poised to descend upon the Cantabri and Astures. This made adequate supervision and administration of the provinces difficult. It was in an attempt to rectify this that Augustus split Ulterior into two parts between 16 and 13 BC. The southern province became Hispania Baetica. Its western limit was defined by the river Guadiana, while the other boundaries and the choice of capital remained the same. Territory to the north and west of this became the province of Hispania Lusitania, with its capital at the newly founded Emerita Augusta (modern Mérida). By 5 BC, however, the territory lying to the north of the river Duero (Gallaecia and Asturia) was added to Hispania Citerior, or Tarraconensis, as it was now called.[2] Tarraconensis was the largest of the three Spanish provinces during the early empire. Moreover, the very rich gold-mines in Gallaecia and Asturia made this province especially important to the emperor. The capital was established at Tarraco (modern Tarragona).

Rome's control of Iberia was founded upon a comprehensive network of roads, many of them military in origin. They followed the course of major rivers like the Ebro, Tagus and Duero, allowing the Romans to break up major tribal confederations. The road known as the *camino de la plata* had a similar origin, being used to contain the Lusitani and, later, the armies of Sertorius in Lusitania. Under Augustus it was extended and became a major trunk-road, linking Asturica Augusta (modern Astorga) in the north and Emerita in the south.[3] One of the most important roads in Spain was the Via Augusta, as it was later called, which joined Spain with Gaul and Italy. An important record of this is engraved upon the two bronze Vicarello cups, which were discovered in Italy in 1852 and provide a list of all the towns and road stations between Rome and Gades (modern Cádiz). The Via Augusta was one of many roads that were crucially important to the Roman administration of the provinces. It was used by the state postal system, and the distances between each town were engraved upon milestones.[4]

The early empire saw the completion of the road system. A large part of its layout is recorded on an important third-century route map called the Antonine Itinerary. Unfortunately, however, archaeological work has yet to provide us with a comparable wealth of data. In most cases the major inter-town roads are preserved only in the alignment of their medieval and modern successors.[5] However, magnificent stone bridges, like those at Alcántara and Alconétar (both in Cáceres province), strongly evoke the scale of the enterprise.

In the early second century, therefore, and again in the late first century BC Iberia was subdivided into a series of large administrative units, or provinces. These were further broken down, and served, by a comprehensive road system. It is in this context that the earliest Roman towns were founded. Initially they were intended as supervisory centres; however, they rapidly became focuses for the agricultural or mineral exploitation of given areas, and the main instruments of local government in the provinces.

Rome's promotion of urbanism in Iberia was a gradual process, achieved in three ways: firstly, by the foundation of towns inhabited by Roman citizens, close to important native towns; secondly, by sponsoring the creation of new native settlements; thirdly, by ceding different degrees of autonomy to native communities. Turdetania (roughly, modern Andalusia) was most suited to this, since major settlements like Carmo (modern Carmona) and Carteia (modern El Rocadillo) had been extensively developed during the Carthaginian occupation (228–206 BC). It is no surprise, therefore, to find some of the earliest evidence for the Roman urbanisation of Iberia in this area. For instance, the earliest Roman town in Spain was at Italica, in Hispania Ulterior, near modern Seville. It was a settlement of wounded soldiers founded by Scipio Africanus in 206 BC. Recent excavations have uncovered traces of the town adjacent to the important Turdetanian settlement of Pajar de Artillo, near modern Santiponce.[6] A similar town was founded by the governor Marcus Claudius Marcellus, in 152 BC, at Corduba on the upper Guadalquivir river. This was a mixed settlement of Romans and Turdetanians, close to a Turdetanian community.[7]

The most important Roman towns were the *coloniae*. These were formal settlements of Roman citizens – in most cases retired legionaries – with individual plots of land. Excavations suggest that one of the earliest *coloniae* in Spain may have been at Emporion (Empúries). It may have been intended as an example of Roman urban planning to be copied in a peaceful and prosperous part of Iberia. It has been suggested that this *colonia* may have been founded by Marcus Iunius Silanus, the governor of Citerior (113 BC),

Detail of the Roman bridge over the river Guadiana at Emerita (modern Mérida). This was probably built in the Augustan period and bears traces of several later reconstructions.

at the end of the second century BC. The Roman garrison building on the plateau behind the Greek port was demolished and replaced by a large monumental complex. This was dominated by a large *capitolium* and enclosed by a porticoed passage on three sides. It overlooked an enormous open space, which served as the forum, or market-place, and small shops were built along its southern face. These buildings comprised the religious and commercial heart of the new town and lay at the intersection of the two main roads, the *cardo* and *decumanus maximus*. The whole town was

Roman gateway, possibly of late Republican date, leading into the *colonia* of Norba Caesarina (modern Cáceres).

enclosed within a monumental stone wall (700 by 300 metres). If the town was a *colonia*, as a recent study suggests, then its inhabitants might have been granted Latin status, an important step on the way to Roman citizenship.[8]

The inhabitants of the *colonia* at Carteia enjoyed similar status. However, the circumstances of this foundation were different. Livy records that it was founded in 171 BC as a special concession by the Roman Senate to the 4,000 sons '. . . of Roman soldiers and Spanish women between whom there was no legal right of marriage'.[9]

The establishment of *coloniae* was part of Rome's attempt to break up the pattern of native settlement and to establish new centres. However, a few Iberian towns were given encouragement, even though there was no formal settlement of Roman citizens. The earliest of these was at Turris Lascutana (modern Alcalá de los Gazules), in Ulterior, in 189 BC. The event was commemorated on a small bronze plaque which records that the governor Lucius Aemilius Paullus decreed that the inhabitants of this site, who had been dependent upon Hasta Regia (modern Mesa de Asta), should formally take possession of the fields and town which they had hitherto occupied.[10] There were similar foundations at Gracchuris (modern Alfaro) and Iliturgis (modern Mengíbar)[11] by Tiberius Sempronius Gracchus in 180/179 BC and at Valentia (modern Valencia) and Brutobriga (location unknown) by Decimus Iunius Brutus in 138–133.[12] Very little is known about the layout and organisation of these towns. However, excavations at Pompaelo (modern Pamplona), founded by Pompey the Great in 75–74 BC, suggest they were small and unimpressive in their early stages.

Until the later first century BC the majority of people not living in the country were in settlements fundamentally unchanged since the Roman conquest. However, it was during the second and first centuries BC that a hierarchy of settlement began to emerge. Based upon the relationship of individual communities to Rome, it was recognised in the degrees of autonomy ceded to different towns. These then served as important centres for the dispensation of justice and the collection of taxes. The Greek settlement at Emporion was recognised as a 'free ally' on account of its long friendship with Rome and was permitted to retain its own laws and internal administration.[13] This arrangement is also reflected in the town's predominantly Greek town plan. Saguntum, Malaca (modern Málaga) and Epora (modern Montoro) had all signed treaties with Rome and were exempted from taxes and interference from the governor; they, too, betray little influence of Roman planning before the end of the first century BC. Gades (modern Cádiz) enjoyed similar privileges and retained traces of its Carthaginian system of government during the first century BC.[14] The layout of the town also retained a strongly Semitic flavour. A Punic-style temple to Melkaart–Hercules–Gaditanus still stood during the reign of Claudius (AD 41–54). The Roman town of Gades was distinct and founded prior to the late first century BC. One prominent local magnate was L. Cornelius Balbus, a close associate of Julius Caesar. He was a notable benefactor of

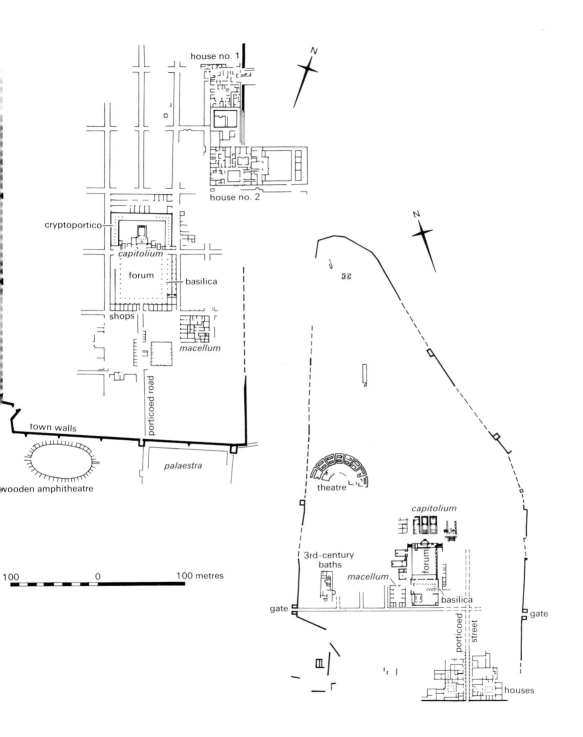

house no. 1

house no. 2

N

N

cryptoportico

capitolium

forum

basilica

shops

macellum

porticoed road

town walls

wooden amphitheatre

palaestra

100   0   100 metres

theatre

capitolium

3rd-century
baths

macellum

forum

basilica

gate

gate

porticoed
street

houses

the town, where traces of a theatre and amphitheatre have been found beneath the modern Barrio del Pópolo.[15]

The commonest form of native town was the *civitas stipendiaria* – a town which regularly paid tribute and other exactions to Rome. The Elder Pliny records that there were 291 such communities throughout Hispania by the early first century AD.[16] Their 'tributary' relationship to Rome is well illustrated by the many Iberian coins which these communities were obliged to mint during the second and first centuries BC, perhaps to pay the legions in Spain.[17] Most of them were similar in size and weight to coins issued at Rome. They carried the names of the issuing communities, spelt out in Iberian or Punic characters; by the later first century BC these had given way to Latin.

The obverses and reverses of Iberian coins from the mints at (*from top to bottom*) Kese, Carmo and Nertobriga.

The magnificent site at Lacipo (near Casares), near Málaga, is one example of the layout of a *civitas stipendiaria*, built on a long, narrow plateau towards the end of the first century BC. The walls and some of the internal buildings are Turdetanian in style and construction; however, traces of a large public building and a monumental marble inscription to the deified Augustus reflect the marginally later, Roman influence.[18] The site at Cabezo de Alcalá (near Azaila), in the lower Ebro valley, exhibits a stronger Roman influence

on its layout before its destruction in 49 BC. Baths, houses and a temple have all been discovered, flanking the roads of this stark plateau town.[19] At a later date the native community at Conimbriga (modern Condeixa a Velha) went to extraordinary lengths to embrace the outward signs of Roman life. The inhabitants levelled the centre of their settlement and built a temple dedicated to the worship of the emperor Augustus within a large forum complex with administrative buildings.[20]

By the mid-first century BC, therefore, few Roman towns had been founded in Spain, and the spread of the Roman way of life was restricted to the Ebro valley, the east coast of Citerior and the greater part of Ulterior. This picture was completely transformed by the mid-first century AD. Between the deaths of Julius Caesar (44 BC) and Augustus (AD 14) legionary veterans were settled in *coloniae* throughout the western Mediterranean. Nine were founded in Baetica, eight in Tarraconensis and four in Lusitania.

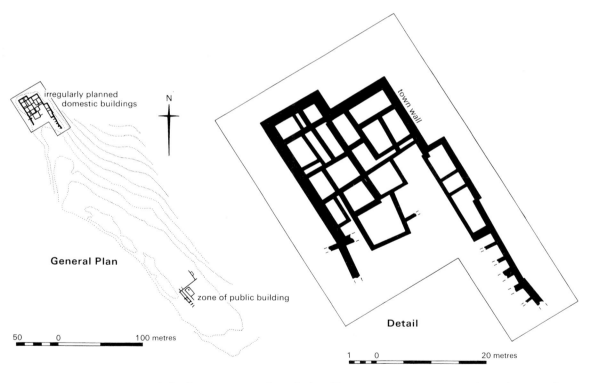

Plan of the hilltown, and *civitas stipendiaria*, at Lacipo (Casares), in southern Baetica.

A further two were founded in Tarraconensis – one a titular colony under the emperor Tiberius (AD 14–31), and the other under Galba (AD 69).

These *coloniae* invariably were rectangular in plan and were surrounded by a circuit of walls. The Augustan *colonia* at Caesaraugusta (modern Zaragoza) covered sixty hectares and was enclosed by monumental stone walls fortified by semicircular bastions. The walls emphasised the town's prestige but also reflected its military origins: the original settlers were discharged veterans of the IIII Macedonica, VI Victrix and X Gemina legions.[21] Barcino (modern Barcelona) was another Augustan military foundation: traces of its walls survive, enclosing an area of 10.4 hectares.[22] Augusta Emerita (modern Mérida) was the most spectacular of all, especially since it was also the capital of Lusitania. One of the best-preserved Roman towns in Spain, it was founded by Publius Carisius in 25 BC with veterans from the V Alaudae and X Gemina legions and was later boosted with a batch of settlers from Rome in AD 69. One of its most remarkable features is the survival of a very extensive stone drainage system beneath the modern town. This has allowed archaeologists to trace the typical Roman 'grid-iron' street plan whereby the town was divided into regular blocks (*insulae*).[23] The colony was also lavished with a huge circus, amphitheatre and theatre for the entertainment of the populace: indeed, the theatre was built by Augustus' famous general and friend, Marcus Vipsanius Agrippa, as is commemorated in an inscription above one of its exits. The most impressive building of all, however, was the temple dedicated to the worship of the emperor, which still stands in the centre of modern Mérida.

The *colonia* founded at Tarraco by Julius Caesar was different. It was installed in a town which had been a centre of Roman power for nearly 200 years. Instead of the imposition of the traditional rectangular plan a Roman forum and a theatre were built near the port on the site of the pre-Roman settlement.

In 44 BC a group of settlers from the poorer parts of Rome were settled in a *colonia* within the Turdetanian settlement at Urso (modern Osuna). This was situated on top of an enormous plateau to the south of Astigi (modern Écija) and enjoyed a stunning view over the surrounding countryside. In 1870 five magnificent bronze tablets were discovered here, which formed part of the town's constitution, or the law of the Colonia Genetiva Iulia Urbanorum of Urso (modern Osuna). This has given us an almost unique glimpse of the guide-lines which Rome laid down for the running of a *colonia*.[24]

The executive body, or *ordo*, was modelled on the Senate at Rome. It was made up of senators (*decuriones*), whose many tasks included supervision of the town's finances and ensuring that all public buildings were properly maintained. They also appointed *patroni* and *hospites* for the *colonia*: these were, respectively, influential people and agents of the community who furthered the town's interests within the province. Every year magistrates were elected as senior executive officers, or duumvirs, who were responsible for most jurisdiction; they were assisted by aediles, who heard less important cases and maintained public order. The Urso charter also states that these magistrates had to pay for public entertainment during their term of office. It seems that the distribution of free food and gifts, and the holding of gladiatorial fights were popular in the town. However, the discovery of a theatre at the site may suggest that the inhabitants also had more cultivated tastes. Clearly, these magistrates had to be wealthy: the charter states that they had to own sufficient land for it to act as a pledge to the colony. This ensured that power in the town remained in the hands of a small oligarchy. The popular assembly had very little power and was limited to electing *decuriones* and municipal priests (*augures* and *pontifices*).

The spread of Roman urbanism during this period was further encouraged by the gradual promotion of all kinds of native settlement to the rank of *municipium*. This meant that all inhabitants of the town were granted Latin status, and upon completion of their office magistrates were granted Roman citizenship. Julius Caesar and Augustus began the process, promoting four Baetican towns, four in Lusitania and seven in Tarraconensis. Claudius (AD 41–54) founded another in Baetica, and Vespasian (AD 69–79) took this process to its logical conclusion by granting Latin status to every community in Spain.[25]

One of the bronze tablets bearing the charter of the *colonia* of Urso (modern Osuna).

Vespasian's measure gave a tremendous boost to the spread of Roman

towns. To date the discovery of inscriptions has confirmed that at least eighty Spanish towns successfully applied for Latin status. The lure of Roman citizenship and the ability to participate in the public life of the empire enticed many local aristocrats into joining the local *ordo* and becoming magistrates, despite the financial and social obligations entailed.

It is no surprise, therefore, to discover native towns ambitiously redeveloping their town centres as soon as they became *municipia*. Baelo (modern Bolonia), for instance, became a *municipium* under Claudius.[26] Earlier buildings were demolished, and the centre of the town was rebuilt on a scale which still impresses today's visitor. The forum is the central feature, built from large limestone slabs and surrounded by public buildings on every side. The municipal lawcourt, or basilica, is situated to the south; the town archives were housed in a small attached building. The local senate house, or *curia*, was located to the west, adjacent to temples of local divinities. On the east side excavations have revealed a row of shops and the edge of a large private house. The whole complex was dominated by three magnificent temples, each dedicated to Jupiter, Juno and Minerva.[27] There was a similar transformation at Conimbriga, in Lusitania, where the

The forum and basilica (background) of 1st-century AD Baelo (modern Bolonia), seen from the *capitolium*.

Augustan complex was replaced by buildings of far greater architectural sophistication. Indeed, this activity occurred throughout the provinces, at towns like Rhode (modern Roses), Baetulo (modern Badalona), Capera (modern Caparra), Aquae Flaviae (modern Chaves) and the small iron-mining town of Munigua (Castillo de Mulva).[28] The inhabitants of the Baetican hill-town of Sabora (modern Cañete la Real) requested permission from the emperor Vespasian to rebuild their town in the lowlands, which were better suited to the regularities of Roman planning.[29]

The internal running of these towns was virtually identical with that of the *coloniae*. Fragments of bronze inscriptions containing the clauses of municipal charters have been found at Emporiae, Clunia (modern Coruña del Conde), Italica, Malaca (modern Málaga), Salpensa (modern Facialcazar) and, most recently, at Irni (near Algamitas, Seville). The last three were Flavian *municipia*, and their charters are amongst the most important examples surviving from the Roman world.[30]

The *coloniae* had set the example of the Roman way of life, while *municipia* had brought it within reach of many provincials. Available evidence suggests that Baetica derived the greatest advantage from this: she far surpassed Tarraconensis and Lusitania in the richness of Roman culture. As Strabo commented during the first century AD, 'the Turdetanians, however, and particularly those that live along the Baetis (Guadalquivir), have completely changed over to the Roman mode of life, not even remembering their own language any more'.[31] Indeed, the latest and most mature example of a *colonia* in Spain was founded at Italica by the emperor Hadrian. It was an entirely new town, built to the north of the earlier settlement. Its enormous public buildings, wide streets and richly decorated houses represent the urban ideal to which most of the earliest Roman towns in Spain had aspired.

By the early imperial period, therefore, Rome had recast the Iberian landscape into a network of semi-autonomous communities: these towns were the administrative cells of Baetica, Lusitania and Tarraconensis. Overall supervision was in the hands of a centralised authority in each province. For most of the Republic the highest authority in each province was the praetor, appointed by the Senate at Rome. He was a senator who governed for one and, later, two years. In the first century BC he was replaced by more senior officials, an ex-consul or ex-praetor. Most of the governor's time was taken up with military campaigns, which provided him with an opportunity to amass considerable booty, build up a large Iberian clientele, and acquire a record impressive enough to enhance his political career at Rome. The governor was also responsible for a wide range of administrative roles, some of which were delegated to his subordinates, the quaestors and prefects. The most important of these tasks was obviously the collection of revenue. After the quaestors had prepared estimates, private contractors, or *publicani*, bid for the contract to collect the *stipendium* (money tax) and *vicensuma* (corn levy) for the governor. After paying the agreed amount, the *publicani* collected the taxes. Such a system was hardly efficient and was open to abuse at every level. For instance, Livy records how in 171 BC delegates from the Spanish provinces visited Rome to complain about the greed of the governors Marcus Titinius, Marcus Matienus and Publius Furius Philus: they had been manipulating the price of grain. The Senate promised to correct their abuses, although the accused managed to evade justice.[32]

Another important duty of the provincial governor was the delegation of justice to the provincials. Invariably, he would visit major towns in the province during the winter months. For example, in the early first century BC Valerius Flaccus, the governor of Citerior, intervened in a land dispute between the Salluiensis and Allavonensis tribes. This is recorded on a remarkable bronze document called the Tabula Contrebiensis, which was found at the town of Contrebia Belaisca (modern Botorrita, Zaragoza) in the Ebro valley.[33] Frequently, however, this kind of work was left to the provincial quaestor: Julius Caesar toured the towns of Ulterior in this role in 68 BC.

After the reorganisation of the provinces by Augustus, this system was broadly retained in Baetica. In theory it was still governed by the Roman Senate. The governor was a proconsul, whose appointment by the Senate was an important stage in his political career at Rome. His main tasks were the delegation of justice and addressing delegations from towns, or the province itself. The financial officer was the quaestor, who was now responsible for the collection of the direct taxes, a tax on produce (*tributum soli*) and a poll-tax (*tributum capitis*), and indirect taxes like the customs tax (*portorium*), the *vicesima hereditatum*, or inheritance tax, paid by Roman citizens, and the *vicesima libertatis*, or tax on the freeing of slaves, established by Augustus. Inscriptions commemorating the quaestor and officials administering those taxes have been found at Corduba and the other provincial capitals. From the beginning of the imperial era the freedom of this official was hindered by the procurator, or official appointed by the emperor to look after imperial property in the province.[34]

On the other hand, Lusitania and Tarraconensis were each governed by a representative of the emperor, the Legatus Augusti Propraetore. He received his instructions from the emperor and served for an indefinite length of time. In directly appointing the governor of Tarraconensis the emperor was ensured control of the Roman legions stationed there. The financial supervision of these 'imperial' provinces was in the hands of the *procurator provinciae*, appointed by the emperor.

Despite all these measures the huge size of the Spanish provinces made the efficient supervision of communities difficult. In the early first century AD, therefore, the Romans brought communities closer together by establishing the centralised Provincial Council, at the capital of each province. Ostensibly this met to promote the Imperial Cult, or state religion (see Chapter 7); however, it was also an important platform for provincials to voice their grievances and to receive instructions from the governor.

Delegates were drawn from a number of judicial districts, or *conventus*, in each province. Each of these had a capital, which was a centre for the annual dispensation of justice by the governor. There were seven of these in Tarraconensis – Tarraco, Carthago Nova, Caesaraugusta, Clunia, Asturica Augusta, Bracara Augusta and Lucus Augusti; four in Baetica – Corduba, Hispalis, Astigi and Gades; three in Lusitania – Emerita, Pax Iulia (Beja) and Scallabis (Santarém).[35]

The peace in the Spanish provinces under the empire was upheld by small garrisons at Corduba, Tarraco and Emerita. There was also a small fleet or mobile land force based at Tarraco, which protected the east coast as far north as Blandae in the first century AD. The main military presence, however, was in north-west Tarraconensis. By the first century AD the Roman army had undergone considerable rationalisation. The legions had begun to assume formal titles, and after the end of the Cantabrian wars (29–19 BC) only the x Gemina ('the twin'), IIII Macedonica (reflecting duty in Macedonia), and the VI Victrix (referring to its victories in Spain) remained

The Augustan provinces of Hispania, showing the *conventus* divisions and capitals, and the road network.

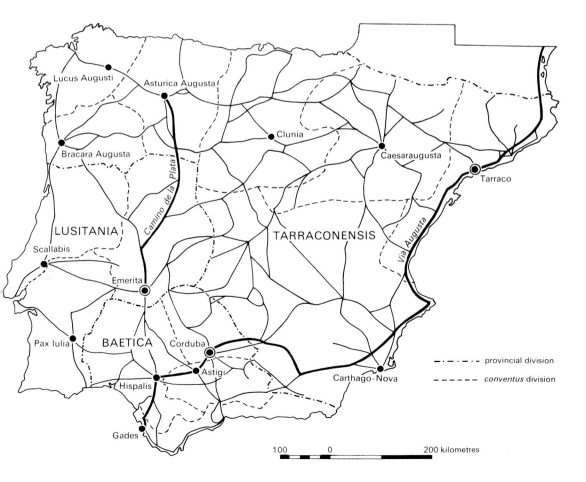

in Hispania. The fortress of the x Gemina has been discovered at Rosinos de Vidriales (Zamora) and was rectangular in plan, covering 18.6 hectares. The fortress of the vi Victrix has not yet been found. However, the discovery of inscriptions defining the territory of the IIII Macedonica suggests that it was located at Aguilar del Campóo: the vi Victrix was probably stationed at Legio (modern León).[36]

The legions now formed a professional army composed of Roman citizens. From the early first century AD, however, many recruits were drawn from the provinces. In Hispania colonies like Astigi, Tucci and Emerita in Baetica and Lusitania provided a ready pool of Roman citizen recruits. They served side by side with Italians in provinces as far away as Britain, the Germanies and Pannonia. From later in the century Spanish recruits were drawn progressively from towns like Segisama (modern Sasamón), Lucus and Asturica, in north-western Tarraconensis. From the middle of the second century AD however, Spanish recruits ceased to serve outside Spain and settled in the vicinity of the legion in which they served at Legio.[37]

Another important change during the late Republic and early empire was the formalisation of allied infantry and cavalry into regular cohorts (500 men apiece) and *alae* (500 men apiece) of auxiliary troops (*auxilia*). These were recruited from non-Roman citizens in the less-Romanised provinces and often took the name of native peoples. In north-western Tarraconensis, for instance, there were units of Astures (Asturum), Callaici (Callaecorum) and Cantabri (Cantabrorum), raised locally and serving overseas. Upon completion of service Roman citizenship was one of the rewards (from the reign of Claudius onwards). The only auxiliary forts known in Hispania have been discovered at La Cidadela (La Coruña) in the third century AD (*cohors* I Celtiberiorum) and at Rosinos de Vidriales (Zamora) which lay on the site of the legionary fortress of the x Gemina, and housed the *ala* II Flavia. A remarkable stone fort has been discovered on the Guadiana, on the border of Baetica and Lusitania, at the Castelo do Lousa (Mourão).[38]

Auxiliary and legionary camps in north-western Tarraconensis were integrated into a road network connecting Bracara Augusta, Lucus Augusti and Asturica Augusta. This was the least Romanised part of Hispania during the early empire, and the garrison protected the imperial gold-mines in Asturia and Gallaecia, as well as keeping the peace. Indeed, an Asturian uprising during the reign of Nero (AD 54–69) was the only serious challenge to its authority. However, there was always a danger that the concentration of these forces in the north-west might tempt a governor of Tarraconensis into challenging central authority. This happened in AD 69 when Servius Sulpicius Galba was proclaimed emperor by the vi Victrix and left Spain with the entire legionary garrison. His venture was shortlived, for he was soon defeated by the emperor Vespasian, who reduced the garrison to one legion, the vii Gemina, henceforth stationed at León.

Between 200 BC and AD 200, therefore, Rome evolved an administrative framework which, as far as possible, was adapted to the size and diversity of Iberia. Peace amongst the Iberians was maintained, and under the control of the provincial governor's staff all communities participated in the exploitation of the country for Rome's benefit.

Most ancient writers saw the Iberian peninsula as a very rich source of precious metals and agricultural produce. In the first century AD Pliny the Elder remarked that '...Next to Italy...I would place Spain...all its productive regions are rich in crops, oil, wine, horses, and every kind of ore...'.[39] Rome was quick to recognise this and, short of means to finance its wars throughout the Mediterranean, lost no time in tapping the mines that she had inherited from the Carthaginians. During the Republic many silver-mines in southern Citerior and Ulterior formed Rome's most immediate source of revenue from Iberia.

Between 206 and 198 BC the Roman state received 6,316 Roman pounds of gold bullion and 311,622 Roman pounds of silver from Spain. Much of the silver came from mines around Carthago Nova, which during the second century BC may have produced the equivalent of 2,500 silver coins (*drachmae*) per day for the Roman state.[40] Much of this was used in Rome's silver coinage, the denarius. Production of denarii rose sharply after the mid-second century BC and reached a peak of 75 million in 90 BC.[41]

The extensive remains that survive today illustrate the huge scale of the ancient workings. At La Fortuna mine, near Mazarrón, galleries were cut up to 1,800 metres along the argentiferous seams. The working conditions for the miners were extremely cramped, and examples of their tools and esparto-grass buckets have been discovered. After extraction the rock bearing silver ore was crushed by stone mills and then washed to remove the surrounding rock. The silver was released from the lead ore by a toasting process called cupellation. At the mine of Las Herrerias no fewer than 276,000 tonnes of slag from such operations have been identified. All mines belonged to the state and were leased out to private contractors, or *publicani*. Exploitation of the mines ended in the second century AD.[42]

Lead was an important by-product of the silver-mines. At Carthago Nova it was formed into ingots weighing up to 35 kg, and was exported throughout the western Mediterranean.[43] These are often stamped with names of private contractors, such as C. MESSI L.F. [CAIUS MESSIUS] and L. PLANI L.F. PUSSINI [LUCIUS PLANIUS], who were of Italian origin, and occasionally also magistrates at Carthago Nova. Sometimes they formed private companies.

The Sierra Morena mountains were another important source of metals. Many mines were worked between the late second and mid-first centuries BC, and again during the first and second centuries AD. In the mid-first century BC mining was disrupted by the civil war of 49–45 BC, during which time Italian mining contractors could have invested their money in forming estates in Baetica, a region where there was to develop large-scale production of olive oil along the lower Guadalquivir in the first century AD. One of the largest Sierra Morena mines is at El Centenillo (modern Baños de La Encina, Jaén).[44] Here two major groups of argentiferrous lead (galena) seams have been discovered. Roman galleries were cut into these for a distance of up to 1,150 metres and depths of up to 200 metres. Large smelting areas were discovered near by; in addition, kilns and baths for the preparation of the silver and lead ores were found, together with store-rooms and the miners' accommodation. There were other important silver-mines at La Loba (modern Fuenteovejuna, Córdoba) and at Diogenes (Ciudad Real). Castulo (Cazlona), the capital of the Oretani, was the major mining centre in this part of Spain. All mining within a thirty-five-kilometre radius of the town was undertaken by a private company. Once the ore was produced it was either sent down the Guadalquivir to Hispalis or Gades, or it was sent overland to Carthago Nova.

Although Rome clearly profited from these mines, the mining contractors also stood to gain substantial profits. Quintus Torius Culleo, a native of Castulo in the first century AD, was probably a mining contractor. On an inscription found at Castulo he recorded that he completely rebuilt the town walls and the road leading from Castulo to the cinnabar mine at Sisapo (Almadén), gave the town the land on which the public baths stood, and remitted 10,000,000 sesterces owed to him by the town. The total value of these gifts has been calculated at 20,000,000 sesterces, the largest recorded private donation in the western Roman Empire.[45]

Rome's need for precious metals grew unabated during the empire. Fortunately, the conquest of northern Lusitania and north-western Tar-raconensis in the late first century BC had opened up vast new resources of gold, silver, copper and iron. From the mid-first century AD onwards Rome concentrated her attentions on these areas as well as the rich silver and iron deposits to the north of Onuba (modern Huelva) and the western Sierra Morena. At the same time the old Republican mines around Carthago-Nova, Castulo and eastern Baetica were gradually abandoned. It is not known whether this was due to exhaustion of the mines, or because they were uneconomic.

The size and large number of Roman gold-mines in north-western Tarraconensis are ample proof of Rome's financial needs during the early empire. A recent survey listed 231 known gold-mines, which cluster in the modern provinces of Asturias and León. Pliny the Elder states that the mines in Asturia, Gallaecia and Lusitania yielded 20,000 Roman pounds of gold per month – a sizeable proportion of the state treasury's income.[46]

Gold in the north-west was found in deposits which were geologically distinct from those of silver in the Republican mines. It occurred either in shallow, or deep, river terrace gravels, or in hard rock deposits. Various techniques were developed to extract the gold ore. The most spectacular, called *arrugia*, is described by the Elder Pliny who witnessed it personally. This method was quite possibly used at the magnificent site of Las Médulas, in the modern province of León. The Romans built two huge water-tanks overlooking the mining area: these were supplied with millions of litres brought to the site from up to twenty kilometres away by six aqueducts,

Aerial view showing the seating-banks at the south side of the Roman circus at Tarraco (modern Tarragona) surviving amongst later buildings.

Pylons and arches of the
Roman aqueduct of Els
Ferreres, near Tarraco
(modern Tarragona).

each two to three metres wide. Tunnels were cut beneath the hill containing the gold deposit until it collapsed into a vast mound of rubble. The Romans then constructed a series of wood-lined canals in front of the rubble: heather was placed inside them. The gates of the water-tanks were opened, and the water rushed over the rubble, collecting the gold particles and depositing them in the canals. They were caught by the heather which was later burnt to release them. A similar system was used for shallower deposits, with the emphasis upon a less spectacular, constant stream flowing through a series of criss-cross gullies. It is not clear who worked these open-cast mines; however, it is probable that in the early days those people who worked the mines were Cantabri, enslaved during the Cantabrian war. All the mined gold would have been collected together, sent by road to Asturica Augusta, and then dispatched southwards to Emerita, Hispalis and Gades, along the road today known as the *camino de la plata*.

This great road passed close to the other great source of metals during the early empire – the mines of Río Tinto, which were scattered over a huge area (85 by 34 kilometres) to the north of Onuba, Niebla and Tharsis. The Romans were mainly interested in silver, although gold, lead, iron and copper are also found here. One of the principal mining settlements was at Río Tinto itself, which is estimated to have produced over 2,000,000 tonnes of silver ore in antiquity. The Roman settlement at Río Tinto, known as Corta Lago, was three-quarters of a kilometre in length. It has yielded the upstanding remains of buildings and, to the north-west, La Dehesa cemetery which contained both rich and poor burials. Early excavations uncovered Roman mining machinery, including a wooden water-lifting wheel and gallery frames. This mine gained especial importance from the Flavian period onwards, and it is probable that silver extracted here was one of the principal sources of bullion for the silver coins (denarii) minted at Rome in the early empire. It has been suggested that an invasion of Baetica by Moorish tribesmen from Mauretania in AD 171 disrupted mining at the site and, as a consequence, caused a shortage of silver coinage from the reign of Commodus (AD 180–92) onwards.[47]

This suggestion does give an idea of the importance of large mines to the imperial government. It is hardly surprising, therefore, that under the early empire Rome soon took steps to ensure greater control over the working of mines. The huge scale of gold-mines in the north-west suggests that they were state-owned and run from the end of the conquest. Indeed, their importance was such that a separate financial official (procurator) was created for Asturia and Gallaecia by the emperor Vespasian. One holder of the post, Lucius Arruntius Maximus, is commemorated on an inscription from Aquae Flaviae. By the second century individual mines were under the control of lessees, freedmen, procurators, who could count upon the assistance of soldiers stationed in the north-west. Elsewhere in Iberia the state only gradually gained control of the smaller and older mines from private contractors. The emperor Tiberius (AD 14–31), for instance, con-

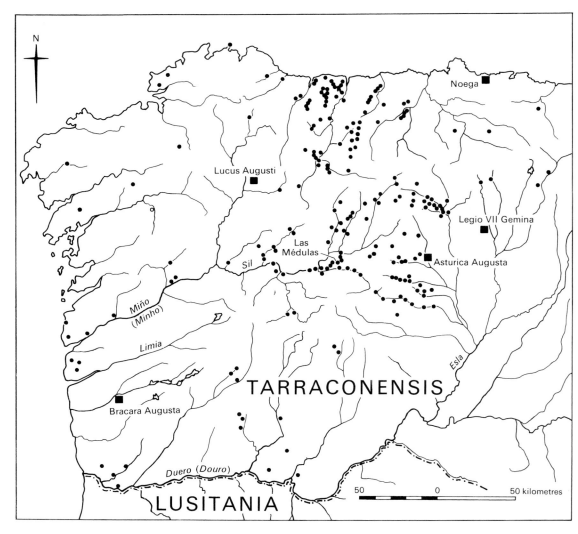

The known distribution of Roman gold-mines in north-west Tarraconensis (after Bird 1984).

fiscated the immensely rich silver-mines of the Corduban millionaire Sextus Marius, after having him executed on a trumped-up charge of treason. The second century saw procurators supervising individual mines, as in the north-west. This is illustrated explicitly by the two bronze plaques discovered at Aljustrel in southern Portugal. Aljustrel was a large source of copper and silver during the first three centuries AD. The plaques date to the mid-second century and contain the regulations of the mining community at Vipasca. These make it clear that the procurator at Vipasca received payments for the right to mine from private contractors, as well as half the ore they extracted. He had an attendant force of soldiers and slaves, and was responsible for the supervision of mining and the overall running of the community.[48]

By comparison Rome's exploitation of Iberia's agricultural resources was less methodical. Classical sources make it clear that when the Romans arrived in Spain the Iberians were producing surplus grain and trading it for luxury items with the Greeks and the Carthaginians. An important change came some time after 175 BC, when the Iberian communities were probably spurred to increase their agricultural output by the introduction of more regular Roman taxation.

The development of a Romanised countryside was hastened by the foundation of Roman towns, situated within their own land, or *territorium*.

The layout and extent of the Las Médulas gold-mine (after Bird 1984).

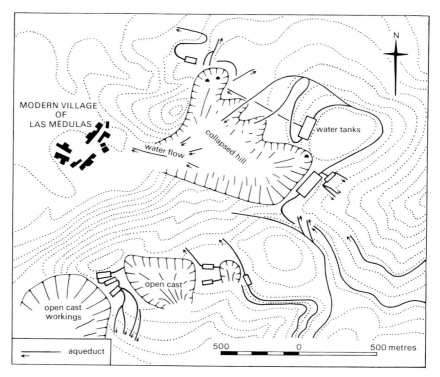

The extent of this territory varied with different towns: the northern limit of Tarraco, for instance, was marked by a triumphal arch at Barà on the Via Augusta. This is more than eighteen kilometres from the town and was originally built in the Augustan period.[49] The western and southern limits are not known but were probably a similar distance from the town.

The *territorium* at Emerita covered a far larger area. A unique description by the Roman writers Frontinus and Hyginus, together with the discovery of boundary stones (*termini Augustales*), demonstrates that it extended 120 kilometres to the east (Valdecaballeros) and 120 kilometres to the south (Montemolín); it also included the town of Turgallium (modern Trujillo) to the north. The veterans were allotted parcels of land measuring 20 by 40 *actus* (710 by 1,420 metres) towards the edge of the territory. The banks of the Guadiana were declared to be public land, while the rest of the territory was turned into communal pasture and woodland.[50]

Coloniae were established on state land, and the land allocated to support the town was often divided up into allotments for the colonists. This system, called 'centuriation', was probably employed at *coloniae* and occasionally *municipia* too. In theory this meant that the land was subdivided into squares of 20 *actus* (710 metres square), whose orientation derived from a prolongation of the main streets (*decumanus* and *cardo*) in the *coloniae*. Land divided in this way was farmed by the original colonists, or lessees, to produce the grain, olives and vegetables needed for payment of tax, or by the *colonia* itself. Moreover, this division of the land into equal blocks and subdivisions aided the compilation of land surveys for taxation. Archaeological work has uncovered traces of centuriation around the Augustan *municipium* and later *colonia* at Italica.[51] Here it has been estimated that the town territory was quite small and divided into 100 *centuriae* measuring 20 by 24 *actus* (710 by 852 metres), with 80 individual parcels of land in each. The centuriation was oriented north-west to south-east and based upon a prolongation of the main street (*decumanus*) of the town.

It is still not clear how widespread centuriation was in Spain. Examples have been identified in the vicinity of such town as Carmo (modern Carmona), at the Augustan *colonia* at Asigi (modern Écija) in Baetica, near Basti (modern Baza), the Augustan *colonia* at Illici (modern Elche), along the Via Augusta between Valentia and Saguntum, and to the south of the Augustan *municipium* at Dertosa (modern Tortosa) in eastern Tarraconensis. However, it would be a mistake to suppose that it was employed in every town. In many parts of the peninsula pre-Roman traditions of land division would have persisted. Columella, for instance, states that in Baetica the *actus* was called the *acnua*, a name recalling the Turdetanian system of land measurement. In the north-west, indeed, where the Celtic tradition was strong, one would expect that pre-conquest land divisions remained in use.[52]

Roman farms, or villas, proliferated from the later second century BC onwards. Surveys along the lower Guadalquivir valley, the upper Ebro basin and along the Catalan coast have located many sites and give us some idea about the intensity of farming. Unfortunately, most of these sites are known to us only as scattered finds of pottery or building materials; however, some have been excavated. Villas at Camallera (Gerona), Sentromà (near Badalona), Constanti (near Tarragona), Hostal Nou (near Balaguer) and La Salut (near Sabadell) in east Tarraconensis were founded between the second century BC and the first century AD.[53] They were essentially farms with rows of large storage jars enclosed within stone walls, with few residential buildings. Other villas, like Vilauba (near Banyoles) and Ca L'Alemany (near Badalona), had more developed residential areas, often decorated with wall plaster.

In north-west Tarraconensis and northern Lusitania the relatively late conquest by Rome meant that villas did not usually appear until after the end of the first century AD. Most of these had a similarly simple layout, like, for instance, the strip-buildings at Las Murias de Beloño (near Gijón) and at Póvoa de Varzim (near Porto).[54] On the other hand, the villa of Prado (Valladolid), near Septimanca (modern Simancas), was on a grander scale with a portico, mosaic floors and heated rooms.

The evidence for southern Tarraconensis and Baetica is less clear. The villas of El Rihuete, Los Ruices and Cabo de Palos (Murcia),[55] near Carthago Nova, recall those further north, having blocks of residential rooms decorated with simple mosaics set into pink concrete. Those at the latter site were enclosed within two adjacent galleries. An early second-century villa discovered near Marbella (Málaga) had a large courtyard (16 by 7 metres) surrounded by a portico decorated with luxurious figured and geometric mosaic floors.

The site of Cabezo de Alcalá (Azaila), an Iberian hillfort whose layout and architecture bear very clear traces of Roman influence prior to its abandonment in the 1st century BC.

These buildings are the only tangible evidence for the many private estates that would have comprised the greater part of the territory around towns, land belonging to the state or in private domains. Surviving inscriptions and literary evidence show that most estates were defined by natural features, which have long since disappeared. There is also little evidence

for the identity of landholders. During the later Republic the Classical sources tell us about resident and absentee landlords, such as Lucius Domitius Ahenobarbus. Much, however, was in the hands of local aristocrats who lived in the towns and profited from the rents paid by tenants on their estates. Inscriptions mentioning one such family group, the Baebii from Saguntum, have been found on many first- and second-century AD sites to the north of Saguntum. In Baetica the family of Lucius Servilius Pollio, from Carmo (modern Carmona), owned olive-growing estates near the town of Arva (modern Peña de la Sal). There seems to be little doubt that the shares of land belonging to such local notables grew through inheritance. Other estates could pass into the control of the emperor, like those of the second-century senator Valerius Vegetus, and were administered by a procurator.

It was against this background that the agricultural potential of the Spanish provinces began to be realised. Grain was one of their most important products during the Republic and early empire. This was especially true of Baetica where it was grown in mixed plantations of vines and olives. In 49 BC the governor of Ulterior, Marcus Terentius Varro, levied a huge quantity of grain from the province for his troops, and milked it again by raising a further 120,000 *modii* from resident Roman citizens. At a later date Gades sent sufficient grain to Rome to be able to alleviate a major food shortage. Grain was also important in north-eastern Tarraconensis, especially amongst communities in the vicinity of Ilerda (modern Lleida) and in the Ebro valley. Olive oil was another major commodity and one for which the Spanish provinces gained great renown during the early empire. Its main production area was the Guadalquivir valley in Baetica, especially between Hispalis and Corduba. Production and export of Baetican olive oil had begun by the middle of the first century AD. By the later second century this had assumed such a large volume that it became a very important element in state supplies to the city of Rome and the army on the frontiers. Moreover, the discovery of stone olive-crushers and oil presses at towns like Baelo, Munigua, Castulo and Tarraco, as well as in rural sites throughout eastern Tarraconensis, confirms that oil played an important role in the domestic economy too. Wine was manufactured in the hinterlands of towns like Emporiae, Iluro (modern Mataró), Baetulo, Barcino, Tarraco, Saguntum, Valentia and Carteia, attracting clientele throughout the western empire. Finally, the rich marine resources of the Iberian coast were also exploited, producing famous, spicy fish sauces during the early empire. Many of the characteristic fermentation vats have been discovered close to ports in southern Lusitania, Baetica and south-eastern Tarraconensis.[56]

By the later second century AD Rome had proved equal to the challenge of taming Iberia and had channelled her tremendous natural resources into underwriting the cost of Roman imperial expansion elsewhere. However, there is another side to the story: the forging of the Spanish provinces also resulted in a unique Hispano–Roman civilisation. This fusion is reflected in architecture, the arts, literature and religion. Let us now pursue this story, beginning first of all with the people and society of Roman Spain. After all, it was their thoughts and actions which made Hispania Baetica, Tarraconensis and Lusitania among the most influential provinces in the western empire during the first and second centuries AD.

FURTHER READING

The boundaries and organisation of the Spanish provinces under the Republic and Early Empire are studied by Knapp (1977), Richardson (1986), Albertini (1923) and Mackie (1983), while an introduction to the road network is provided in Roldán 1975. The possible role of Italian mining contractors in developing olive-oil producing estates in Baetica is studied by C. Domergue, 'Rapports entre la zone minière de la Sierra Morena et la plaine agricole du Guadalquivir à l'époque romaine', *MCV* 8 (1972), as are the gold-mines of north-west Spain, in 'Introduction à l'étude des mines d'or du nord-ouest de la péninsule ibérique dans l'antiquite', *Legio VII Gemina* (1970); Bird (1972) and Jones and Bird (1972) provide further details. Archaeological evidence for urbanism in Iberia is collected together in A. Balil, 'Casa y urbanismo en la España antigua III', *Studia Archaeologica* 20 (1973), and by others in *Symposion de Ciudades Augusteas. Bimilenario de Zaragoza*, 2 vols (Zaragoza, 1976), and is the subject of studies by scholars like Le Roux (1975, 1977). Galsterer (1971) looks at the status of privileged towns, while English translations of their charters are given by Chester Johnson *et al.* (1961) and González (1986); J. González, 'Tabula Siarensis, Fortunales Siarenses et Municipia Civium Romanorum', *Zeitschrift für Papyrologie und Epigraphik* 55 (1984), 55–100, discusses an important bronze document from Siarum, which sheds light on the character of *municipia*. P. Le Roux and A. Tranoy, 'Villes et functions urbaines dans le nord-ouest hispanique sous domination romaine', *Portugalia* IV/V (1983–4), 199–214, look at the character of urbanism in the north-west. Roman villas throughout Spain and Portugal are listed and discussed in Gorges 1979 and Fernández Castro 1982, while Ponsich (1974, 1979) and M. Prevosti, *Cronologia i Poblament a l'area rural de Baetulo* (Badalona, 1981) adopt regional and local approaches to the study of rural settlement. The most comprehensive work on the organisation and development of the Roman army in Hispania under the Empire is Le Roux 1982, while Jones (1976) explores its involvement in gold-mining in the north-west. The camps of the x Gemina and Ala II Flavia Hispanorum at Rosinos de Vidriales are the subject of a study by R. Martín Valls *et al.*, 'Sobre los Campamentos de Petavonium', *Studia Archaeologica* XXXVI (1975), and that of the Cohors I Celtiberorum at Cidadela (Coruña) by J. M. Caamaño, 'Excavaciones en el campamento romano de Cidadela (Sobrado dos Monxes, Coruña)', *NAH* 18 (1984), 235–54.

— 4 —

SOCIETY IN ROMAN SPAIN

T he inhabitants of pre-Roman Spain and Portugal had their own beliefs and customs; Rome never sought to impose her own values on these peoples. Hispano-Roman society was, in many ways, the result of a self-generated fusion of Roman and native. It came about, above all, through the involvement of the native landed aristocracy in the Roman system of self-government in the towns and their eventual participation in all the other social and political opportunities which the empire offered. This was not, however, an even process, because the slowness of the Roman conquest meant that by the first century AD native traditions were stronger in the newly conquered north-west than in the more Romanised south and east of the peninsula.

Romans and natives

Prior to the middle of the first century BC few Italians or Romans lived permanently in Iberia. They were mostly officials, merchants, shipowners, tax or mining contractors and money-lenders, at towns like Tarraco, Carthago Nova and Gades. At the same time there was a steady trickle of unofficial settlement by discharged Roman and Italian soldiers in the more peaceful parts of Iberia. Indeed, it should be remembered that between the late third and early first centuries BC there were rarely fewer than two legions (no fewer than 4,200 men each) and a large complement of Latin allies serving in Iberia every year. Towns like Hispalis and Corduba, as winter quarters for the army, were natural focuses for such settlement, giving Turdetanian communities in the Guadalquivir valley direct contact with the Romans from the earliest years of the conquest. One recent estimate suggests that there may have been as few as 30,000 Romans permanently resident in Iberia prior to the mid-first century BC.[1] These

settlers banded together into small, but powerful, communities (*conventus civium Romanorum*) which safeguarded Italian landed and commercial interests during periods of unrest. In time these became more influential and frequently acted as a 'bridge' for the promotion of native communities into Roman *municipia* and *coloniae*.

After the middle first century BC the number of resident Italians dramatically increased. Many were veteran legionaries settled as part of a conscious policy by Julius Caesar and, to a much greater extent, Augustus to demobilise veteran soldiers of the Civil Wars of 49–45 BC and 31 BC.[2] They were grouped together in formal settlements of Roman citizens (*coloniae*), consisting of between 2,500 and 6,000 men and their families. Augustus established several of these in Hispania Ulterior Baetica,[3] Hispania Citerior Tarraconensis[4] and Hispania Lusitania.[5] For his part Caesar founded the Colonia Genetiva Iulia Urbanorum at Urso (modern Osuna) which, as its name suggests, comprised men and their families from Rome.

The growth of Roman citizen communities and the deliberate installation of large groups of Roman citizens in native communities in south and eastern Spain diluted the social fabric. The distinction between Iberian and Roman was further broken down by granting Latin rights and Roman citizenship to individuals. In 90 BC, for example, Cnaeus Pompeius Strabo (the father of Pompey the Great) granted Roman citizenship to a well-deserving band of Iberian cavalry from Salduba in the Ebro valley.[6] The recent discovery of a remarkable bronze document, the Tabula Contrebiensis at near-by Contrebia (modern Botorrita), indicates that communities in the lower Ebro valley were partly Romanised by this time.[7] Alternatively, provincial governors might grant Roman citizenship to individual families in the way that Pompey the Great promoted Lucius Cornelius Balbus of Gades.[8] Nevertheless, this was rare, and it is only from the mid-first century BC onwards that a deliberate policy of making Romans out of Iberians is evident. Either the status of *municipium* was granted to a native community, or Roman citizenship was granted directly to people living in communities with the status of *colonia*.

The more advanced native communities in Iberia gradually became centres of Roman social customs and the Latin language. A few traces of pre-Roman social organisation may have survived into the imperial era. Ibero-Turdetanian names (*cognomina*), like those of Lucius Antonius *Antullus* from Gades[9] and Marcus Pompeius *Icstnis* from Ipsca[10] (modern Baena), are attested during the early empire, suggesting that some traditions still lingered in Baetican communities. The survival of late Carthaginian (neo-Punic) burial rites at towns such as Baelo (modern Bolonia) and Carmo (modern Carmona) is further evidence of this. Another pre-Roman tradition was *hospitium*: this was a form of reciprocal hospitality between communities and was usually formalised by exchanging inscribed tablets. Examples have been discovered at Lacilbula (modern Grazalema), Iptuci (modern Prado del Rey) and Ugia Marti (modern Cabezas de San Juan) in Baetica and at Emerita

Statue of a man, of Republican date, wearing a toga, discovered at Tarragona.

C·LAECANIO·BASSO·
Q·TERENTIO·CVLLEO·
NE COS
CLVNIENSES·EX·HISPANIA
CITERIORE·HOSPITIVM·FE
CERVNT·CVM·C·TERENTIO
BASSO·C·F·FAB·MELANATE
ETRVSCO·PRAEFECTO·ALAE
AVGVSTAE·LIBERIS·POSTERIS
QVE·EIVS·SIBI·LIBERIS·POSTERI
SQVE·SVIS EGERVNT·LEG
C·MAGIVS·L·F·OAL·SILO
T·AEMILIVS·FVSCVS

Bronze plaque from Clunia
(modern Coruña del Conde)
recording a pact of
reciprocal hospitality.

(modern Mérida) in Lusitania.[11] Larger towns like Emerita and Ucubi are recorded accommodating poorer towns, like Iptuci, to whom they would have shown financial generosity and whose interests they would have protected.[12]

In the north-west of the peninsula and certain parts of Celtiberia native survival was much stronger. There had been virtually no Italian immigration prior to the conquest of the area between the late second and first centuries BC, and subsequent settlement was predominantly military in character. Towns like Asturica Augusta (modern Astorga), Bracara Augusta (modern Braga) and Lucus Augusti (modern Lugo) were initially administrative centres and a source of Roman customs and the Latin language. Prior to the granting of Latin status to communities in the north-west by Vespasian (AD 69–79) there was no mechanism for the large-scale 'Romanising' of the natives, apart from enlistment into the Roman auxiliary forces.[13] As a result, pre-Roman social traditions survived until the third century AD.

The strong Celtic heritage in this rugged part of Iberia hindered the advance of Roman customs and lent a distinctive flavour to local Hispano-Roman society. The area was divided up into large confederations, such as the Cantabri, Callaici and Vaccaei, composed of peoples like the Orniaci, Lemavi, Paesici and Zoelae, who lived in scattered hilltop settlements (*castros*). These peoples, in turn, were subdivided into clans containing individual families, which formed the basic unit of society. In the *conventus Asturicensis* and *Cluniensis* the clan system persisted under the Latin name *gentilitates*.[14] The names of many of these have survived in inscriptions, the most important of which comes from Asturica Augusta.[15] It is a bronze plaque recording two pacts of *hospitium*: the first, dating to AD 27, was between the *gentilitates* of the Desonci and Tridiavi of the Zoelae people; the second, in AD 152, records a pact between the same *gentilitates* of the Zoelae and those of the Orniaci. In the *conventus Bracaraugustanus* and *Lucensis* a similar clan system existed, although it was known here as the *centuria*.

Further evidence for the slow penetration of Roman customs comes from a study of personal names. In the north-west nearly 900 Roman inscriptions have been discovered: they show that while Latin names were common at major centres like Asturica and the fortress of the VII Gemina legion at Legio (León), during the first two centuries AD, native names persisted at towns like Bracara, Aquae Flaviae (modern Chaves) and in the countryside.[16] Very un-Roman names like Ableca and Acondus were therefore passed on to a new generation born under Roman rule, while others gave their children Latin names in an attempt to integrate them into the Roman way of life.[17]

Hispano-Roman society had complex origins. Cultural differences between the peoples of Hispania had been broken down by limited, but dominant, Roman settlement in towns and in the countryside. Moreover, the grant of Roman citizenship and Latin rights to native communities during the first century BC encouraged the spread of Roman customs and social values throughout the peninsula at the expense of earlier, native, traditions.

Hispano-Roman society

The most commonly recognised face of Roman society is slavery.[18] This had been practised by the Carthaginians in Iberia before the arrival of the Romans; but there is no doubt that the conquest of the peninsula during the last two centuries BC brought about a dramatic increase in its scope and scale. Classical sources often tell us about large numbers of vanquished Bergistani, Lusitani, Arevaci and Cantabri being sold in the slave markets at towns in Mediterranean Spain and overseas. After this source dried up in the late first century BC, the markets remained active with a traffic in people from inside and outside Hispania. Some individuals were born into slavery, while others could be sold into slavery by their impoverished families seeking to pay debts.

The study of inscriptions shows that most Spanish towns had a significant slave population. To be a slave meant having no legal rights, not being able to own property, have a recognised family or choose a home or work in a chosen profession. At Carthago Nova (modern Cartagena) a local guild (*collegium*) employed its slaves to build the foundations of a shrine financed by its members.[19] Others were employed by towns and the state itself as a cheap, but often skilled, labour force. Alternatively, public slaves could be used as a kind of police force, as at Nescania (modern Cortijo de Escaña) in Baetica.[20] The more educated slaves (frequently Greek-speaking) were often employed as doctors, teachers, accountants and messengers. The public slave Graecinus, for instance, was an archivist at Astigi (modern Écija).[21] Others were employed privately, or in semi-skilled trades, like Agathocules, the glass-blower, from Tarraco,[22] and Pelagius, the carpenter, from Sasamon (Segisama).[23] Many others worked as domestics and servants at the wealthier homes in towns.

Luxurious villas staffed by large numbers of slaves, as in central Italy, are largely absent in the Spanish provinces of the late Republic and early empire. The agronomist Columella, himself from Gades, tells us that small groups of rural slaves were used for menial work on large estates, and were supervised by a slave or freedman overseer (*vilicus*) and other staff. One such *vilicus*, Sabdaeus, is known from Corduba. Columella also recommends

Tombstone of a 41-year-old slave-woman, Specla, from Italica (*CIL* II 1156).

that the *vilicus* should 'call over the names of the slaves in the slaves' quarters, who are in chains, everyday, and make sure that they are carefully fettered and also whether the place of confinement is well secured and properly fortified'.[24] An important bronze inscription from Lucus Dubiae Fanum (modern Bonanza), in Baetica, records a slave called Dama doing different work. Acting on behalf of his owner, Lucius Titius, he formalised a contract for the purchase of the Baianus farm, in the district of Olbensis, from one Lucius Baianus.[25]

The day-to-day working of the mines was another field of labour dominated by slaves. This practice extended back to the Republic, when slaves were used as cheap labour by contractors of large mines. The most explicit evidence for this comes from clauses in the law of the mining district at Vipasca in Lusitania during the first two centuries AD.[26] These make it clear that slaves were common at the mines and employed on the more menial tasks. For instance, they used to collect slag for resmelting from the person who had bought the contract from the relevant official. If slaves stole mineral ore from any of the mines, then they were sold, with the proviso that they be kept in chains and never be allowed to return to another mining community.

Slavery was not a caste system, and if a slave managed to accumulate sufficient savings, then he would be able to buy his freedom from his master. He did, however, retain obligations to his master who, in his turn, looked after his ex-slave's interests. This left some room for warmth in the relationship between a freed-slave (*libertus*) and his old master. At Emerita, for example, the freedwoman (*liberta*) Paccia Glycera put up a tombstone to her 'well-deserving' patron, the sixty-five-year-old Paccius Fortunatus.[27]

After being given their freedom, freedmen were able to pursue careers in those fields open to them. These were restricted because of social discrimination by free-born people and excluded any of the municipal magistracies, a career in the army, or joining the equestrian and senatorial orders. On the other hand, as many freedmen came from the Greek-speaking east and were well-educated, they were able to work in professions of importance to the state and the emperor. Ulpius Aelianus, for example, was the freedman procurator of the mines at Vipasca during the reign of Hadrian (AD 117–38), and the imperial freedman Marcus Ulpius Eutyches was *procurator metallorum* at Albocolensis in Gallaecia in the mid-second century AD.[28] By contrast Marcus Ulpius Gresianus, an imperial freedman from Mentesa Oretanorum (modern Villanueva de la Fuente, Ciudad Real), was successively archivist for the inheritance tax in the provinces of Gallia Lugdunensis, Gallia Aquitania and Hispania Lusitania.[29]

The careers of many socially ambitious freedmen culminated in an appointment as one of the six annual *seviri augustales* at their home towns. These *seviri* were quasi-magisterial priests who formed part of an association (*collegium*) which fostered the cult of emperor worship. This semi-religious cult encouraged the unity of towns, *conventus* and province within the framework of the empire. *Seviri* appeared at towns throughout Baetica, southern Lusitania and eastern Tarraconensis during the first century AD. One of their main conditions of office was that they should contribute 500 denarii to the municipal treasury, and that during their tenure they should bestow public banquets, sacrificial altars, public shows and other gifts upon the community. At Segida Restituta Iulia (modern Zafra) in northern Baetica Lucius Valerius Amandus and Lucius Valerius Lucumus were gratefully acknowledged for building part of the arena wall of a chariot-racing circus.[30] In such a way the *seviri* were visibly honouring the concept of imperial unity, contributing to the status of the town, and at the same time enhancing their own status in the community. Indeed, the personal status of these men could be enormous. Lucius Licinius Secundus, a freedman of the great general Lucius Licinius Sura, was simultaneously *sevir* of Barcino and Tarraco during the second century AD. He was singularly honoured with the dedication of over twenty statues to himself in the forum at Barcino, by other *seviri*, the guild of the Assotani, the town council of Barcino, the town council of Ausa (modern Vic), and such close friends as Caius Granius Felix and Caius Herennius Optatus.[31] It comes as no surprise, therefore, that tremendous wealth and prestige acted as a springboard for freedmen marrying into the families of the free-born or the wealthier knights. In this way descendants of a slave could enter the higher echelons of society within one or two generations.

In the Roman world most free-born people were domiciled in their town of birth. Epitaphs and other kinds of inscriptions provide us with the occasional glimpse into their everyday lives. During the first two centuries AD working people in many professions frequently banded together in social clubs, or guilds (*collegia*).[32] Unlike modern trade unions the *collegia* did not have a political role; indeed, this was expressly forbidden by successive emperors. Instead, they provided their members with a form of corporate identity and protected some of their personal interests. This was often assured by a *collegium* adopting an influential patron. At Corduba the guild of municipal builders offered a formal contract of patronage to their chosen patron, Iulius Caninus, in AD 348. Many guilds also adopted a protective deity; the guild of road-surface workers at Tarraco chose the goddess Minerva.[33] The construction workers (*fabri*) and canvas makers (*centonarii*) were the most important urban guilds and were often banded together to act as municipal fire brigades. They have been attested at towns like Tarraco, Corduba and Miranda where many buildings were constructed out of inflammable wood and mudbrick. The most famous example is the *corpus centoniarum* of Hispalis, which had 100 members and was founded with the personal approval of the emperor Antoninus Pius (AD 138–61).[34] Other *collegia*, like that of the fishermen and fishmongers at Carthago Nova,[35] cobblers at Uxama (modern Osma),[36] lamp-wick makers at Igabrum (modern Cabra)[37] and copper refiners at Hispalis[38] give us an idea of the variety of the more important professions in Hispano-Roman towns. Guild

Skilfully composed mosaic decorating the mansion of a member of the urban rural aristocracy at Emporiae (modern Empúries).

members met periodically at special premises, one of which has been identified beneath the Rambla Nova at Tarragona (ancient Tarraco): this may have belonged to the *collegium fabrum*.[39]

Rural landowners also formed associations, known as *centuriae*. Invariably they had a patron and protected the interests of their members from the local aristocracy whose large, expanding estates threatened their livelihoods. An inscription from Arva (Peña de la Sal) in Baetica records a dedication by the Oresis, Manenesis, Halos, Erquesis, Beresis, Arvaboresis, Isinensis and Isurgutana *centuriae* to Quintus Fulvius Carisianus, their elected patron.[40] The *collegia* of land-surveyors from Arva, Obulco, Munigua and Carmo are known to have banded together with the *centuriae* of their respective towns and to have made a dedication to the goddess Ceres Frugifera at Carmo.[41]

If we are to discover how free-born Spaniards came to participate in the political and cultural life of the Roman Empire, then we must know how the aristocracies of Hispano-Roman towns were formed. Individual members can be readily recognised from epitaphs and commemorative inscriptions recording their roles in, and membership of, the councils (*ordines*) of *coloniae* and *municipia* throughout the provinces. All were Roman citizens and many prominent families, like the Aelii Hadriani, the family of the future emperor from Italica, were probably descended from those Italian families who had settled in Iberia during the Republic.[42] Others from Carthago Nova, Illici (modern Elche) and Tucci (modern Martos) were of indigenous origin and had been made Roman citizens during the Republic. There was a later admixture of resident foreigners, who emigrated to the main towns of southern and eastern Spain during the first three centuries AD. These people were an important component of the municipal aristocracies in eastern Tarraconensis, especially that of Tarraco. This was implicit in Tarraco's pre-eminent role as the centre of the provincial Imperial Cult and the Provincial

Council. The fine collection of Roman inscriptions from the town suggests that most of these *incolae* came from the *conventus Carthaginensis*.[43]

From the first century AD onwards large, wealthy family groups monopolised the prestigious town magistracies in the more urbanised southern and eastern parts of the peninsula. The Cornelii, for instance, played a prominent role at Tucci, Obulco and Anticaria (modern Antequera) in Baetica,[44] as did the Baebii at Saguntum in Tarraconensis.[45] The fine quality of life enjoyed by such people is reflected in their enormous mansions, still to be admired at towns like Corduba, Emerita and Italica. The main source of their wealth was agricultural land. Indeed, candidates for town magistracies needed sufficient property and wealth to free them from other responsibilities and to devote most of their time to new duties. This land may have been held close to their home town but was frequently scattered throughout the Spanish provinces. It was rented out to tenant farmers, while the agricultural produce of the estates was sold in neighbouring towns for cash. Wealth accumulated in this way was an important means of social advancement and often enabled individuals to enter the equestrian and senatorial orders at Rome. Status was achieved by lavishing costly benefactions on one's home town. The main motive for this public munificence was local patriotism, born out of an intense rivalry between Spanish communities. Inscriptions in prominent places on monuments show that during the first two centuries AD this was responsible for many of the theatres, baths, temples and roads which still grace many Spanish and Portuguese towns.

The Roman bridge over the river Tagus at Alcántara (Cáceres), built by the architect Caius Iulius Lacer, and dedicated to the Emperor Trajan by native communities in AD 106.

The consul Lucius Minicius Natalis recorded on a large marble inscription that he had built a large public bath complex, with porticoes and piped water, on his own property at his native Barcino.[46] These baths may, perhaps, be identified with a large complex recently discovered beneath the Plaça de Sant Miquel in the heart of modern Barcelona.[47] Alternatively, an inscription from Emporiae records that Caius Aemilius Montanus, aedile and duumvir at the town, paid for the construction of a temple and statue to the Tutela. Recent excavations have uncovered the remains of what may have been this temple, at the north-western corner of the Roman forum.

Financial settlements on the urban community were another kind of benefaction. At Hispalis, Fabia Hadrianilla left a bequest of 50,000 sesterces in her will, which yielded an annual income at 5 or 6 per cent. This was spent on food for 21 free-born girls (40 sesterces each) and 22 free-born boys (30 sesterces each) belonging to a local youth club (*collegium iuvenum*). The money was to be distributed twice a year on the birthdays of herself and her husband.[48] Another inscription records how Lucius Caecilius Optatus, a centurion of the VII Gemina legion, gave 7,500 denarii to the community of Barcino.[49] Interest at 6 per cent was used to pay for an annual boxing match (costing 250 denarii) on 10 June and a donation of olive oil (costing 200 denarii), to be used in the public baths on the same day. Optatus imposed

Large mudbrick building at the heart of Contrebia Belaisca (modern Botorrita). Its function is unknown, although the collapsed colonnade in front may reflect Roman architectural influence of the late Republican period.

Marble bust of a man, from Tarraco, 2nd century AD.

the condition that his freedmen should be exempted the obligations of the sevirate priesthood. If this were not met, then he stipulated the transfer of the money to Tarraco, where it would be dispensed in the same way.

Public banquets and the distribution of cash gifts were other forms of munificence. At Siarum (modern Utrera) in Baetica one man promised to distribute three denarii to each decurion, two to each *sevir*, and one to every

Marble head of a woman, from Tarraco, 2nd century AD.

citizen and resident on his birthday over a twenty-year-period. For a select few the reward of such sustained public service was to serve as a priest (*flamen* or *pontifex*) for the Imperial Cult at one's home town or as a high priest of one of the three provinces. All these posts were reserved for Roman citizens and held by men (and occasionally women) who had served as magistrates on local town councils.[50] At Obulco (modern Porcuna) Caius Cornelius Caeso held a magistracy (aedileship) followed by the post of *flamen*, that of a more senior magistrate (duumvirate) and then priest (*pontifex*) of the town.[51] Lucius Caecilius Caecilianus of Tarraco had an even more spectacular career: he was elected duumvir three times before becoming the *flamen* of Tarraconensis in the early second century AD.[52]

In a sense, therefore, there was a career structure, and ambitious people in search of high social status and political achievement might occasionally progress from membership of their town councils to the position of provincial *flamen*. The holders of the latter post came both from major and minor towns; a few went further. After one year's service a *flamen* would be in his thirties and eligible to join the equestrian order: this was the first step in a political career based at Rome itself. There is no doubt that the *flamen*-elect incurred major expenses throughout his career. For instance, Caius Marcius Cephalonius, an aspiring *flamen* from Lacipo (near Casares) in Baetica, promised to pay out 4,000 sesterces if he were appointed.[53] The *pontifices* Lucius Blattius Traianus Pollio and Caius Fabius Pollio paid for different parts of the early imperial theatre at Italica.[54]

Members of municipal aristocracies accrued considerable social prestige as a result of such gestures. This, together with their accumulated wealth, was the key to their participation in the wider political life of the empire. The most successful could join either the order of knights (the equestrian order) or the more distinguished senatorial order. Knights from Hispania are known as early as 81 BC,[55] but are not common until the second half of the first century BC. They came from towns like Gades and Italica, serving in financial posts. They possessed considerable wealth, needing a minimum property qualification of 400,000 sesterces. Under the early empire the equestrian order became a ready source of officials directly serving the emperor and by the mid-first century AD a hierarchy of posts had developed. Thus a knight would have to serve in a military post, followed perhaps by a spell in the Praetorian Guard at Rome. He then served in different financial positions (procuratorships) in the provinces and crowned his career by holding some of the prestigious prefectures. During the early empire knights from Baetican[56] and Tarraconensian towns[57] held many posts in the imperial administration. Some, like Publius Acilius Attianus,[58] served as the Praetorian Prefect at Rome, while others, like Caius Turranius Gracilis,[59] obtained the Prefecture of Egypt. These and other positions were of vital importance to the security of Rome and the emperor. Knights were recruited from people selected by the emperor, and this virtually presupposed political contacts, or patrons, at Rome. For instance, the Younger Pliny wrote to the great jurist Javolenus Priscus at Rome in the late first century AD about Voconius Priscus, from Hispania Tarraconensis: '... his father was distinguished in the order of knights; ... his mother comes from a leading family. He himself recently held a priesthood in Hither Spain.... What is most important is that you should like him; for though you grant him the highest office in your power, you could give him nothing better than your friendship ...'[60]

Vibius Paciaecus was one of the first Spaniards to be made a Roman senator.[61] He became a legate of the dictator Lucius Cornelius Sulla in 81 BC and owned large estates near Carteia (El Rocadillo) in Hispania Ulterior. By the later first century BC many others had been admitted into this distinguished order. All of them came from Ulterior, not least the family of the Cornelii Balbi. The elder Lucius Cornelius Balbus was immensely wealthy and owned estates near his home town of Gades, throughout Italy, as well as houses in Rome itself.[62] Under the early empire such enormous wealth was an even more important requirement for membership of the exclusive senatorial order than it had been for the order of knights. The minimum property qualification was one million sesterces, and membership was either inherited from father to son, or was bestowed upon chosen knights by the emperor himself. The young senator then embarked upon a succession of offices, starting with a financial post (quaestorship) in the provinces, followed by a legal post (praetorship), and more responsible posts as pro-praetor – either in command of a legion, or as the governor of a minor province. Subsequently he held one of the two major magistracies at Rome (the consulship), followed by postings as governor of the more important senatorial or imperial provinces.

During the first half of the first century AD senators from Hispania firmly established their influence at Rome. The majority came from Baetica. The family of the Annaei, from Corduba, were amongst the most powerful in the Senate, with Lucius Annaeus Novatus attaining the consulship and governorship of the province of Achaia (mainland Greece).[63] However, the 'golden age' of Spanish senators was between the late first and late second centuries AD, when senators from towns in Baetica and eastern Tarraconensis exercised strong influence in the Roman Senate.[64] Indeed, one of their number, Marcus Ulpius Traianus (Trajan), the acting governor of Upper Germany, was chosen by the reigning emperor Nerva (AD 96–8) to be his successor. Trajan (AD 98–117) was of Italian colonial stock from Baetica and was the first provincial to be emperor of the Roman world. He was succeeded by his relative, Hadrian (AD 117–38), who probably came from Italica.[65] During their reigns Hispano-Romans comprised nearly a quarter of all new admissions to the Roman Senate. Some of them, like Lucius Iulius Ursus Servianus (from Italica), Lucius Minicius Natalis (from Barcino) and Lucius Licinius Sura (from Tarraco), were instrumental in Trajan's conquest of the new province of Dacia (Romania).

Such people were at the pinnacle of Hispano-Roman society, leading a life far removed from the more mundane day-to-day concerns of most provincials. For the more privileged members of society these began with a sound education and ended with competition for magisterial office and the management of their estates. As early as the end of the second century BC the great teacher Asclepiades of Myrlea, in Bithynia (northern Turkey), taught grammar amongst the Turdetani in Ulterior.[66] Later the renegade general Sertorius set up free schools for the sons of local chieftains at Osca

Marble head of the Emperor Hadrian from Tarraco.

(modern Huesca) in Citerior. By the early empire education had become sufficiently well established for the province of Tarraconensis to produce the most famous Roman writer on education – Marcus Fabius Quintilianus, or Quintilian. He was born at Calagurris (modern Calahorra) in AD 33 and, as holder of the Chair of Rhetoric at Rome, taught such people as the Younger Pliny and the nephews of the emperor Domitian (AD 81–96). His most important work, however, was a twelve-book treatise entitled 'The Education of the Orator'.

There was no concept of compulsory state education in any of the western Roman provinces. Primary education between the ages of seven and eleven was either conducted at the homes of wealthier families or, for people of more modest means, in small rooms in public buildings. For most of the urban poor and isolated rural communities there was no education at this or any other level. The syllabus consisted of practice in reading, writing and numbers. The child was taught by a *magister ludi*, several of whom are attested at the mining community of Vipasca in Lusitania. The method of learning involved the memorising and repetition of facts, leaving little room for the development of critical ability.

For most children the conclusion of primary education at about eleven years of age marked the end of their academic careers. For those of the wealthier families instruction continued at home. The syllabus concentrated upon Greek and Latin literature together with a smattering of physics, history, geography and astronomy. Teachers of Latin and Greek literature are known throughout Hispania. For instance, Lucius Memmius Probus, *grammaticus latinus* from Clunia, was paid a salary for his work by the town of Tritium (modern Tricio) in northern Spain.[67] Higher education was intended as a preparation for public speaking, one of the most important assets for a public career. Training comprised public debates between students, or individual speeches, under the instruction of rhetors and orators. There were schools of rhetoric throughout Hispania, at Gades, Collippo and Tarraco, the last of which was run by a professor from Baetica.[68]

Lucius Annaeus Seneca the Elder (55 BC–AD 40) was one of the more famous Roman rhetors. He came from Corduba and collected together ten books on speeches and debates. His son, Lucius Annaeus Seneca the Younger, was famous for his involvement in court intrigues at Rome. In AD 49 he became tutor to the young Nero at the request of the empress Agrippina and upon Nero's accession in AD 54 became his principal adviser. He eventually fell from favour. In AD 65 Seneca, together with his nephew, the noted epic poet Lucan, were implicated in a conspiracy against Nero and forced to commit suicide. Seneca also produced twelve philosophical treatises and some works of drama based upon legendary Greek characters. Martial, on the other hand, provided light relief. He was born at Bilbilis (Cerro de la Bámbola, Calatayud) in central Tarraconensis in AD 40 and wrote some 1,500 epigrams on frivolous and scatological topics. Lucius Iunius Moderatus Columella and Pomponius Mela made a more scientific contribution to Roman culture. The former was an agronomist from Gades who wrote a treatise on trees and a very important manual (*De Re Agricultura*) on agriculture in the mid-first century AD. Mela, from Tingentera in Baetica, was a geographer who produced the first geographical treatise in Latin, entitled 'Description of Places' (*Chorographia*).

Given the absence of even the crudest form of general education in Hispania, such cultural achievements would have meant very little. People spent much of their free time at the public entertainment provided in the towns. The charters of towns like Urso show that by the end of the Republic public games had become institutionalised and celebrated annually. They were also sponsored by private individuals in commemoration of imperial birthdays and religious anniversaries. The most dramatic games took place in the amphitheatre and circus. Amphitheatres have been discovered outside the walls of many towns in modern Spain and Portugal: those at Tarraco, Italica and Emerita are amongst the most spectacular. At Italica the amphitheatre held some 25,000 spectators who probably would have come from smaller local communities as well as Italica itself; entry was usually free. In fulfilling their official duties magistrates were obliged to sponsor games at least once a year, as, indeed, did provincial high priests of the Imperial Cult. The Urso charter tells us that duumvirs had to spend a minimum of 2,000 sesterces and the aediles 1,000 sesterces, both being assisted by similar sums from the town treasury. The same was probably true at Italica. The games in the amphitheatre lasted four days, consisting of animal baiting and gladiatorial combats. In the latter gladiators fought either mock contests with blunted weapons or battles to the death. The bullfights of today are, in some ways, heirs to this tradition.

Epitaphs of gladiators survive at Gades, Emerita, Barcino and Tarraco. At Corduba most examples commemorate heavily armed fighters, such as Faustus, a slave from Alexandria in Egypt. He died after twelve fights, at the age of thirty-five.[69] The heavily armed charioteer Ingenuus, from

The Roman amphitheatre at Emerita (modern Mérida).

Germany, managed to win twelve victory palms before dying at twenty-five.[70] At Emerita there is an epitaph to Cassius Victorinus, who was a lightly armed gladiator and is represented with his characteristic net and trident.[71] An even more extravagant form of entertainment was the staging of mock naval battles (*naumachiae*) in the larger amphitheatres. The arena was flooded, and specially trained gladiators fought each other on board ships. An inscription records that Annius Primitivus sponsored *naumachiae* at Balsa (modern Tavira) in Lusitania.[72]

Chariot races were also organised at municipal and provincial level, as illustrated by inscriptions from Arunda (modern Ronda), Astigi (modern Écija) and Tucci (modern Martos).[73] The circus was usually situated outside the town: the magnificent example at Emerita was one of the largest in Hispania and at full capacity held 30,000 spectators, all of whom were admitted free of charge. Chariot races whipped up tremendous excitement among the populace at provincial capitals and lesser towns, like Toletum (modern Toledo) in Tarraconensis. Nor, indeed, was it restricted to the lower classes: the senator Lucius Minicius Natalis Quadronius Vetus from Barcino was himself a keen charioteer and took part in the Olympic Games at Corinth in the early second century AD.

Theatres offered their audiences rather more eclectic entertainment. Plays by Roman and Hispano-Roman playwrights were occasionally staged, although the discovery of a mime-artist's epitaph at Tarraco[74] reminds us that the repertoire of the theatre varied.

The inhabitants of towns and the larger villas found a different form of relaxation in public and private baths. Examples of these have been discovered throughout modern Spain and Portugal (see Chapter 6). The bathers mixed socially while moving through a succession of attractively decorated cold (*frigidarium*), warm (*tepidarium*), hot (*caldarium*) and steam (*laconicum*) rooms, like those in the baths to the south of the forum at Conimbriga. There were also facilities for boxing and wrestling.

The abundance of these establishments reflects the importance attached to hygiene by Roman town planners in Hispania. Extensive drains, serving public and private buildings, have been discovered beneath the paved streets of towns like Emerita, Caesaraugusta, Italica and Emporiae. By modern standards, however, hygiene was still poor and medical science rudimentary. Roman medical practice was based largely upon Greek traditions, and few major innovations are known. In Roman Spain Classical sources frequently cite the value of various natural cures: Baetican olive oil for liver complaints and other ailments, linseed oil from Gades for eye pains, crystalline salt from Baetica to soothe other eye complaints and painful haemorrhoids.[75] In addition, excavations at towns like Emerita, Toletum, Baelo and Pallantia (modern Palencia) have yielded many fine examples of medical instruments like surgical scalpels, knives, scissors, trepans and vaginal specula.[76] Most doctors in Hispania were slaves of freedmen of Greek origin. Some, like Philumenus from Segobriga (Cabeza del Griego), and P. Sicinius Eutychus from Dianium (modern Denia), were public doctors.[77] Others, however, were specialists: Albanius Artemiodorus was an eye-specialist at Gades. Quite often the sick and the elderly had recourse to health spas like Aquae Bilbilitanorum (modern Alhama de Aragón), Aquae Flaviae (modern Chaves) and at Alanje in Badajoz, where they could bathe in spring water or inhale its vapours.

Much of the available medical skill was undoubtedly limited to the wealthier households in the town or in their country villas, leaving the great majority of the population susceptible to disease and infection. Sources record the widespread havoc caused by pestilences like bubonic plague which ravaged other provinces like Germany and Italy in the aftermath of the wars against the Marcomanni on the Danube frontier in the late second century century AD. Teeming ports like Gades and Carthago Nova would have been especially vulnerable to diseases brought by ships from other parts of the Mediterranean. Unfortunately, causes of death are rarely recorded on tombstones, so it is not known whether an individual died through disease, accident or natural causes. An epitaph from Conimbriga (modern Condeixa a Velha) in western Lusitania is typically vague. It was set up by Arquia Helena to her daughters Helena, Festiva and Augustina, since all three had died at the same time, aged thirty-three, eighteen and five respectively.[78] The study of bones holds great potential in this field, although to date the rich Spanish and Portuguese evidence has not been tapped.

Roman society was as hierarchical in death as it was in life. According to their means, each member of society coped with death by trying to perpetuate their memory amongst the living. People were apprehensive of the unknown after death and feared the loss of individuality that they had enjoyed during their lives. The extraordinary variety of tombs discovered throughout Hispania is partially explained by this attitude.

During the Republic and early empire the dead were cremated and the ashes buried in cemeteries outside the walls of towns. People of modest means could ensure themselves satisfactory burial by joining a funerary club (collegium funeraticium). In principle, this would consist of a group of people who paid an initial entry fee and a monthly contribution.[79] After death the heirs of the deceased were paid the money owed and made arrangements for the funeral themselves. If the deceased had died intestate, then the funeral was organised by the collegium. These funerary clubs are known throughout Hispania. One of the best-known examples is attested on a tombstone discovered at Carmo in Baetica. It records its members paying for the burial and tombstone of a twenty-three-year-old man called Quietus.[80] Close by a communal mausoleum (columbarium) was discovered, in which members of funerary clubs were often interred. This example consisted of a rectangular rock-cut chamber (10.3 by 6.3 metres), whose walls were provided with forty-eight niches. These held the ashes of the deceased and their names were inscribed below.[81] The layout of the *columbarium* allowed ritual funerary banquets to take place during the days of observance immediately after burial and later. One half of the chamber accommodated couches for the bereaved family, while the other held a hearth for the preparation of food, a well and an altar. Burial clubs were formed by people from every walk of life: for instance, a group of labourers at Tarraco, worshippers of Hercules at Dertosa (modern Tortosa), and slaves belonging to a gladiatorial association at Corduba.[82]

Wealthier people were able to afford private burials and tombstones and usually left provision for this in their wills. The heirs of Marcus Aurelius Marinus, for example, paid for his burial and tombstone at Olisippo (modern Lisbon) according to the terms of his will.[83] Many of these tombstones bore standardised epitaphs, mentioning friends, relatives or a plea that the tomb be left undisturbed. Occasionally, however, the epitaph might consist of a

A commemorative limestone statue-pedestal set up in honour of Caius Licinius Minicianus by his mother Licinia Crispula, from Tarraco (*RIT* 462).

long declamation to the passer-by, or a touching address to the deceased. One of the most moving examples was addressed by a father to his thirty-year-old son, Aper, at Tarraco. It concludes: '... Oh, grief! Oh, lamentation! Where shall I seek you meanwhile, my son? I shed these tears for you, poor me, ... Even light fails me; my limbs are limp from sorrow.... Now I see no light, for I have lost you, my son.... Good-bye for ever more, dearest son.'[84]

After the deceased had been laid out and prepared for burial, a coin was sometimes placed beneath the tongue to pay Charon, the ferryman, for passage across the river Styx, which divided the worlds of the living and the dead. The body was then taken to the cemetery and cremated — either in an oven or in a special ditch: examples of both were discovered at Carmo. Relatives collected the ashes into a cinerary urn, which was placed in the tomb alongside everyday utensils for use in the afterlife. Early imperial cemeteries discovered to the west and south of the Roman town of Emporiae provide us with some clear examples.[85] In the simplest cases ashes were placed inside pottery cinerary urns or, occasionally, small lead caskets: these were sealed with lids and placed in a plot in the cemetery. Burial goods were frequent and included imported fine tablewares for eating meals, some food (snails and oysters), personal rings and other jewellery, boxes of make-up and other beauty aids, lamps to light the darkness of the underworld, and glass phials to hold the tears of mourners present at the funeral. The discovery of a lead curse-tablet in each of three burials in the Ballesta cemetery was more unusual. These tablets were written backwards and were meant to bring misfortune down upon the heads of two imperial legates (Titus Aurelius Fulvus and Lucius Marcius Rufus), one imperial procurator (Maturus) and three other, unknown individuals. After these goods had been placed inside, or next to, the cinerary urn, the tomb was filled with earth and the tombstone positioned. Similar tombs are known throughout Hispania, most notably in the south-east cemetery at Baelo and that outside the north-east gate at Castulo.

Certain types of burial were restricted to particular classes of society. For instance, the distinctive loaf-shaped *cupa* burials which are common at Barcino seem to have been preferred almost exclusively by slaves or *liberti* of Hellenic or African origin.[86] The deceased was not cremated but placed instead at the bottom of a deep shaft which was back-filled and surmounted by a small collection of household articles for the afterlife. These, in turn, were covered by a stone or mortar cover (*cupa*), which bore the name of the deceased in a cartouche. Several of these can still be seen in the second- and third-century Roman cemetery at the Plaça de la Vila de Madrid, in modern Barcelona.

The wealthiest members of society ensured their place in posterity by building imposing mausolea for themselves and their families. A good example is the tomb of the Voconii family, discovered immediately to the south-east of Emerita.[87] It is a low rectangular stone building (2.6 by

3.8 metres), entered by a low door: above this the visitor can still see the epitaph dedicated by Caius Voconius Proculus to his father, mother and sister. Inside, rectangular niches were cut into the three facing walls, with *loculi* to hold the ashes of the dead; a fine portrait of each of the deceased was painted above the *loculus*. Altogether more elaborate were the stone mausolea, like those of the Atilii at Sadaba and Lucius Aemilius Lupus at Fabara.[88] Both were elaborately decorated, that at Fabara being planned in the form of a small temple. The hypogea at Carmo embody a different, indigenous Ibero-Turdetanian burial tradition adapted to Roman practice. The so-called 'Quadrangular Mausoleum' was built below ground level and approached down a narrow shaft: this led into a rectangular burial chamber (2 by 1 metres). The walls were pierced by six *loculi*, and a stone funeral couch ran around the inside.

One of the most impressive mausolea discovered in Roman Spain can still be seen at Carmo. It was carved out of the bedrock and planned in the style of a luxurious town house, with an enormous patio (24 by 17.5 metres) surrounded by a double portico. The principal burial chamber was also rock-cut and consisted of a domed ante-chamber, off which opened several

Tomb of the Voconii family at Emerita (Mérida).

niches. The monument was built in the early first century AD, probably for the family of Lucius Servilius Pollio. An inscription to Servilia Pollio, a close relative, was discovered inside.

The tall stone funerary towers built along the Mediterranean coast and in the Ebro valley during the later Republic and early empire were heirs to a different tradition. The most famous is the Torre dels Escipions, which is to be found a few kilometres to the north-east of Tarragona, by the side of the Via Augusta. It has a rectangular plan and consisted of three tall superimposed sections, capped by a small pyramid: the central section is decorated with two figures flanking the epitaph.

This portrait of Hispano-Roman society shows us how wholly Roman it had become by AD 200. We have seen how this developed in its early stages, gathering momentum with the large-scale settlement of Italians in south and east Spain during the later first century BC. During the first two centuries AD Hispano-Roman society developed into a hierarchy modelled upon that at Rome and serving Rome's own needs. This was a complex process, whose detailed understanding lies well outside the scope of this book but must surely be a very fruitful area for future research. The emergent Hispano-Roman society was focused upon a network of self-

The mausoleum of L. Aemilius Lupus at Fabara (Zaragoza).

governing communities, run by wealthy landed élites of Italian and native origin, and underscored by a huge majority of free-born people and slaves in towns and in the country.

FURTHER READING

Roman emigration to and settlement in Iberia during the later Republic is discussed in Wilson 1966, Brunt 1971 and Knapp 1977. Dyson (1980–1) compares the distribution of family names and the activity of governors in Iberia during the Republic, while C. Castillo, 'Stadte und personen der Baetica', *Aufsteig und Niedergang der römishen Welt* II.3 (1975), 601– 54, and Rodríguez Neila (1973, 1981) examine the composition of local families in Baetica and their role in local government. The strong persistence of Celtic social organisation in north-western Iberia is explored in Caro Baroja 1970, Albertos Firmat 1975 and Tranoy 1981, while the impact of Roman upon native is examined in Le Roux and Tranoy 1973. Epigraphy is the greatest source of information for the organisation of Hispano-Roman society, and among the best recent studies are those by Alföldy (1975), *IRC* (1984), *IRPC* (1982) and P. Le Roux and A. Tranoy, *Inscriptions romaines de la province de Lugo* (1979). D'Ors 1953 is still, perhaps, the best commentary upon the older and more important inscriptions from the Iberian peninsula. The Emperor Hadrian is probably among the most widely known natives of Roman Spain and is given a sympathetic treatment by S. Perowne, *Hadrian* (1960), while his achievements as Emperor are discussed by different scholars in *Les Empereurs romains d'Espagne* (Paris, 1965). The Emperor Trajan is discussed in R. Syme, *Tacitus* (1958), while Seneca the Younger is the subject of an excellent biography by M. Griffin, *Seneca: A Philosopher in Politics* (1976). The study of cemeteries is an important source of evidence for our understanding of Roman society, with Almagro 1955 and Bendala 1976 remaining amongst the best: J. Toynbee, *Death and Burial in the Roman World* (London, 1971) provides a broad framework for this kind of evidence.

— 5 —

INDUSTRY,
TRADE
AND TRADERS

The archaeological evidence for Hispania's rapid economic growth during the Republic and early empire is dramatic and reveals that her agricultural products came to dominate the markets of the western empire.[1] During the early years of the Roman conquest, the Romans found the Iberian peninsula not only an almost unlimited source of wealth — such as gold, silver, grain and slaves — but also an enormous market for their own agricultural products. However, by the first century AD the volume of olive oil, fish sauce (*garum*) and wine produced in Hispania was sufficient to satisfy home markets and to find one of its greatest markets in Italy and at Rome itself. At the same time, the growth of flourishing urban markets stimulated a vigorous trade in ceramics, textiles and building materials within the Spanish provinces.

There is little doubt that the Iberians were ready customers for imported goods. Livy noted that during the early years of the Roman conquest those Iberians living in the vicinity of Greek Emporion (modern Empúries) 'were glad to do business with the Greeks, and wanted to purchase the foreign goods which the Greeks imported in their ships and to dispose of the products of their own farms'.[2] The discovery of pottery and other luxury goods from Greece, the eastern Mediterranean, Carthaginian Ebusus (modern Ibiza) and North Africa at many sites along the Mediterranean coast shows that the larger Iberian communities had developed a flourishing exchange network before the arrival of the Romans. Italian imports, however, were largely absent.

As a result of the Roman conquest the Iberians had to increase their agricultural output in order to pay the Roman taxes and rents. Grain was their main product, and once this was sold on the open market the Iberians received sufficient coinage to pay their taxes and buy some of the newly available Italian luxuries. Central Italian wine produced in Latium, Etruria and Campania was especially popular. It was carried in tall pottery containers, or amphorae, known to archaeologists as the Graeco-Italic and Dressel 1. Similarly, a wide range of fine tablewares (known as Black Glaze and Thin-Walled pottery) were produced in the same areas. All of these have been found in large quantities at native settlements and Roman sites in Mediterranean Spain. They were imported initially by Italian merchants (*negotiatores*) and contractors meeting contracts to supply the Roman legions campaigning in central and western Iberia. Thus Dressel 1 amphorae have been discovered at the camps of Scipio Aemilianus' legions, which still surround Numantia, the Castra Caecilia (near modern Cáceres) in Lusitania, and at the Roman camp of Almazán (Soria).[3] These men had rapidly assessed the potential of the Iberian market, while the possession of Italian wine and pottery was seen as highly prestigious by the Iberians. Hence a vigorous exchange was built up between the Romans, Iberians and Turdetanians of Mediterranean Spain. This grew in range and intensity during the later second and early first centuries BC, reaching a climax with the appearance of Roman towns and settlements as major markets towards the middle of the first century BC.

Thereafter the picture rapidly changes. In Chapter 4 we saw how the landed aristocracies of towns in eastern Tarraconensis and Baetica had begun to accumulate considerable wealth and power by the late first century BC. Archaeology is now providing evidence that shows them investing capital in their estates to produce cash crops for sale at budding urban and rural markets in Hispania and overseas.

Towards the middle of the first century BC wine was being produced at estates along the east coast of Tarraconensis – between Blandae (modern Blanes) and Tarraco – in sufficient volume for the surplus to be exported to local towns, such as Baetulo (modern Badalona) and Emporiae. The wine was carried in amphorae known as the Laietana 1.[4] Examples have been discovered in excavations at Baetulo bearing the name of one of the estate owners, Caius Mucius, stamped on the rim. Ten or twenty years later the scale of wine production had grown and spread to many estates scattered along the coasts of Tarraconensis and Baetica. It was carried in a new, 22-litre, amphora, known as the Pascual 1. The kilns which manufactured these have been discovered in the vicinity of major towns. Name stamps are still quite rare; however, they do show that the production and marketing of wine were profitable enough to attract the interest of wealthy landowners like Marcus Porcius, who probably held estates near Baetulo, and Caius Mussidius Nepotis.[5] Indeed, one of these amphorae was stamped with the name of the Roman consul for AD 14, Cnaeus Cornelius Lentulus Augur.[6] This distinguished senator had been given large estates in coastal Tarraconensis by the emperor Augustus and started producing wine carried in these containers. However, they disappear from the archaeological record in the early first century AD. This is probably due to the confiscation of all the senator's property on his death in AD 25. Some of it was claimed by the Vibii Serenii family, while the rest was seized by the emperor Tiberius (AD 14–37). Pascual I amphorae were exported in considerable quantity to ports like Tarraco, Barcino, Iluro, Emporiae and Baetulo, where a tavern full of these, ready for sale, was discovered outside the walls.[7] They were also exported overseas. Nine shipwrecks laden with these amphorae have been discovered along the coast of north-eastern Tarraconensis and Gallia Narbonensis (Provence), suggesting that this was the main trade route,[8] which has been confirmed by the discovery of many examples on land sites in the area and up the river Garonne as far as Burdigala (modern Bordeaux) in Gallia Aquitania. There was a lesser trade beyond Burdigala to southern Britain, and east of Narbo (modern Narbonne) to Ostia, the port of Rome.

Between the reign of Tiberius and the early second century AD the volume of wine production grew dramatically. The very best *cru* came from vineyards in the vicinity of Lauro (modern Llerona del Vallès), to the northwest of modern Barcelona. Both Pliny[9] and Martial[10] fulsomely praise wines produced throughout Laietania and in the vicinity of Tarraco. Spanish wine was now transported in larger, 26-litre, amphorae, known as the Dressel 2–4, which were produced at kiln sites all along the Mediterranean coast as far as Lucentum (modern Alicante) and at Carteia (modern El Rocadillo), near Gibraltar.[11] They are stamped with the names of the potters who produced them. Iberian names, like Andoxus, Cissus and Sosibia, are rare, and most name stamps refer to slaves or freedmen with Greek names like Acanthus and Philomusus, and Latin names like Clarus and Rusticus. The study of name stamps from kilns such as Can Pedrerol and Can Tintorer (both near Barcelona) suggests that potters often co-operated in the production of individual amphorae.

Emporiae, Iluro, Barcino, Tarraco and Saguntum were the main ports through which the wine was exported. Emporiae had at least two harbours, both of which have now silted up. The largest (500 by 200 metres) was situated between the Greek town (Neapolis) and the offshore island (Palaiapolis), now covered by the medieval village of Sant Marti d'Empúries: it was protected from the prevailing winds by a magnificent stone and concrete mole which still stands today. Ships would have entered the harbour through a narrow gap to the north-east. The other harbour lay three kilometres to the south-east at Riells-La Clota, by the mouth of the River Ter.[12] It was much larger (1,000 metres long) and was used between the second century BC and the sixth century AD: remains of a large port building have been discovered nearby, at the Puig del Corral d'en Pi. The wine amphorae would have been loaded on to ships in harbours such as these and then ferried up the coast towards southern Gaul, Liguria, Ostia and Rome. This route could be hazardous, and some fourteen wrecks of ships carrying them have been discovered. There was a short cut, which involved navigating the treacherous straits of Bonifacio, between Sardinia and Corsica. A ship (the *Sud-Lavezzi 3*) laden with nearly 200 Dressel 2–4

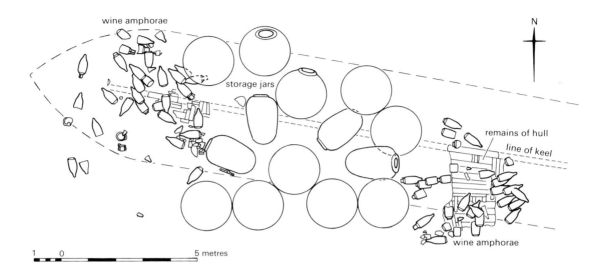

wine amphorae

storage jars

N

remains of hull

line of keel

wine amphorae

1   0   5 metres

amphorae foundered on a bed of rocks here in the early first century AD.[13] Despite these perils wine from Tarraconensis and Baetica claimed a much larger market than before, with clientele scattered along the coasts of North Africa and Italy, and in Germany, southern Britain and northern Gaul. In southern Gaul it suffered from the strong competition offered by local wine. Little is known about the merchants (*negotiatores*) engaged in this flourishing trade, although two people who may have been involved, including Quintus Ovilius Venustianus, are known from Tarraco and Iluro.[14]

For reasons that still elude us the wine industry in Tarraconensis and Baetica practically disappeared by the end of the second century AD. However, as an industry it was dwarfed in size by the production of olive oil in Baetica between the late first and late third centuries AD. Whereas Tarraconensian wine had been produced exclusively for a civilian market, much Baetican oil was bought by the state to satisfy its own needs. In antiquity, olive oil was used extensively in cooking (as it still is in Mediterranean countries), medication and as a body toner by athletes. Moreover, it was widely used as one of the few means of lighting. Small quantities of oil were poured inside a pottery lamp and lit by a wick. Such lamps are common at most urban and rural sites throughout the empire.

Olive oil was produced on large estates along the river Guadalquivir between Hispalis (modern Seville) and Corduba (modern Córdoba), and transported in globular amphorae known as the Dressel 20.[15] At least seventy-one kiln sites manufacturing these have been discovered in the Guadalquivir valley, along the banks of the Guadalquivir, the Genil, or clustering inland near local towns. At one site, El Tejarillo, near the Roman town of Arva, five kilns were built in a row: one of these was excavated and found to consist of a rectangular block (14 by 8 metres) subdivided into a service area and firing chamber.[16]

Plan showing the Diano Marina wreck with its cargo of wine amphorae (Dressel 2–4) from Tarraconensis and large storage jars from Italy.

Recent work on the extraordinarily rich written records preserved on the amphorae and stone inscriptions has provided a startlingly clear insight into the organisation of this major industry and how its products were traded.[17] Firstly, the ownership of the estates where the oil was produced and the organisation of the amphora kiln workshops (*figlinae*) are reflected in name stamps on the rims or handles of the amphorae. Indeed, they also record how kilns and estates changed hands during the second and third centuries AD – a reflection of the great political importance of olive oil to the state and the fortunes that were to be gained from it.

One amphora kiln workshop, the *figlina Virginensis*, was located between the Roman towns of Naeva (modern Cantillana) and Ilipa (modern Alcalá del Río), to the south west of modern Brenes. From the amphora stamps found here it is clear that there were five individual kilns at work until the later second century AD: each had its own name, like VIR I, VIR II, and so on. Moreover, the amphorae often bear the stamp C.Q.V., which is an abbreviation of the estate owner's name, Caius Quintus Virginius. It has been calculated that his estates would have comprised between 325 and 465 hectares of olive groves. Towards the end of the second century his name was replaced by that of an unidentified person, I(?) S(?). This individual had acquired both Virginius' estates and the amphora kiln workshop, running the latter in a different way. Henceforth each kiln was identified by the name of individual potters, like Augustalis, Callistus, Hermes, Milo and Romulus, all of whom were probably freedmen.

The above therefore shows how an olive-producing estate and its *figlina* could pass from one private owner to another. A few kilometres to the east, in the neighbourhood of Arva, a group of four kilns (at Guadajoz, Adelfa, Juan Barba, El Villar Tesoro) have been discovered. In the mid-

Upper half of a Dressel 20 amphora from Baetica, bearing a *titulus pictus* and name-stamp (after Rodríguez Almeida 1981).

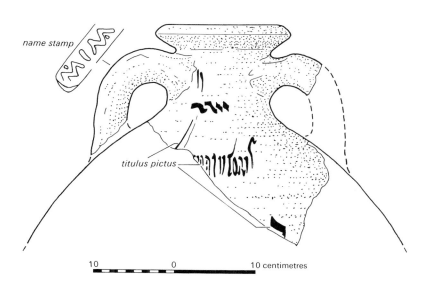

name stamp

titulus pictus

10   0   10 centimetres

second century AD these manufactured Dressel 20 amphorae carrying oil from the estates of Lucius Servilius Pollio (indicated by the stamp LSPBOEQ) and Marcus Servilius Pollio (indicated by the stamp M.S.P.). Members of this family came from Carmo (modern Carmona), to the south (see Chapter 4). During the reign of the emperor Septimius Severus (AD 193–211) many estates were confiscated from prominent landowners in Baetica, as they had supported his rival, Clodius Albinus, in a counter-bid to become emperor. It seems that the property of Lucius Servilius Pollio was also confiscated and divided up amongst new owners. Henceforth the amphora kilns manu-factured vessels carrying olive oil produced on the estates of people like L. Lae (?) Africanus, whose names are imperfectly known.

In the vicinity of Axati (modern Lora del Río) stamps on amphorae manufactured at the *figlinae* of Barba, Ceparia and Grumense reflect how these workshops and their surrounding estates passed from private to imperial ownership during the reign of the emperor Septimius Severus and his sons in later second to early third centuries AD. The original owners' names have not yet been deciphered and are known only in abbreviated form, like Mu(?) S(?) and F(?) P(?) R(?). In the first decade of the third century olive oil produced on them formed part of supplies requisitioned by the state (the *annona*) to feed the urban poor at Rome, officials in Rome and Italy, and the legions along the Rhine, Danube and British frontiers. Special officials (*conductores olearii*), like Earinus, Leopardus and Asiaticus (known on stamps from these kilns), were employed by a special institution called the Kalendarium Vegetianum and contracted to buy amphorae from these

The mouth of the firing chamber of a Dressel 20 amphora kiln at El Tejarillo, near the Roman town of Arva.

figlinae. This tight state control over the manufacture and packaging of Baetican olive oil was relaxed by the emperor Alexander Severus (AD 222–35), and the ownership of the estates and workshops passed to the private ownership of the Aurelii Herculae family.

All of these remarkably clear changes in land ownership vividly underline the importance of Spanish olive oil to individuals and the state. It comes as no surprise, therefore, to find that the filling, sealing and exporting of oil amphorae were also carefully monitored by imperial authorities in Baetica. The process is recorded on a series of notations painted on the necks and shoulders of many amphorae in red ink (*tituli picti*). Thus, one amphora from the wreck of a Roman cargo ship (the *Saint-Gervais 3*), which sank close to Massalia (modern Marseilles) in Gallia Narbonensis in AD 149, recorded the following:[18]

XXCVS [$85\frac{1}{2}$ Roman pounds]	The weight of the empty amphora
L(ucius) Antoni(us) *Epaphrodit*(us)	The name of the trader (*mercator*)
CXCVS [$195\frac{1}{2}$ Roman pounds]	The weight of the olive oil
Ac(cepi)*t G. Primus* [registered by Primus]	Registration
Charitianum Aeliae Alian(ae) *LVIIS* [from the estate of Charitianus, owned by Aelia Aeliana]	The oil was from the estate of
CXCVS (ponderavit) *Anice*(tus) [Anicetus weighed the oil at $195\frac{1}{2}$ Roman pounds]	The name of the person who weighed the olive oil

The notation therefore records that the merchant Lucius Antonius Epaphroditus bought 71.29 litres of olive oil from Aelia Aeliana's Charitianus estate, and that it was sealed in an amphora which was registered by Primus. It formed part of a consignment which would then have been loaded on to a boat – probably at the river port of Astigi (modern Écija) on the Guadalquivir.

During the first stage of their journey amphora cargoes were loaded on to river barges at different ports along the Guadalquivir. Thus an epitaph to one Caius Aelius Avitus was set up at Hispalis by a group of barge-hands from the river ports of Canania (modern Alcolea del Río), Oducia (modern Tocina) and Naeva.[19] Very little is known about the layout of such ports. However, the possible remains of a quay wall built from large stone blocks have been discovered at the port of Celti (El Higuerón, at Peñaflor). Similar remains, jutting out into the Guadalquivir, were discovered at Naeva. Passage along the river was not free, and boats laden with olive oil and other cargoes would have incurred an entrance tax (*portorium*), rated at $2\frac{1}{2}$% of the total cargo value, at each port. An inscription from Ilipa, dedicated to the Chief Financial Officer (Procurator) of Baetica in AD 195, was set up by Irenaeus who was an imperial slave responsible for collecting such tolls at Ilipa.[20]

Once the barges arrived at Hispalis they were loaded on to large seagoing ships for the second stage of their journey. Hispalis was the major port along the Guadalquivir and had direct access to the sea. Unfortunately, nothing is known about the layout of the harbour, although it would have had its fair share of warehouses and merchants' offices. Julius Caesar informs us that Hispalis was also a centre of shipbuilding: indeed, a small wooden boat (10 by 1.2 metres) was discovered a short distance downstream, near Puebla del Río.[21]

The large seagoing ships were owned by wealthy landed men (*navicularii*) or their freedmen. In the context of Baetican olive oil this lucrative business was dominated by large families like the Fadii, Valerii, Segolatii and Olitii from Gallia Narbonensis.[22] Amphorae shipped by them have been found at Rome with their names painted on the sides. *Navicularii* were middlemen who acted in their own interests and chose to invest some of their wealth in the risky business of sea transport. The writer Petronius caught something of their spirit in his *Satyricon*, when he put the following speech into the mouth of Habinnas, one of Trimalchio's dinner guests: 'I wanted to go into business ... I built five ships, I loaded them with wine ... and I sent them to Rome. You'd have thought I ordered it – every single ship was wrecked. In one day Neptune swallowed up 30 million. I built more boats, bigger, better and luckier ... I loaded them again with wine, bacon, beans, perfumes and slaves. ... In one voyage I carved out 10 million. I immediately bought back all my old master's estates. I built a house, invested in slaves and I bought up the horse trade . . . I retired from business and began advancing loans through freedmen'.[23] As olive oil was so important to the Roman state, *navicularii* and barge-men were paid for transporting it to Rome, or other destinations, by an official known as the Assistant to the Prefect of State Supplies (*adiutor praefectus annonae*). Indeed, a corporation of boat-towers from Hispalis set up a commemorative inscription to one such official, Sextus Iulius Posessor, in AD 161–9. He had supervised the supply of olive oil from Hispania and Africa earmarked for the *annona*.[24]

Once the ship had been loaded with its cargo it would have sailed down to the mouth of the Guadalquivir, past the lighthouse at Turris Caepionis (modern Chipiona) and out into the open sea. The journey between Hispalis and Ostia, the port of Rome, probably lasted about one week. However, it was a voyage fraught with danger, and many ships never reached their destination. One sank off the coast of Gallia Narbonensis, near modern Port-Vendres (ancient Portus Veneris), during the reign of the emperor Claudius (AD 41–54). It had carried a mixed cargo of olive oil and fish-sauce amphorae, kitchen pottery, glass and metalwork, which was scattered over the seabed together with fragments of the rudder and anchors.[25]

Merchants were the other middlemen between the olive-oil producers and their clients. They bought and sold contracts for consignments of olive oil, a wide range of other products and shipping-space throughout the empire. Such a lucrative business was monopolised by large families who

The huge mound of southern Spanish oil amphora fragments at Monte Testaccio, Rome.

had commercial offices in Baetica and in those provinces with the largest markets. Rome was one of the most important of these. The huge volume of Baetican olive oil consumed there is dramatically illustrated by the enormous hill of mostly Dressel 20 amphora sherds, called Monte Testaccio, which still towers fifty metres above the banks of the Tiber.[26] It has been calculated that this represents as many as forty million amphorae, implying some 2,000 billion litres of olive oil! One of the most famous oil-merchant families were the Aelii Optati from Celti (modern Peñaflor), near Hispalis. The discovery of an epitaph dedicated to Quintus Aelius Optatus, as well as stamps and *tituli picti* from Gaul and Rome, are witness to the family's far-flung commercial interests during the second and third centuries AD. The D. Caecilii were another important family, who originated from Astigi (modern Écija) and traded in oil for over sixty years between the late first and middle second centuries AD. D. Caecilius Optatus is recorded on a commemorative inscription from Astigi, *tituli picti* from Monte Testaccio and an inscription from Rome, where he was a merchant (*diffusor*) in Baetican oil.[27] He would have represented his family's commercial interests in offices for Spanish merchants in the famous 'company square' (*piazzale delle corporazioni*) at the heart of Ostia.

Maps illustrating the distribution of Baetican oil amphorae around the western Mediterranean – apart from Baetica and Rome – emphasise the importance of markets in Italy and southern Gallia Narbonensis and along the coasts of Spain and Portugal. It comes as no surprise, therefore, to find that Cassius Sempronianus, a *diffusor olearius* from Olisippo (modern Lisbon) in Lusitania, resided at Oducia for a while during the early second century

AD.[28] He might well have been acting on behalf of clients in Lusitania.

Baetican olive oil was produced in great volume until the third century. As a result of the trading network already discussed, Dressel 20 amphorae have been discovered at sites as far apart as Alexandria in Egypt, Carthage in North Africa, Basle in Switzerland, Budapest in Hungary and York in England. However, in the course of the third century olive oil from Africa Proconsularis began to undercut this dominant market position. Excavations at Ostia have shown how African oil amphorae rapidly displaced those from Baetica, so that by the fourth century most of Rome's oil requirements came from Africa and not Baetica. With the loss of this market Spanish olive oil was now directed mainly towards military markets in Pannonia, Germany and Britain.

Other important Spanish products to capture extensive overseas markets were the various fish sauces which were manufactured at large installations along the south coast of Lusitania, Baetica and Tarraconensis during the first two centuries AD (see Chapter 3). These were piquant delicacies which were to be consumed sparingly, like the modern 'Gentleman's Relish'. All the fish-sauce factories were situated on the sea-shore, so that adequate fish supplies and access to major ports were assured. Moreover, it ensured that the extremely putrid smell generated during production was kept away from the residential areas of towns like Baelo. Upon arrival at the factories the heads, entrails, eggs, soft roes and blood of the fishes were removed: tunny and mackerel were the favoured species. These were then laid, alternately with layers of salt, in characteristic square vats. The brine in the

Large town houses and installations producing fish sauce at Baelo (modern Bolonia).

salt then evaporated over about three weeks: the process could be hastened by placing the mixture in jars inside a specially heated room with a raised floor (hypocaust).[29] One example has been discovered at the fourth-century AD *garum* factory at Rhode (modern Roses), in north-eastern Spain. Salt clearly played a vital role, and it comes as no surprise to find that a major production centre like Carthago Nova (modern Cartagena) should be only sixty kilometres to the south of such large modern salt-pans as Las Salinas de Torrevieja.

Once the fish sauce was ready it was packed inside a variety of pear-shaped amphorae known as the forms Beltrán I, II, III and IV. They frequently bear name stamps and *tituli picti* so that, like the Baetican oil amphorae, they provide precious information about the trade in fish sauce.[30] Clearly its production and trade were controlled by private individuals, or corporations, and destined primarily for private consumption; there was no state involvement. Thus the production of one variety of fish sauce (*garum*) at Carthago Nova was controlled by the 'Association of Garum Producers' (*garum sociorum*) and is known to have been shipped to Pompeii, in Italy. A *titulus pictus* found on an amphora at Augusta Raurica (modern Augst), in the Roman province of Germania Superior (roughly Switzerland), mentions a manager (*vilicus*) called Fronto, who ran a *garum* factory in Hispania.[31] The amphorae themselves were produced independently at kilns which have been discovered in the vicinity of such places as Gades (at Puerto Real), Onuba (at Huelva) and Carteia (at Algeçiras). Stamps on the handles mention the names of Roman citizens like Lucius Octavius Caesius, Caius Fuficius Antonius and Claudius Socius, on whose estates the amphorae were manufactured. None, however, were as eminent or wealthy as those producing the Baetican oil.

A *titulus pictus* from Augst (Augusta Raurica) in Switzerland, on a southern Spanish *garum* amphora, which mentions Fronto, the manager of a *garum* factory.

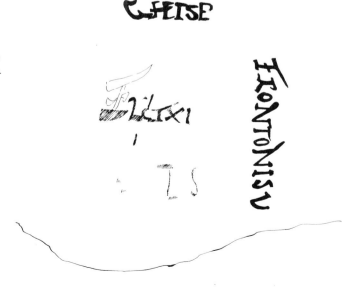

Fish-sauce amphorae were exported from major ports such as Gades, Carteia, Malaca and Carthago Nova to markets in Tarraconensis, Gaul, Britain, the German provinces and Italy. Indeed, it was especially popular in the capital, where, Pliny tells us, two measures of *garum* could fetch as many as 1,000 denarii. *Tituli picti* on fish-sauce amphorae often advertised the variety of condiment they contained: for example, 'best-quality *liquamen*', 'second-class *muria*' and 'Malagan *muria*'.[32] The distribution of fish sauce was in the hands of a few, very wealthy families. One of the largest of these were the Numisii, who seem to have originally come from Carthago Nova. However, in the first two centuries AD branches of the family held magistracies at Lacipo (near Casares), Italica, Corduba, Emerita, Ossonuba, Ipsca (modern Baena), Gades and Tarraco. The names of freedmen Marcus Numisius Nicerotis and Lucius Numisius Silonis have been found on *garum* amphorae at Rome, while Lucius Numisius Agathermes was known as a 'merchant in produce from Hispania Tarraconensis' (*negotiator ex Hispania Citeriore*) at Ostia. On the other hand, there was still room for individuals — like the 'fish-sauce merchant' P. Clodius Athenius from Malaca — in what was clearly a very profitable trade.[33]

A lesser Baetican product which still managed to claim a substantial overseas clientele was a range of very fine table-pottery, known as 'thin-walled wares'.[34] Delicate bowls and cups were the commonest forms and can be readily distinguished by their fine finish and barbotine decoration, which takes the shape of pine scales, rouletting and running stags. The pottery was very common in Baetica and Gallia Narbonensis during the first century AD but considerably rarer along the coasts of Tarraconensis and Italy; a few examples have also been discovered in Africa Proconsularis, Gaul and Britain. Despite its obvious appeal to townsfolk in these areas, such pottery had little intrinsic value and was probably one of the many subsidiary cargoes on ships such as the Port-Vendres wreck, which were mainly filled by amphora-borne goods. Cargo space would have been bought by merchants specialising in ceramics.

Neither this nor Spanish red-gloss fine wares (*terra sigillata hispanica*) could compete in appeal or volume with the imported red-gloss fine wares. In the first half of the first century AD South Gaulish Samian (or *terra sigillata*) from the great production centre of La Graufesenque (Millau, Languedoc), in Gallia Narbonensis, captured the markets of coastal Tarraconensis. Later in the century, these were superseded by an even more prolific range of orange-gloss fine wares, known as African Red Slip, which were produced in the provinces of Africa Proconsularis and Byzacena and dominated all Mediterranean markets until the sixth century AD.

However, there is no doubt that during the first two centuries AD wine, oil, fish sauce and ceramics from the Spanish provinces captivated a large clientele throughout the western empire. Both production and trade in these profitable businesses were monopolised by those large families with sufficient landed wealth to underwrite costs. In the early third century the state briefly intervened, although only to be assured that its own regular needs were met. No less remarkable was the rapid development of internal trade within the Spanish provinces. Archaeological research in recent years has begun to reveal the first details of highly organised pottery industries which, for the most part, served markets within the provinces of Baetica, Lusitania and Tarraconensis.

The earliest of these were the 'thin-walled wares' manufactured at Emerita during the first century AD. Eleven varieties of bowls, cups and flagons were produced at kilns in the *colonia*, and decorated with very characteristic rouletting and applied barbotine crescents. The similarity of some of the Emeritan forms to those current in central Italy suggests that Italian potters might have been at work in those workshops. The distribution of this pottery was limited to western Baetica and Lusitania. Moreover, the clientele was very varied: examples have been found at the Valdoca mining settlement of Vipasca (modern Aljustrel), the town of Conimbriga (modern Condeixa a Velha), the mines of Río Tinto (Huelva) and the *municipia* of Italica and Munigua.

Nevertheless, the scale of production was limited. This was not the case with the red-gloss wares known as *terra sigillata hispanica*. These were manufactured on an enormous scale and are found at sites throughout Baetica, Lusitania and Tarraconensis.[35] Most of the forms in this repertoire are copies of south Gaulish *terra sigillata*. The bowls and cups were decorated with floral – and, to a lesser extent, animal – scenes, while the platters and dishes were left plain. The decorated forms were manufactured in special moulds and, prior to firing, were covered in an extremely fine orangey-red slip. The shapes of some jugs and vases were locally inspired.

Terra sigillata hispanica was manufactured at two main centres, between the middle first and middle second centuries AD. The most important of these was focused on the *municipium* of Tritium Magallum (modern Tricio), a few kilometres to the south of the river Ebro in central Tarraconensis. Excavations have uncovered major workshops in its immediate vicinity, at Bezares, Arenzana de Abajo, Baños de Río Toba and Najera.[36] The complex at Bezares was subdivided into two parts by a wall. On one side was a small circular kiln with adobe walls, used to fire the *hispanica* pottery, together with a rectangular one for the firing of tiles. On the other side was a small reservoir, built from stone and tiles, for the preparation of the clay, and an area for the drying of newly made pottery prior to firing. This workshop manufactured moulds for decorated bowls as well as the bowls themselves, since the stamps for individual decorative motifs were found on the site. The other production centre was at Andújar (near Los Villares del Caudillo), on the banks of the Guadalquivir, in eastern Baetica. Here too kilns have been found. All four were circular (2 to 3 metres in diameter), with perforated floors supported by a central pillar. In addition, a large dump of misfired pottery and poor-quality products was found near by.

Apart from these two centres there were lesser, and often imitative, pottery workshops producing *terra sigillata* at Illiberis (Granada), in Baetica, and at Bronchales (Teruel) and Abella-Solsona (Lleida), in eastern Tarraconensis. These were probably located on the estates of enterprising, wealthy landowners, and operated for only a short period in the later first and second centuries AD. Finally, isolated *terra sigillata hispanica* moulds have been discovered close to towns in central Tarraconensis, like Clunia (modern Coruña del Conde), Uxama (modern Burgo de Osma), Pompaelo (modern Pamplona), Termes (modern Tiermes) and Caesarobriga (modern Talavera de la Reina), and in coastal Tarraconensis, near Barcino (modern Caldes de Montbui) and Gerunda (modern Gerona). In this case the moulds were probably bought by local potters who would have then produced their own *terra sigillata hispanica* for extremely limited local markets.

Hispanica from the main production centres was often stamped with the names of the managers of many workshops producing the pottery. The stamps are small (some inscribed within small cartouches, or circles) and found on the inside of the plain forms, and amongst the motifs of decorated forms. To date about 137 workshop managers' names have been identified. A minority, like Accunicius, Miccio and Nemettus, were clearly native people of Celtic extraction, while others, like Karacter and Petronius Eros, were slaves or freedmen with Greek names; the majority, however, were Roman citizens with Latin names such as Aemilius Fronto and Lucius Curtius. Thus the stamps provide us with a good cross-section of people involved in a low-status occupation: indeed, none of the workshop managers working around Tritium Magallum seem to have held local magistracies, or even to have been members of the municipal aristocracy. The workshops were probably located on the estates of local landowners, whose names have not survived.

Merchants specialising in ceramics probably handled the distribution of *terra sigillata hispanica*. Products from around Tritium Magallum had by far the widest distribution, claiming urban markets in all the Spanish provinces but especially Lusitania. They would then have reached villas, unless an individual estate produced its own *hispanica*. Eastern Tarraconensis, by contrast, imported little of this. Its markets were satisfied by a local *hispanica* but were dominated by imported south Gaulish *terra sigillata* and African Red Slip ware. The strength of local production at Andújar meant that products from Tritium Magallum were rare in Baetica too.[37] Indeed, *hispanica* from Andújar was rarely exported outside Baetica; the exception was Mauretania Tingitana (modern Morocco), with whom Baetica had a long tradition of cultural contact.[38] Generally, *hispanica* was rarely exported overseas, although occasional finds have come to light at towns in Gallia Aquitania and Narbonensis, Mauretania Caesariensis (modern Algeria) and at Ostia in Italy.

The production and distribution of these ceramics speak eloquently of the strength of internal trade within the Spanish provinces during the first two centuries AD. They are also representative of the trade in perishable commodities, like foodstuffs, which have not survived in the archaeological record. Nevertheless, these ceramics were still luxuries, and their availability would have interested only the wealthier Hispano-Romans living in the towns or on country estates. However, the manufacture of textiles for clothes, coverings, and blankets was a basic requirement for every member of the population. Indeed, one has only to look at the enormous range of garments illustrated on mosaics and tombstones to realise how important this industry would have been in Roman Spain. Unfortunately, textiles rarely survive at archaeological sites.

However, literary evidence shows that production of the two main raw materials — wool and flax — was common throughout Hispania. The flat and arid central *meseta* of Tarraconensis was the ideal environment for large flocks of sheep, and writers like Livy, Martial and Pliny often allude to the thick woollen blankets produced there during the Republic and early empire. Baetica was also noted for its very fine-quality wool due, in no small way, to people like the uncle of Columella, who carefully recounts how his uncle bought some coloured wild rams imported to Gades from North Africa. Having tamed them, he mated them with his own ewes, then mated their offspring with fine-woolled ewes from Tarentum, in southern Italy. In the space of three generations Columella's uncle had produced rams whose wool embodied the softness of their mothers and the fine colours of their fathers and grandfathers.[39] Quite often the wool was collected by pulling it out in tufts after the sheep had been without food for three days. More frequently, however, long (25–30 cm) iron shears were used. Examples of these were discovered at Emerita's eastern cemetery, while others came from the Romanised Castro of Montesclaros, in the conventus Lucensis and the late Roman cemetery at Fuentespreadas (Zamora).[40] After shearing, the fleece was cleaned prior to the conversion of individual fibres into thread.

By contrast, flax was produced in predominantly coastal and fluvial areas in all three provinces. Classical sources mention the fine quality of that produced in the vicinity of towns like Emporiae, Tarraco, Saetabis (modern Játiva), Gades, along the Guadalquivir valley, up the coast of Lusitania, and in the territory of the Zoelae people in north-western Tarraconensis. The most famous variety, esparto grass, was grown on the hills and plains around Carthago Nova. It was used by local peasants for making sandals, bed mattresses, clothing and baskets; however, it was also prized throughout the Roman world for use in ships' rope and rigging. To date only one small production centre has been excavated: it lies at El Cuatrón (Farasdués, Zaragoza), in the vicinity of Caesaraugusta.[41] This unique site comprised three interconnecting, stepped tanks cut into bedrock by the side of the river Agonia. In each of these flax stalks were placed, weighed down by stones, and a constant supply of tepid water ran over them. After a short period in the sun they were pressed dry by a special machine: recesses for its upright beams were discovered adjacent to the tanks. After the remains of the sheath of the flax plant were raked away, the fibres were exposed and then refined. Pliny tells us that every 50 Roman pounds of flax yielded 15 Roman pounds of fine combed flax.[42]

Strabo and Pliny inform us that flax from north-western and eastern Tarraconensis and wool from Baetica were exported in their raw state. Most of it, though, was used to make articles of clothing on rural farmsteads and in the towns. Little of what must have been a very widespread industry survives. Scraps of cloth were found attached to the back of some mirrors from a first-century tomb at Carmo (modern Carmona), while other pieces were discovered in the huge early Christian cemetery at Tarraco. However, the discovery of terracotta loom-weights at farmsteads and villas through-out Hispania clearly underlines the importance of weaving as a domestic industry. On the larger estates weaving was often supervised by the wife of the baliff: as Columella notes, 'At one moment she will have to visit the loom and impart any superior knowledge which she possesses, or, failing this, learn from one who understands the matter better than she does'.[43] Textiles produced in this way were probably used on the estate. On the other hand, large-scale commercial production took place in the towns. At the Ibero-Roman settlement of Cabezo de Alcalá, for instance, nearly 400 loom-weights were discovered in first-century BC occupation debris. Moreover, inscriptions tell us about the existence of a weaver at Tarraco and a seamstress at Corduba.[44]

Most finished textiles were plain and undecorated. However, the clothes worn by wealthy members of the town aristocracies, magistrates, knights and senators were brightly coloured as a sign of their high status. Examples of clothes worn by the seated magistrates are illustrated on the mosaic of the Muses from Arroniz (Navarra). The dye industry was therefore import-ant, and in the Roman world there were specialists producing individual colours: the *cerinarii* produced yellow, the *flammarii* red, the *crocotarii* saffron, the *purpurarii* purple, and so on. The cochineal insect was one important source of red dye in Hispania, often being used to colour the cloaks of generals. The main sources of purple dye were the *murex* and *purpura* shells which infest the Mediterranean coastline of Spain, and the Atlantic coastline between the Algarve and the river Minho. No dye production centres have yet been discovered, and it may be that out of the fishing season the fish-paste factories along the coasts of Lusitania, Baetica and Tarraconensis were used. The molluscs were caught by fishermen, and the dye was extracted at a seaside factory by the *purpurarii*. The *purpuraria* Baebia Veneria lived and worked at Gades, while the slaves Diocles and Diotimus were *purpurarii* based at Corduba. These people would have sold the dye either to a workshop specialising in the redyeing of old clothes (*offectorium*) or to one where new clothes were dyed (*infectorium*). One of the latter existed at Obulco (Porcuna), in inland Baetica, where a freedman called Liberalis worked as a dyer.[45]

The provision of fulling workshops for the cleaning and brightening of old and dirty clothes, would have been another aspect of the textile industry

Houses and workshops sharing a single building-lot (*insula*) at the Roman town of Celsa (modern Velilla del Ebro). The Casa de Delfines lies beyond.

in Roman Spain. The dirty clothes were placed in vats filled with a mixture of water, saltpetre and urine, whose ammonia acted as a detergent. The urine was often collected from passers-by in foul-smelling receptacles on the pavement adjacent to fulling workshops; one recalls Martial's uncharitable comment that 'Thais smells worse even than a grasping fuller's long-used crock ... '![46] After bouts of washing in running water, beating and drying, the colours of the clothes could be enhanced by exposing them over a brazier of burning sulphur and given extra sparkle by rubbing special sands into them. From the bronze tablets discovered at the Vipasca mining district in Lusitania it is clear that fullers serving this community were contracted to use the facilities there. The same was probably true in the fulling workshops in towns throughout the peninsula. A magnificent bronze inscription from Segisama (modern Sasamón) informs us that, hardly surprisingly, the fullers themselves were men of low status: Bebbius Voloddus was a free-born fuller, while Elenus was probably a slave. Similarly, Flavus, a fuller from Caldas de Vizela, in Lusitania, was probably a freedman.[47]

The textile industry was therefore of considerable importance. Items were produced mainly for local markets, like *terra sigillata hispanica*, and very little was exported. Indeed, evidence for clothing dealers in Hispania is virtually non-existent, with only one known at Corduba.[48] The same is true for the small-scale iron and copper smelting which took place at towns and many villas throughout Hispania. Many of the iron implements and bronze fittings discovered at these sites would have been produced locally. A small iron-smelting workshop was recently discovered in a first-century BC industrial quarter beneath the car park immediately to the south of Emporiae: its floors were littered with slag, and the workshop was equipped with two small roasting kilns.[49] Other kilns and debris have been discovered at Munigua (Castillo de Mulva) and Onuba (modern Huelva).

Most of the building stone, tiles and bricks which supplied the essential needs of the larger towns and villas throughout Hispania were obtained from local sources. Archaeological research in this field is still in its infancy, although the potential is enormous. Large limestone quarries have been discovered close to many Roman towns in Spain and Portugal – at the hill of Montjuic near Barcino, Velilla del Ebro near Celsa, El Médol near Tarraco, at Antequera near Anticaria, at Luque near Ipsca (Baena), and so on. Travertine was quarried at Albox, near Baria (Villaricos), and granite in the vicinity of Iulia Traducta (modern Tarifa) and Guilena, near Hispalis and Italica.[50]

It is impossible as yet to estimate the relative importance of these limestones and granites to local and imported marbles. The main problem is that to date only a few of the major ancient marble quarries have been located in Iberia. One of the better known of these lies at Almadén de la Plata, some sixty kilometres from Hispalis on the Italica to Emerita road. The ancient quarries are located in the Covachos hills and are still being worked today, yielding a white marble with darkish veins and a bluish variety with darker stripes. The workings were open cut, and the marble released by working downwards and outwards in blocks against the face of the hillside. Individual blocks were removed by driving dry wooden wedges into holes along the lines of desired fracture, and then wetting them so that they expanded and split away from the surrounding rock. Traces of this activity have been found at Almadén and at El Médol, near Tarragona. An inscription from Almadén mentions the existence of a *pagus marmorarius*, suggesting that the quarry may have formed part of a special administrative district, focused on a town near the quarry.[51]

Quarries were probably under private ownership during the Republic and the empire, although it is possible that some near Italica and Tarraco were owned by the emperor. A few kilometres to the north-east of Tarraco limestone quarries have been discovered at Els Munts (near Altafulla) and Els Capellans (near Torredambarra) and may have been imperial property.[52]

Both are in the immediate vicinity of the enormous maritime villa complex at Els Munts and were undoubtedly exploited by the owners. The villa was probably run by a certain Caius Valerius Avitus. Moreover, an inscription from near-by Tarraco also makes it clear that during the reign of Antoninus Pius (AD 138–61) Avitus had been deliberately transferred to the *colonia* from Augustobriga (modern Agreda) in central Tarraconensis. A bronze stamp bearing his name was discovered at the site.[53]

The actual working of quarries was in the hands of freedmen and slaves, like Hermes, who was engaged in marble work in Lusitania; similarly, L. Aemilius Quartius was a stone-cutter from the vicinity of Clunia (modern Coruña del Conde).[54] Their profession was highly skilled, and the dressing and finishing marks of their chisels, claws and hammers can be seen on many building blocks, inscriptions and sculptures.

The trade in building stone and marble decoration in Hispania must have been on an enormous scale.[55] Little is known of the mechanics of distribution, although the range of different marbles and stone in the larger towns was enormous. For instance, marble for the ambitious building programme at Italica came from sources as far afield as Almadén de la Plata, Alconera (near Zafra), Macael (Almería), Antequera (Seville), Coín (Málaga) and Estremoz (to the west of Terena) in Baetica, and from Buñol (to the west of Játiva) in Tarraconensis. In addition, large quantities of Numidian, Phrygian and Egyptian marble were also used. Emerita exploited the neighbouring quarry of Carija for its white marble, while importing limestone from quarries in the vicinity of San Pedro, fifty-one kilometres from the *colonia*.

By contrast, the production and distribution of bricks and tiles were far more localised. Both were specifically Roman innovations in an Iberian context and used extensively on buildings in towns and villas throughout Hispania. In some cases they were manufactured by individual estates to satisfy their own needs. For instance, a stamped brick found in the vicinity of Villajoyosa (the site of a large Roman *municipium*), in eastern Tarraconensis, tells us that Felicius was manufacturing bricks on the estates of Lucius Lucretius Servilius Gallus Sempronianus, a third-century Spanish senator. His family was based at Villajoyosa, where one of their number is known to have rebuilt the market building (*macellum*).[56]

More often bricks and tiles were produced on estates for clients in local towns or surrounding estates. One such workshop has been discovered at Llafranc, on the coast to the south of Emporiae.[57] Some seventy-eight tiles, covering an area of 28.5 square metres, had been laid out to dry in the sun in neat rows; they had not even been fired in the kiln before the workshop was abandoned. In its heyday, the kiln had produced tiles, local wine amphorae and plain kitchen pottery for various clients. Again the stamps on the tiles reveal the names of some of these clients. A number were produced for a certain Quietus and discovered in different buildings at Emporiae. Tiles manufactured for Primus were also discovered at Emporiae, as well as at the large villa at Camp de la Gruta, a short distance to the south. Other workshops' tiles were stamped with the name of the owner of the estate on which they were produced. For instance, tiles produced on the estates of Lucius Herennius Optatus were marketed all along the east coast between Tarraco and Gallia Narbonensis: the workshop has been traced to the villa of Torre Llauder, near Iluro. Other workshops of bricks and tiles have been discovered in central Tarraconensis (that of Antonius at Alcalá de Henares) and in north-western Tarraconensis (that of Protius at Asturica Augusta).[58] By contrast, tiles were also produced for contracts to supply the army: tiles stamped with the name of the legionary garrison in Hispania, the VII Gemina, have been found in the fortress at León, in the north-west.[59]

Examples of bricks have given us an insight into the day-to-day running of such workshops. One found near Conimbriga, in Lusitania, has a stamp which records that Maelo, one of the workers achieved his daily production quota of bricks. Furthermore, a graffito on an unfired tile from Valentia (modern Valencia) was etched by a workshop manager, Julius, and states that a certain Anthemius had paid for the 803 tiles sold to him; after receiving the tile, the owner of the workshop had added that he disagreed with the bill![60]

Very occasionally tiles and bricks were imported to Hispania from private and imperial estates in Italy. Examples have been discovered at a number of sites along the east coast, including Iluro and Tarraco. An even rarer import was of bricks stamped IMP AUG. These were used exclusively in the baths at Baelo and had been manufactured at an imperial brickworks at the fort of Gandori in Mauretania Tingitana (modern Morocco); otherwise the fort sold its products to Mauretanian towns like Tingis (modern Tangiers) and Tamuda (modern Thamusida).[61]

Between the second century BC and second century AD, therefore, Hispania was transformed from being a net importer of luxury goods into a dynamic exporter of wine, olive oil, fish sauce and ceramics to an extensive but often select clientele at Rome and throughout the western empire. The east coast of Tarraconensis, Baetica and southern Lusitania were thus integrated into the web of commercial currents linking the provinces of the western Mediterranean. Production of these commodities was intertwined with the emergence of a wealthy and sophisticated Hispano-Roman aristocracy, which fully participated in the public life of the towns and the empire as a whole. In the interior of Tarraconensis and Lusitania, meanwhile, the production and local marketing of fine tablewares were a response to the demands of the more insular, but equally sophisticated, clientele. Towards the end of the second century AD Hispania embarked upon a period of slow but profound social and economic change: one of its most vocal expressions is the apparent breakdown of these complex commercial relationships. Its consequences will be discussed in Chapter 8.

FURTHER READING

The role of trade in the ancient economy is studied in M. Finley, *The Ancient Economy* (London, 1973), Hopkins in P. Garnsey, K. Hopkins and C. Whittaker, *Trade in the Ancient Economy* (London, 1983), ix–xxv, and 'Taxes and Trade in the Roman Empire', *JRS* 70 (1981) and A. Jones, *The Roman Economy: Studies in Ancient Economic and Administrative History* (1974). J. Rougé, *Recherches sur l'organisation du commerce maritime en Méditerranée sous l'empire romaine* (1966). West 1929, Van Nostrand 1937 and J. M. Blázquez, *Economía de la Hispania romana* (Madrid, 1978) and A. Balil, 'Economía de la Hispania romana (s.I–II d.c.), *Studia Archaeologica* 15 (1972) are important early studies. Amphorae are an important source of archaeological evidence, and Beltrán (1970) and D. Peacock and D. Williams, *Amphorae and the Roman Economy* (London, 1986), provide good introductions to the Spanish forms. Local wine amphora production and export is studied in *El Vi a l'Antiguitat. Economia, Produccio i Comerç, al Mediterrani Occidental* (Badalona, 1987), while the fish industry of southern Spain is looked at by Ponsich and Tarradell (1965) and D. Peacock, 'Amphorae and the Baetican fish industry', *Antiquaries Journal* 54 (1974), 232–44. The production and export of Baetican olive oil is the subject of two important conference volumes, *Producción y Comercio del Aceite en la Antigüedad. Primer* (Madrid, 1981) and *Segundo* (Madrid, 1983) *Congreso Internacional.* Its supply to forts along the Rhine frontier is studied in Remesal 1986. J. Price, 'Glass vessel production in Southern Iberia in the first and second centuries AD: A survey of the archaeological evidence', *Journal of Glass Studies* 29, (1987), 30–9, provides an introduction to a neglected area of archaeology in Iberia. Syntheses of regional ceramic production are comparatively rare, although Mayet (1975, 1984) and Garabito Gómez (1978) have set high standards. By contrast to the publication of raw data, the study of processes in the production and exchange of ceramics in Iberia, in the manner of D. Peacock, *Pottery in the Roman World; an ethnoarchaeological approach* (London, 1982), are rare. The trade in local and imported building stone is discussed in Canto 1977–8, while M. Mayer, J. Alvárez and I. Roda, 'La importación del mármol en la época romana. El ejemplo de Ventimiglia y su contraposición con el litoral norte de la Tarraconense', *Quaderni* 10.11.12, (1987), 497–523, provide a more specific study. M.-J. Sánchez *et al., Portus Illicitanus. Datos para una sìntesis* (Alicante, 1986), is a rare attempt to study the remains of a Roman port in Iberia.

EARLY ROMAN ARCHITECTURE

odern Spain and Portugal have a rich heritage of Roman buildings, sculpture, mosaics and wall-paintings. In many ways they embody traditions and concepts that were totally alien to Iberia. In the late first century BC the great Roman architect Vitruvius stressed the fundamental importance of layout, order, proportion, symmetry and stylistic perfection in architecture.[1] This principle is borne out by many surviving buildings in Spain and Portugal, although it stands in sharp contrast to pre-Roman architecture in Iberia. Initially Roman architectural and artistic concepts were introduced to a few Roman administrative sites, like Italica, Emporiae and Tarraco. Then, between the late first century BC and the mid-first century AD, they spread throughout the Spanish provinces, evolving a specifically Hispano-Roman identity. This was to persist, fundamentally unchanged, until the later third and fourth centuries AD.

Rivalry between Iberian communities in the third and second centuries BC found renewed expression during the later Republic and early empire. The new public and private buildings, brightly coloured mosaics and wall plaster are all outward signs of Spanish towns competing with one another for prestige and status. As far as their finances permitted, communities strived to be more Roman than their neighbours. The *coloniae* and other communities like Italica and Saguntum were foremost in this: they had a long tradition of Roman settlement and were dominated by families of Italian descent. Their self-consciously Classical taste determined artistic and architectural styles, as their architects drew upon models from different parts of Italy, North Africa and the eastern Mediterranean. At the same time other buildings were tempered by the regional traditions of Hispania.

The major public buildings at the *coloniae* and older Roman settlements in Hispania were at once the hallmarks of Roman civilisation and, at the same time, the most alien to earlier traditions. Nowhere is this contrast clearer than at Emporion where about 100 BC the new Roman town was founded on the plateau behind the Greek port. The religious and commercial heart of the new town was defined by the building of a large (63 by 38 metres) formal market-place (forum), dominated by an awe-inspiring temple (*capitolium*) to the Capitoline gods Jupiter, Juno and Minerva.[2] This complex was on a far larger scale than the agora in the adjacent port or, indeed, open areas in any of the neighbouring Iberian settlements, and is the earliest known example of this Roman architectural type outside Italy. The complex was symmetrical about a south-north axis, and on approaching it through the south entrance the visitor directly faced the altar and *capitolium* at the north end. The temple was therefore its most prominent feature: it was specially raised on a rectangular (19 by 9 metres) platform (*podium*) built from loose stones and earth set within a casing of sandstone blocks. The shrine itself (*cella*) was a square room set back towards the rear of the podium and surrounded by engaged columns on three sides, and free-standing columns on the fourth. The columns were capped by leafy Corinthian capitals and supported the architrave, frieze, cornice and, ultimately, the tiled roof. All these elements were strictly symmetrical and proportional, and would have been aesthetically satisfying. Religious ceremonies were conducted at the small altar in front of the temple, and by climbing the steps immediately behind it the priests gained access to the images of the Roman deities in the *cella*.

Frontal view of the Roman temple at Evora (modern Ebora), showing the steps leading up to the main platform (*podium*).

The ground in the immediate vicinity of the *capitolium* was a sacred precinct (*temenos*). In an attempt to demarcate this and provide a spectacular backdrop to the temple a two-storey portico (*cryptoporticus*) was built at

the north end of the complex. The columns of the portico and the temple were covered in a white stucco which dazzled the eyes of the worshippers. The lower storey of the cryptoportico was set below ground level and was used to store temple property, while the upper storey allowed easy communication from one side of the precinct to the other.

The enclosed area to the south was used as a market-place. Merchants and local farmers would have exchanged goods in temporary stalls in the square, or in stone rooms (*tabernae*) running along its south side. At Emporion the architect therefore directly planted alien architectural concepts into an area of older, and different, traditions. Indeed, some of the closest parallels for the complex are at Gabii (Latium) and Minturnae (Campania) in central Italy.

During the first century BC complexes like the one at Emporiae became grander and more ambitious. The most important change was the appearance of a long porticoed hall (basilica) within the scheme. This may have derived from the Greek *stoa* (portico) but at Rome had developed into a covered aisled hall to house the lawcourts and other official business. By the Augustan period these halls had become an integral part in the planning of new town centres. However, the layout of Emporiae's earlier forum and *capitolium* hindered this: in the Augustan period the east side of the forum was therefore demolished, and a small basilica was squeezed in, as well as the assembly room (*curia*) of the town council. This change altered the whole character of the forum. Commercial premises were moved out, and the area now became an administrative centre. The inner edge of the forum was converted into a monumental porticoed passage way, while a series of small temples clustered along the north side in the shadow of the *capitolium*. The official character of the forum is illustrated by the discovery of marble statues and inscriptions dedicated to local notables, like Lucius Caecilius Macer, and patrons of the town, like Cnaeus Domitius Calvinus. The statues themselves are typical examples of Roman 'official' art produced locally. The trunk and legs of a man wearing the official Roman toga were carved first, with no attempt at individuality. Later a personalised head was added, together with bright yellow bronze arms. Finally, the statue would have been painted to make it lifelike. Unfortunately, no heads survive from Emporion; however, contemporary heads from Tarraco show that they would have been executed either in the exaggeratedly realistic style of the late Republic or in the more idealised Hellenistic style of the Augustan age.

Architects at Emporiae therefore adapted the basilica to fit in with the pre-existing forum as far as possible; however, it broke the axiality of the earlier scheme and denied the architect the freedom of using any of the new developments in Roman architecture. At the provincial capital of Tarraco the architect was able to embark upon a more radical scheme. Excavations in the 1930s uncovered the great basilica of the Augustan forum in the lower part of the town near the port: the forum itself still

Comparative plans of different kinds of Roman public and domestic buildings in Spain and Portugal.

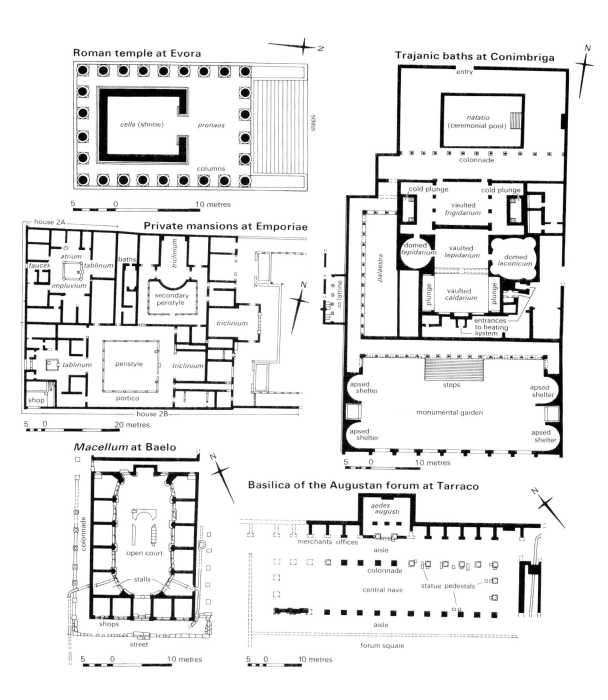

Roman temple at Evora

cella (shrine) pronaos

columns

steps

5 0 10 metres

Trajanic baths at Conimbriga

entry

natatio
(ceremonial pool)

colonnade

cold plunge cold plunge

vaulted
frigidarium

domed
tepidarium

vaulted
tepidarium

domed
laconicum

palaestra

latrine

plunge

vaulted
caldarium

plunge

entrances
to heating
system

apsed
shelter

steps

apsed
shelter

monumental garden

apsed
shelter

apsed
shelter

5 0 10 metres

Private mansions at Emporiae

house 2A

fauces

atrium

tablinum

baths

triclinium

impluvium

secondary
peristyle

triclinium

tablinum

peristyle

triclinium

shop

portico

house 2B

5 0 20 metres

***Macellum* at Baelo**

colonnade

open court

stalls

shops

street

5 0 10 metres

Basilica of the Augustan forum at Tarraco

aedes
augusti

merchants' offices

aisle

colonnade

central nave

statue pedestals

aisle

forum square

5 0 10 metres

remains buried beneath the streets of modern Tarragona.[3] The basilica is a long covered hall constructed from small stones set in mortar, and is still visible today. The interior is divided into a central nave and surrounding aisle by over twenty-four limestone columns with Corinthian capitals, some of which have been reconstructed. A small square room (*aedes augusti*) opens into the basilica from its northern side. Its floor is still covered with bright and finely cut marble slabs (*opus sectile*), and in antiquity the entrance to this ceremonial room was framed with small columns. The central nave was studded with large marble pedestals for statues dedicated to emperors and senators like Raecius Taurus Gallus and formed part of a gallery of individuals and deities closely identified with the imperial house. Several of these sculptures have survived – there is a very fine head of a youngish Marcus Aurelius (AD 161–80) carved locally in a white marble. The slightly upraised eyes are delicately sculpted, and the hair has been carefully worked with a drill.

The layout of this basilica was novel in Hispania, and its closest parallels are to be found at Herdonia and in the basilica built by Vitruvius himself at Fanum, both in Italy. The great initiative and financial patronage required for such a scheme suggests that it was undertaken by the town council. Nevertheless, it was not beyond the scope of private citizens. At Saguntum, for instance, the immensely wealthy Cnaeus Baebius Geminus is thought to have paid for the building of the forum.[4]

Further experimentation took place with the institutionalisation of the Imperial Cult and the need to build suitably impressive monuments. In the later first century AD a vast complex for the provincial Imperial Cult was built at Tarraco. Above all it was intended as a dramatic political statement about the strength and unity of the communities of Hispania Tarraconensis within the framework of the Roman Empire.[5]

The hill of the upper town was cleared of whatever military or civilian buildings had stood there previously and a gigantic terraced complex was built within the old Republican walls. The hillside was cut away at its lowest point to allow a large (340 by 116 metres) chariot-racing circus to be built longitudinally: it completely filled the wide space between the Republican walls on either side of the hill. Immediately behind it the level of the hillside was raised by nearly twenty metres and covered by an enormous rectangular space (300 by 120 metres), or forum, for assemblies of the provincial council. This, in turn, abutted another, raised, rectangular enclosure (140 by 120 metres), at the rear of which was the temple of Rome and Augustus. Much of this complex survives in the narrow medieval streets of Tarragona.

The circus and provincial forum were supported by a myriad of connecting vaulted tunnels and galleries. Indeed, the success of the whole enterprise relied upon these and, ultimately, upon the use of concrete. One of Rome's great technological advances, this had been introduced in the capital as early as the second century BC. The builders added smallish stones to a mixture of lime, sand and water and then laid it in continuous layers,

Reconstructed layout of the late 1st-century Imperial Cult complex at the upper town of Tarraco (modern Tarragona). The photograph (*below*) shows that much survives in the modern street plan.

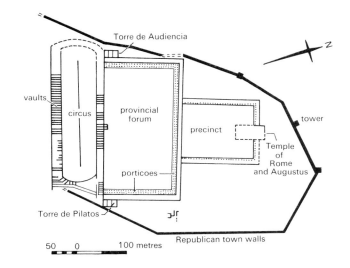

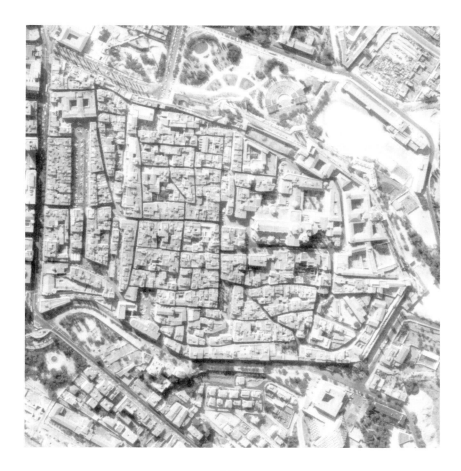

between wooden shuttering, or planks. Once the concrete had hardened, the shuttering was removed and the wall remained free-standing. The wall was faced with small stone blocks, and in this way the builders slowly built up the wall, supporting themselves on wooden scaffolding: recesses (putlog holes) for the horizontal beams are often still preserved on walls throughout the complex. They also supported the wooden arches upon which the concrete vault was actually built. Traces of shuttering on vaults can still be seen at various points in the Calle Trinquet Nou and beneath the Archaeological Museum. Other research has brought to light the arcaded southern façade of the circus, which was covered with local limestone blocks and decorated with engaged pilasters.

In antiquity entry to the provincial assembly place was probably restricted to those actually taking part in important deliberations. They entered by way of narrow stairs inside two magnificent towers at either side of the south façade of the enclosure; these still survive and are known as the Torre de Audiencia and the Torre de Pilatos. Inside the enclosure ran a monumental double portico, which consisted of two free-standing colonnades and engaged pilasters on the inside: some of these are still to be seen on the east face of the Torre de Pilatos. There may also have been a large triumphal

Engaged portico on the southern angle-tower (Torre de Pilatos), of the provincial forum at Tarraco (modern Tarragona).

arch standing at the centre of the south side, overlooking the circus. The basilica – or meeting hall – for delegates to meetings of the provincial imperial cult has not yet been discovered. However, the discovery of many statue bases to priests of the cult (*flamines*), like Quintus Porcius Vetusinus of Iuliobriga (modern El Retortillo) and Caius Virius Frontinus from the *conventus Lucensis*, suggest that it lay on the south side. The uppermost terrace was the most sacred precinct of the temple of Augustus and was surrounded on at least three sides by a monumental portico. The limestone shell of the temple has survived, together with a wealth of exquisite marble decoration, carved in a style and quality comparable to that of the forum of Augustus at Rome itself. Especially fine examples are the huge roundels (*clipei*), each decorated with a horned head of Jupiter Ammon.

This whole enormous enterprise was symmetrical about an axis which ran from the temple of Augustus, down through the middle of the triumphal arch, to the south side of the circus below. There is no doubt that it was intended to impress visitors with the power and might of the Roman state. When viewed from the sea, the great cult centre would have acted as a shimmering backdrop to Tarraco, inexorably leading the eye up to the temple of Augustus at its summit.

The imperial cult centre at Emerita (modern Mérida) seems to have been a more modest affair. The temple of Augustus still stands in the centre of modern Mérida, although it is now known incorrectly as the temple of Diana.[6] It was much larger (40.75 by 21.9 metres) than the small temple at Emporiae, and some thirty fluted marble columns ran around its sides on the rectangular podium. Excavations within have revealed fragments of the large bronze cult statue together with a small bronze statue of the spirit (*genius*) of the Roman Senate. However, as at Tarraco, marble decoration retrieved from the site shows a very close stylistic affinity to that from the forum of Augustus at Rome. This suggests that in both cases marble sculptors and quite possibly architects, surveyors and other specialists from the capital were present.

The forum built in the new town at Italica represented a complete break with these traditions. That great Hellenophile, the emperor Hadrian, seems to have been the driving force behind the planning of this new quarter, immediately to the north of the old *municipium*. He wanted to honour his birthplace,[7] and on his visit to Hispania in AD 122–5 may well have been accompanied by a large retinue of skilled labourers, surveyors, architects and other craftsmen. In the heart of the new quarter a large area was marked out (108 by 80 metres) and within it a high walled enclosure was built from concrete. A number of large niches (*exedrae*) with apsidal vaults opened off this wall on to the enclosed forum area, while a porticoed gallery ran around its inner face. The whole of the interior was then decorated with thin slabs of gleaming marble. This forum was a monumental, enclosed meeting-place, although without temples or basilicas. Like many fora of the imperial age, it was also used as a centre of ostentatious display where wealthy inhabitants

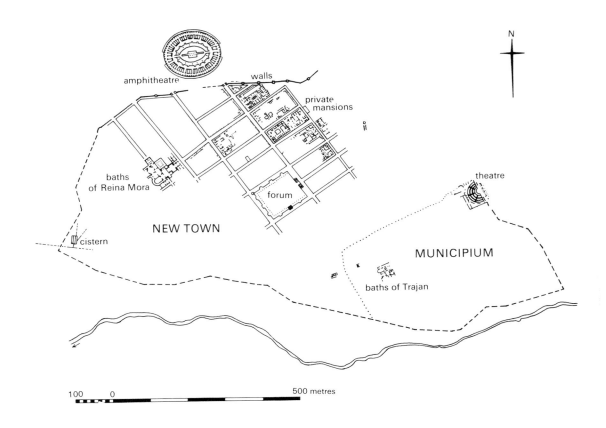

could set up inscriptions boasting their deeds and the gifts which they had bestowed on the community. Marcus Cassius Caecilianus, for example, recorded how he paid one hundred pounds of silver for raising four statues. This extraordinary building is unique in Hispania. It recalls the layout of the Hadrianic library at Athens and market-places (agoras) in Asia Minor and can thus be seen as a reflection of Hadrian's taste for things Greek.[8]

In the privileged Roman towns, therefore, architects designed buildings which expressed Roman religious, administrative and commercial requirements, and experimented with the different artistic traditions prevailing in Italy and the eastern Mediterranean. The wealth and patronage of their wealthy citizens ensured that these Spanish towns were in the forefront of Roman architectural development in the western empire. This is especially evident in other public buildings, like baths, theatres, amphitheatres and circuses, where architects successfully exploited concrete to produce some truly accomplished buildings.

A good example is the baths of La Reina Mora, built in the new town at Italica during the reign of Hadrian (AD 117–38). This big complex (78 by 57 metres) was built entirely from concrete, faced with specially manufactured bricks, like the many buildings still standing, for example at

Plan of Italica (Santiponce) showing the relationship of the earlier *municipium* to the later, mid-2nd century new town.

Ostia. The rooms were arranged axially, running north-east to south-west, with the main architectural emphasis upon two large and adjacent square, vaulted rooms leading into a large cold plunge-bath (*frigidarium*). This was nearly twenty-two metres long and ended in a graceful apse. It provided access to a large hall with a nave, two aisles and a double portico. A gymnasium (*palaestra*) and heated room were amongst many other features of this complex. These baths were richly decorated, with stucco, painted wall plaster, mosaic floors and marble columns, although little of this survives today.[9]

Theatres, amphitheatres and circuses were equally new to the architectural traditions of Iberia. Effectively, they were monumental settings for the mass and frequently brutal entertainment that was so much a feature of Roman urban life. Most of the surviving theatres in Spain and Portugal date to the first and second centuries AD. Wherever possible the architects took advantage of the topography and literally carved the great semicircular auditoria (*caveae*) out of the hillsides. This was partially for convenience but also helped to ensure the near-perfect acoustics needed for theatrical performances. The seating banks were raised on a series of concentric

The imposing 2nd-century AD stage-building (*scaenae frons*) of the great theatre at Emerita (modern Mérida).

concrete vaults which followed the contours of the hillside. This would allow spectators to file in and out of the auditorium as quickly as possible. This system was employed at all the major theatres, like those at Italica, Emerita, Tarraco, Saguntum and Acinipo (modern Ronda La Vieja),[10] and in each case its success must be attributed to the efficiency of Roman concrete. Once the concrete infra-structure was complete, long concentric rows of benches were installed; these were either cut from local stone or, as at Tarraco and Italica, carved from marble. The semicircular orchestra could be covered with large marble slabs, occasionally – as at Italica – bearing the name of a great patron of the theatre. The stage building (*scaenae frons*) behind was usually decorated with a rich array of marble sculptures, although such embellishments often took place later.

The sculptures from Tarraco and Italica are amongst the richest to have been found in Hispania. Most represent members of the imperial family. At Tarraco, for instance, two exquisitely carved white marble heads of young princes of Augustus' family were found, together with two colossal, headless men wearing togas who have been identified as Augustus and Claudius. Even more impressive are two magnificent torsos of second-century emperors wearing richly decorated breastplates. The immense *scaenae frons* at Emerita has proved to be an inexhaustible source of every kind of sculpture, including portrayals of Pluto and Proserpina, the god and goddess of the underworld. However, perhaps the finest piece of all is a veiled

The cavea, *orchestra and stage of the early Imperial theatre at the* municipium *of Italica (modern Santiponce). Most of these elements are of 2nd-century AD date, although the building was first constructed in the Augustan period.*

Statue of a Roman emperor in military dress, from the theatre at Tarraco (modern Tarragona).

head of the emperor Augustus: it embodies his youth and authority in a Hellenised style and was probably carved by sculptors brought from Rome itself.

Amphitheatres and circuses were even more ambitious works of architecture than theatres, impressing us more by their sheer size than by any aesthetic qualities. One of the earliest amphitheatres in Hispania was built outside the south wall of the Roman town of Emporiae during the late first century BC. It consists of low stone and mortar walls, supporting wooden seating tiers. Another example is to be found at Carmo (modern Carmona), in Baetica, although this was completely rebuilt in stone at a later date. By the first century AD, amphitheatres had become much more sophisticated and relied heavily upon the use of concrete. At Tarraco, the architect took advantage of the natural slope between the Via Augusta and the sea below, on the north side of the town, and cut the western side of the arena from the living rock. However, the north, east and south sides were built up artificially upon a massive concrete raft. The stone seating banks were then built up on top of this, as in the theatres, on top of supporting vaults which radiated outwards from the arena. They were then connected by a series of concentric vaults and stairs. The situation of the amphitheatre ensured that spectators making their way to their seats along the eastern side enjoyed a magnificent view over the Mediterranean below. The arena was covered by sand, and beneath this were concealed two intersecting passages covered by wooden planks which enabled gladiators, animals and machinery to move from one side of the arena to the other. The only concession to aesthetics was the treatment of the outer façade of the amphitheatre. The architects' challenge was to contain any spreading by the bulk of the concrete seating platforms and, at the same time, to render the building pleasing to the eye. At Italica, this was achieved by encircling the amphi-theatre with a series of brick and concrete arches, running between upright pylons decorated with engaged pilasters.[11]

Circuses were built in a similar way, perhaps as early as the first century AD. The superb example at Emerita consisted of two parallel stone and concrete walls running around the long, oblong arena. The space between them was filled with many concrete vaults running perpendicularly around the arena: these supported the seating banks. At the straight end of the circus was a monumental starting-gate consisting of two parallel rows of stone pylons supporting a monumental façade. The outer wall of the circus was decorated with an arcade and engaged pilasters, in the same way as amphitheatres.

Roman architects at these great centres successfully combined the strictly functional with the aesthetic in amphitheatres and circuses. This is an important aspect of their genius which can be appreciated even more readily in other works of engineering. Aqueducts are the best-known examples of this genius, reflecting the extraordinary importance that the Romans attached to a steady water-supply to their towns. One of the main sources of Emerita's industrial water-supply has been discovered at the Lago de Proserpina. It consists of a large Roman dam blocking off a tributary of the river Aljucén. A concrete channel carried the water from this source for six kilometres to a special desilting tank (3 by 3.6 metres) close to Emerita. The terrain between the tank and the *colonia* dips quite sharply, and in order to maintain the gentle gradient and speed of water flow the magnificent

The arcaded façade of the circus at Tarraco (modern Tarragona).

aqueduct of Los Milagros was built during the reign of the emperor Hadrian. It has a maximum surviving height of twenty-eight metres and still strides boldly across the countryside for nearly 350 metres. Consisting of tall, square (3 metres square) pylons which support the water channel, it is linked by three tiers of graceful arches. Again the key to the success of this daring enterprise was the use of concrete which, in this case, was faced with ashlar blocks. The aesthetic appeal was improved by leaving a rusticated finish on the lower part of the buttresses and separating the other courses at intervals with thin courses of bright orange tiles.[12]

The first-century AD aqueduct of Els Ferreres at Tarraco is perhaps even more remarkable, as concrete was hardly used in its construction. The aqueduct is the surviving portion of a channel which relayed water from the river Gaià, ten kilometres away, to the residential and administrative zones of Tarraco. Indeed, the early medieval Arab geographer Al-Makkari recorded that in his day it still carried enough water to power all the stone mills in the town. Four kilometres to the north of the town the channel crosses a gorge on top of a monumental twenty-five-arch arcade, which at its deepest point is supported by a lower and sturdier row of eleven arches. The maximum height of this impressive monument is twenty-six metres. The water channel was made from concrete, while the aqueduct itself was built from large honey-coloured limestone blocks (*opus quadratum*), with a rough 'rusticated' finish.

Spain and Portugal are also fortunate in having a large number of surviving Roman bridges. One of the finest examples is the magnificent bridge which still straddles the river Guadiana in front of Emerita.[13] This is 792 metres long and is built from concrete faced with large stone blocks. The first of its three great spans consisted of twenty-two arches built upon enormous, wide piers and ran to the edge of the south bank. A second span ran from here to an island at the centre of the river, while a third covered the remaining distance to the town: all three spans shared the same construction

The aqueduct of Los Milagros, on the outskirts of Emerita (modern Mérida).

technique. The central island was incorporated in the scheme as a huge mid-river quay. It was surrounded by a substantial stone and concrete wall, which described a great wedge shape, over 150 metres long. The sharp end of the wedge pointed up-river, in such a way that the island acted as a breakwater against the violent winter floods, as well as a mooring for river barges. Other impressive bridges are still to be found along the course of the major trunk-road between Emerita and Asturica Augusta.[14]

A rather more unusual survival is the great Roman lighthouse at La Coruña, on the north-western tip of Tarraconensis. It is one of the few monuments in Roman Spain whose architect is known to us – Sevius Lupus, from Aeminium (modern Coimbra), in northern Lusitania. His great masterpiece still proudly stands to a height of thirty-four metres, alerting ships to the treacherous shallows in the area. The present façade was built in the late eighteenth century but encloses most of its Roman predecessor. The Roman lighthouse was modelled closely upon the great Pharos at Alexandria, in Egypt. Careful investigation has revealed that Lupus' work comprised a central square block built in three storeys: each of these consisted of two pairs of connecting vaults. In antiquity this central core was surrounded by a ramp, which wound around it and, in turn, was enclosed by an outer wall. Nothing survives of the great lantern.[15]

These great engineering works were essentially practical. The Roman architects used their great ingenuity to create architectural forms which adapted the landscape to suit their own, broader purposes. In public building they drafted architectural forms from Italy and the rest of the empire to the centres of the new *coloniae* and their major towns. Under the early empire these were political statements enhanced by an astonishingly fine array of imperial portraits in prominent places.

There was a similar evolution in domestic architecture, although this was influenced more by personal wealth and taste. The earliest known Roman houses in the *coloniae* of Roman Spain date to the first century BC. Their layout was a direct transplantation of the classic atrium and peristyle houses which flourished in Etruria, Latium and Campania in second- and first-century BC Italy. The House 2A at Emporiae is a classic example of the type. It is a large (27 by 24 metres) private house (*domus*) which lies on the corner of a large building lot (*insula*) on the eastern side of the Roman town.[16]

The building is broadly symmetrical and displays most of the rooms of a traditional Roman house. Now, as in antiquity, one enters from the road by way of a narrow passage (*fauces*) and arrives in a large hall (*atrium*). Its most prominent feature is a square pool in the centre of the room (*impluvium*). In antiquity the roof above would have been open to the sky, allowing sunlight to spill through into the hall; it also served to collect rainwater, which filtered down from the *impluvium* into a large cistern below floor level. The roof itself was supported by columns at each corner of the *impluvium*: the red-painted stumps of these are still visible. On its far side is a large reception room (*tablinum*) where, in his role as an influential

patron, the owner of the house would have received his clients. A dining-room (*triclinium*) and various bedrooms (*cubicula*) bordered the other sides of the atrium. These rooms were all decorated with wall-paintings, some of which still survive today. One of the best preserved consists of a series of abstract panels, simply decorated in black, red and brown. One of the rooms had a concrete floor, while the *tablinum* was suitably decorated with a black and white mosaic arranged in a satisfying arrangement of squares and rectangles. The very Roman character of the house and its decoration contrasts with its construction technique. As in most of the large houses at Emporiae, the lowest parts of the walls are built from stone and mortar, while the upper reaches were made from mudbrick. This technique is very durable and had a long tradition in many parts of Hispania.

At a later date the building lot was more than doubled in size and extended over the line of the old town wall. The old building (House 2A) was now incorporated into a huge new mansion (House 2B), which successfully combined old traditions with new fashions. Foremost among these was an enormous garden surrounded by a portico (peristyle). In antiquity the portico would have been covered, keeping guests cool in the hot summers and sheltered from the winter rains and winds. Enclosed gardens of this kind were a Greek idea introduced to Rome during the second century BC. One large dining-room (*triclinium*) and a few smaller rooms opened off the portico. The dining-room faced west and would have been used during autumn and spring. Moreover, it was on exactly the same axis as the entrance of the mansion so that guests looking back in that direction would have enjoyed a subtle vista of alternating dark and light, relieved by coloured wall-paintings. Another novelty was the installation of a small, private bath suite consisting of four interconnecting rooms.

In mansions like this it is important to remember that the gardens, *tablinum* and atrium were considered to be rather more public than private. They were frequented by clients, officials and acquaintances, so that the more luxurious they appeared to be the more the prestige of the owner was enhanced. On the other hand, the bedrooms, dining-rooms and baths were closed off by wooden partitions and remained strictly private. Indeed, some of these rooms were decorated by portraits of distinguished family members. Other parts of the house, like the south-western corner of House 2B, were let as shops, providing the owner of the house with an outlet to sell the produce of his country estates, or could be rented as a concession to a small trader.

The large mansions at the new town of Italica were planned and immaculately built according to new architectural traditions of late first- and early second-century Italy. This new style is epitomised by the Casa de la Exedra, which was a two-storey mansion built adjacent to the town wall.[17] It covers some 3,000 square metres and is built entirely from brick-faced concrete, like contemporary houses at Roman Ostia. The old concept of atrium and peristyle was abandoned in favour of greater privacy. The mansion is divided into four major parts. Firstly, there is a large entrance (*vestibulum*) flanked by minor rooms, as well as some small shops (*tabernae*) which opened on to the porticoed pavement outside. A high-class toilet had also been installed, and displays a black and white mosaic floor depicting pigmies spearing birds and fishes. The second part of the house was a self-contained garden surrounded by a vaulted portico. The floor of the latter is still covered by coloured mosaics with geometric motifs. Opening off the portico is a large summer dining-room (*triclinium*) and a series of smaller rooms, one of which had a sumptuous *opus sectile* floor. The third part of the house was also self-contained and comprised various service rooms, a kitchen, and a private bath suite with raised floors; all these rooms were arranged around a patio with a rectangular water pool. Immediately to the north was a long (40 metres) patio (*dromos*), which terminated in a tall semi-domed niche (*exedra*). This patio may have been used for vigorous exercise, or as a running track by an owner who was clearly keen to get his daily exercise. Parallel to this was a long sunken passage way (*cryptoporticus*).

There were equally luxurious houses throughout the new town, and the modern visitor is struck by the profusion of mosaics throughout. They are all multicoloured and far more sophisticated than those at Emporiae. One of the most charming examples depicts thirty-seven different varieties of birds in brightly coloured square panels. Another from the same house displayed a beautiful head of Bacchus, the god of wine, within a central roundel set against a carefully executed geometric background.

One can imagine some of the wealthier families of Italica, like the Ulpii and Aelii, proudly leaving their old mansions in the cramped conditions of the old *municipium* of Italica and laying claim to plots in the new town. However, it is somewhat ironic that after building such luxurious and costly up-to-date mansions as these, walls began to settle and structures subsided. The architects responsible for the planning of the new town had not fully appreciated the unstable soil conditions at the site, so that within a generation the mansions, baths and the new forum were all abandoned. Some families — like that which owned the Casa de la Exedra — put on a brave face and retained their houses for about fifty years before abandoning them; others cut their losses and presumably moved back to the older town.

Excavations at *coloniae* like Barcino, Cathago Nova and Illici (modern Elche) provide graphic evidence of how mansions were continually enlarged, adapted or rebuilt during the first two centuries AD. However, it is at Emerita where their fully developed form can best be appreciated. Vast mansions have been discovered to the north of the amphitheatre (La Casa del Anfiteatro) and within the town at the Calle Sagasta and Huerta del Otero. The mid-second-century Casa del Mitreo, outside the walls to the south of the town, is one of the most spectacular examples. All the standard features are evident — an atrium with *impluvium*, at least two peristyles, a series of sunken rooms and rooms decorated with sumptuous mosaics and wall-paintings. One of the largest mosaics (48.5 square metres) graced the floor of a room claimed by some scholars as a meeting-place of a group of Stoic philosophers. Among the images are the celestial forces, namely the celestial triad (Saeculum, Caelum and Chaos), the family of Titans (Polum), the rising sun (Oriens) with bright gold rays emerging from his head, the clouds

The peristyle and adjacent rooms in a luxurious mansion (Casa del Anfiteatro) adjacent to the Augustan amphitheatre at Emerita (modern Mérida).

(Nubes) and the four winds (including Boreas and Zephyrus). Further down are personifications of terrestrial forces like the mountains (Mons), snow (Nix) and probably the Seasons. The bottom part of the mosaic is dominated by the maritime forces, like the rivers (Nilus and Euphrates), and aspects of the sea (Oceanus, Pharus and Navigius). The Greek conception of cosmic forces was embodied in these 'Romanised' figures executed with such a fine attention to detail. The whole ensemble reflected the ubiquity and stability of the Roman Empire which, in turn, reflected the universe in one harmonious and eternal unity. The room was also decorated with a series of painted panels emphasised by diamond-shaped lozenges and circles.[18]

All the houses discussed above belonged to the very wealthy senators, knights and *decuriones* discussed in Chapter 4. It would be a mistake to believe that all inhabitants of the *coloniae* and major towns lived in such splendour. As Vitruvius wrote 'we have to plan the different kinds of dwelling suitable for ordinary householders, for great wealth or for the high position of the statesman'.[19] Indeed, more modest houses have been discovered at Tarraco, Illiberis (modern Granada), Barcino and many other *coloniae*. One of the best examples, however, is the Casa de los Delfines at Celsa (near Velilla del Ebro), in the Ebro valley.[20] Excavations have uncovered a building lot occupied between 36 BC and the abandonment of the *colonia* in AD 58. During the earliest phases of occupation the lot was partitioned between two colonists' families. At the beginning of the first century AD the house incorporated both building lots. The core of the house consisted of a traditional Italian atrium, which was entered from the outside by a passage (*fauces*), and off which opened a small *triclinium, tablinum* and a couple of bedrooms. Pink concrete floors were laid in the *tablinum* and in one of the bedrooms, the decorative motifs including an interlocking Greek-key design with a central emblem flanked by four dolphins. A large ceremonial dining-room (*triclinium*) was built adjacent to these rooms. Both areas opened on to a large patio, in the centre of which was a water tank, slightly at odds with the symmetry of the rest of the house. The garden lay to the south and was enclosed by a simple portico and three ranges of service rooms. One of these has been identified as the kitchen – with its oven still in place – and another as a small animal pen.

This house is earlier than the more sumptuous mansions in the other *coloniae*, and is thus lacking some of the more fashionable embellishments. The layout is unambitious and practical, and may well have been designed by one of the citizen colonists themselves rather than a recognised architect. This was quite a common practice, which clearly met with Vitruvius' approval: 'I can find nothing but praise for those householders who, in the confidence of learning, are emboldened to build for themselves.'[21]

This survey of public buildings and private houses has shown us how quickly the traditional Italian influences became rooted in the art and architecture of the *coloniae* and major towns. Most of their inhabitants were Roman citizens of Italian origin who sought to live in familiar surroundings within an alien environment. In time the wealthier élite embarked upon political careers which took them to Rome and many different parts of the empire. This exposed them to a variety of different artistic and architectural fashions which are reflected in their houses and public buildings. In their turn these served as models for the developing indigenous towns throughout Hispania between the late first century BC and the second century AD. The initiative lay in the hands of the local aristocracies, to whom the new Roman architectural and artistic styles had become as prestigious as imported Italian wines and luxury goods had been to their forebears. The degree of sophistication with which a particular architectural or artistic form was adopted was tempered by the availability of skilled architects and craftsmen. Both were attracted to the surer patronage offered by the larger and richer native towns like Clunia (modern Coruña del Conde), Conimbriga (modern Condeixa a Velha) and Toletum (modern Toledo).

The smaller towns drew more upon local architectural traditions, constructing public buildings which embodied a mixture of Roman fashions and native techniques. Thus at Arcobriga (Monreal de Ariza) , in the Jalón valley, local architects seem to have tried to imitate the great Augustan basilica at Tarraco. They constructed a long (31 by 7.6 metres) basilica with a single line of columns running down the centre and a small room (5.33 by 4.4 metres) opening off the rear wall. Here the similarity ends, since the basilica was built entirely from local stone with no trace of the elaborate marble decoration which graced its counterpart at Tarraco.

The inhabitants of Munigua (Castillo de Mulva) in Baetica went to extraordinary lengths to transform a sanctuary at the centre of their small town into an impressive copy of the great temple of Fortuna at Praeneste (Italy).[22] The Claudian town centre at Baelo (modern Bolonia) was equally sophisticated, although its architects had clearly drawn upon North African traditions; southern Baetica and the North African coast had a long tradition of close cultural contact. The three temples to Jupiter, Juno and Minerva stand together in a row overlooking the forum. The layout recalls the *capitolium* at Emporiae. The forum itself is a rectangular paved area, with a major temple half-way along its western edge. A basilica occupied its southern side, with a colossal white marble statue of the emperor Trajan standing at its eastern end. The emperor is represented wearing a toga and has sockets for arms. The head was detachable and, being a little clumsy and stylised, was almost certainly carved by local sculptors.[23]

In this complex the relationship between the temples, forum and basilica is more reminiscent of the Augustan forum at Leptis Magna in Tripolitania (modern Libya) than at any of the Spanish *coloniae*. Similarly, the construction technique of the walls, built from irregular stone courses sandwiched between stone uprights (*opus Africanum*), was Carthaginian in origin. The limestone columns from the temples and the forum portico were either crude imitations of Roman orders, like the Corinthian, or were carved in a style which clearly betrays the Turdetanian architectural traditions of the area. On the other hand, the adjacent market building (*macellum*), with its characteristic central space and *tholos*, was clearly influenced by south Italian prototypes.[24]

The great forum at Conimbriga, first laid out in Augustan times in a Lusitanian settlement, was heir to a totally different tradition. While the temple of Rome and Augustus was added during the Flavian period,[25] original features included rows of shops filling all three sides of the forum. Close parallels for this complex are to be found at Lugudunum Convenarum (modern Saint Bertrand de Comminges), in south-west Gaul, and at Iader (modern Zadar) in Dalmatia. The source of the architect's inspiration, however, was probably northern Italy. A number of white marble statues of the imperial family adorned the forum area, although they are too mutilated for easy identification. Nevertheless, the sophistication of the whole ensemble and especially its Augustan predecessor is surprising, given that Conimbriga was a native, Lusitanian site with no recorded settlement of Roman citizens.

Amphitheatres, theatres, circuses, bridges and aqueducts were also adapted as architectural forms in towns and country areas. Theatres are known at such regional centres as Segobriga (Cabeza del Griego) and Bilbilis (Cerro de la Bámbola near Calatayud),[26] where they were largely rock-cut. On the other hand, the Roman theatre at Olisippo (modern Lisbon) was graced with a stage building similar to that at Emerita. Circuses were less common. One of the most spectacular was built at Toletum in the later first century AD. It is still possible to see the great concrete vaults and arena wall of a building that was similar in size and layout to the great circus at Emerita. By contrast the circus at Mirobriga (modern Santiago do Caçem) probably supported wooden seating banks.

It was in building bridges and aqueducts that local municipalities often succeeded in producing some of the finest works of engineering to have survived from Roman Spain. One of the most spectacular bridges to be found anywhere in the Roman Empire lies at Alcántara (Cáceres), in eastern Lusitania, on the Norba (Cáceres) to Igaeditani (modern Idanha la Velha) road. It still carries the roadway some forty-five metres above the river Tagus. It is borne aloft by six symmetrical arches which are anchored to the floor of the gorge by powerful pylons: a triumphal arch marked the mid-point of the bridge. The Alcántara bridge embodies a mastery of concrete as an architectural and engineering medium, and was faced with large rusticated ashlar blocks. It was dedicated in AD 106 to the emperor Trajan by regional communities like the Igaeditani, Lancienses Oppidani, Arabrigenses and the Banienses Paesures. The architect of this great masterpiece was a man called Caius Iulius Lacer: he completed his work by dedicating a small temple to the emperor, with the assistance of his friend, Curius Laco.[27] This still stands at the end of the bridge.

One of the most magnificent aqueducts in Roman Spain was built by the inhabitants of Segovia, in central Tarraconensis, perhaps during the first

century AD. Water was channelled for eighteen kilometres to the town from the Río Frío (near Fuenfría) in a concrete channel. At the outskirts of the town the water was fed into a distribution tank and then into another channel. This still zigzags through the narrow streets of modern Segovia, borne aloft by 119 arches built entirely from large, coarse blocks (*opus quadratum*). Over the last stretch, before the medieval Castillo de Segovia, the ground drops away sharply (the modern Plaza del Azoguejo), and a much taller row of arches on top of narrow pylons effortlessly carries the water channel and its supporting arches. The aqueduct was designed to ensure that the $1\frac{1}{2}$ per cent gradient necessary to maintain the constant flow of water was maintained.

All these buildings reflect how provincials accepted the formalities of Roman public life. The profusion of Roman-style bath-buildings and private houses, however, suggests that Roman customs were absorbed into the social and private lives of Hispano-Romans. By the end of the first century BC a Roman-style bath-house had been built at the settlement of Cabezo de Alcalá (modern Azaila).[28] It comprises an oblong dressing-room (*apodyterium*), warm room (*tepidarium*), hot room (*caldarium*) and a circular room for a large stone water-basin (*labrum*). The rooms were heated by hypocausts and floored in pink concrete decorated with pink tesserae in simple geometric patterns.

Concrete vaults supporting seating-banks at the circus of Toletum (modern Toledo).

By the early first century AD bath-buildings were amongst the repertoire of standard public buildings in the rapidly developing Hispano-Roman communities like Conimbriga. A fine example is the small, but fairly sophisticated, complex built at the south-east corner of Baetulo (modern Badalona) in the mid-first century AD.[29] The decoration and layout were simple, with a block comprising a large hot room (10.85 by 5.85 metres), a warm room, dressing-room, cold room (*frigidarium*) and plunge pool, adjacent to a walled exercise area (*palaestra*). The covering of the hot and warm rooms was achieved by means of a number of parallel brick and tile arches over each room. This comparatively primitive system of vaulting points to the absence of mature concrete technology at Hispano-Roman towns before the mid-first century AD. However, it was later used to spectacular effect at the near-by spa town lying beneath Caldes de Montbui. Here the *frigidarium* of the large bath complex is still covered by a magnificent concrete vault, supported upon low arches.

By the second century AD the development of bath-buildings had taken on a momentum of its own. At Conimbriga the Augustan baths were replaced by an enormous complex during the reign of the emperor Trajan.[30] This was far more ambitious and influenced by the contemporary baths at Rome itself. The complex was divided into three main units. The first of these was a large, rectangular, ceremonial pool around which people passed to gain entrance into the main bath-building. It was undecorated and bordered by a long colonnade. The pool abutted the second unit, which incorporated a huge, cold plunge bath, one square warm room and one round warm room, and one hot room with two plunge baths. This central unit was symmetrical about a north-south axis, with architectural innovation lying in the architect's masterful control of its large covered spaces. A principal concrete vault ran the full north-south length of the building, and there were also two lesser vaults over the east and west sides of the cold room as well as the large, domed *laconicum* and *tepidarium*. Domed hot rooms were a second-century introduction to Hispania which have also been discovered at the Roman spas at Noega (modern Gijón), on the Cantabrian coast, and at modern Alanje (near Emerita). Indeed, at Alangè the cupolas are still standing, and the interior is lit by a circular hole (*oculus*).[31]

On the western side of the Conimbriga baths was a small porticoed exercise area (*palaestra*), which gave access to a large public toilet (10.6 metres long). The third and final element in this complex was a monumental garden, built in the form of two long, parallel areas with tall apsed shelters at either end. From a monumental façade at the bottom of the garden clients enjoyed a spectacular view over the deep gorge of the Dos Mouros river and the olive groves beyond.

Bath-buildings were therefore rapidly adopted by Hispano-Roman towns and by the middle of the second century AD had become almost as sophisticated as those in the *coloniae* and other towns with a tradition of

Italian settlement. One can detect a similar evolution in the layout of wealthy town houses.

During the early first century BC houses at Cabezo de Alcalá were built by architects clearly inspired by Roman-style houses at coastal towns like Emporiae and Tarraco. One example (Casa 5c) was a long, narrow building (9 by 16 metres) with stone footings and mudbrick walls. One enters through a narrow passage (*fauces*), which leads into a square, covered atrium.[32] A *tablinum* and several other rooms opened off it. Other rooms were demarcated by wooden partitions which have long since vanished. A larger house (Casa 2D) (25 by 24 metres) consisted of a large *triclinium*, service rooms and kitchen, built around a central patio, or courtyard. The floors of both houses consisted of beaten earth or pebbles.

By the second half of the first century AD far more elaborate houses were planned and built in Hispano-Roman towns. At Baetulo, for example, a huge house in the north of the town, was sumptuously decorated with fine-quality mosaics and painted wall plaster. At the centre of the atrium floor (10.6 by 9 metres) the square *impluvium* was decorated with a black and white mosaic.[33]

The Casa del Aqueducto at Termes, in central Tarraconensis, was heir to a different tradition and may have belonged to one of the local notables, like Titus Pompeius Rarus. Here the architect actually cut the walls of the *domus* from the bedrock.[34] Excavations have uncovered a large square peristyle surrounded by a colonnade, off which opened a series of large rooms and an apsidal *triclinium*. All the walls were covered with painted wall plaster: indeed, one room boasted a scheme of painted white columns interspersed with imitation mottled marbled panels, echoing styles in first-century BC Italy. By contrast Roman town houses discovered at Numantia, a short distance to the west, were smaller and very poorly decorated. Nevertheless, many still bear the unmistakable signs of Roman planning. Clearly the desire to appear Roman was sufficiently strong to affect towns like Numantia, which had no legal privileges and a long history of antipathy to Rome.

The maturity of Hispano-Roman domestic architecture is represented by the great palatial mansions at Conimbriga.[35] These were built outside the town walls towards the end of the second century AD. Their architects may have been influenced by developments at the new town of Italica, although the absence of an imposed street grid permitted more experimentation. The focus of each of the largest two mansions was a spacious, rectangular, porticoed garden, which was laid out with due regard to the overall symmetry of the house and flanked by a large entrance hall (*vestibulum*) at one end and a monumental dining-room at the other. At the eastern mansion a large L-shaped fish-pond enclosed the *oecus*, while at the southern mansion a series of secondary gardens opened off the *oecus* together with a narrow apsed garden and colonnade further to the east. This residence also excelled in having a small, but sophisticated, bath suite. A large, square entrance hall led directly into a succession of seven round and hexagonal heated rooms with raised floors. It also provided access into an apsidal room with a cold plunge bath. Brick-faced concrete, however, was not used, and the walls in all these houses were built from the traditional stone, mortar and mudbrick.

The mosaics are one of the most impressive features of these houses. Over 15,000 square metres of brightly coloured pavements have been discovered in this part of Conimbriga. The many mosaics at the southern mansion give the modern visitor an insight into the tastes and social milieu of its owner. Those on the floor of the great peristyle reflect an awareness of Classical mythology, even though the figures themselves are clearly of local inspiration.[36] In one of the eight great roundels forming the main artistic focus of these mosaics Perseus clutches the head of Medusa Gorgon and offers it to a sea-monster: in another, damaged, roundel Bellerophon spears a winged Chimaera. In one of the *cubicula* near the peristyle the central (6 metres square) emblem was decorated by a circular medallion flanked by four panels. These form a continuous narrative, in which two hunters in short-sleeved tunics lead their horses and dogs to hunt down a wild boar. They are eventually successful, and their hunt seems to symbolise the victory of virtue over violence, chaos and death. The central medallion depicted a beautiful four-horse chariot, driven by a victorious charioteer, racing through a celestial vault peppered with red and yellow stars. This represented the spirit of the successful and virtuous man becoming one with the splendid astral divinities. The owner of the house was clearly a man with strong Classical preferences. However, the awkward jux-

Head of Oriens from the 'cosmological mosaic' at Emerita (modern Mérida).

tapositioning of themes and the rather clumsy figures show that he was satisfied by what aristocrats in the *coloniae* would consider to be a clearly provincial style.

By the later second century, therefore, the architecture and decoration of Hispano-Roman towns had developed an identity of their own. Native architects wasted no time in drawing upon the Roman architectural conventions so blatantly adopted in the *coloniae* and older towns; they adapted them to suit the prevailing local artistic and architectural traditions. Country villas were an extension of this development since in architectural terms they were essentially urban houses transplanted into a rural setting.

From the second century AD onwards the urban aristocracy probably spent increasingly more time on their country estates and less in the towns. However, as they were unwilling to forsake all the comforts and luxuries of their town-based existence, they started to build large stately homes with supporting farms. These villas are quite rare before the later second century, when they started to replace the modest farm houses (*villae rusticae*) throughout Hispania. The villa of La Cocosa (Badajoz), near Emerita, is one of the best-known examples, probably laid out in the mid-second century AD. The heart of the villa was a large, rectangular peristyle (7 by 13 metres), supported on twenty columns, and was almost identical with those in town houses at Emerita. It was surrounded by a series of square rooms (some of which are clearly bedrooms with mosaic floors), a large *oecus* with black and white geometric mosaic floor, and a small bath on the south side. In the fourth century the house was enlarged and, as in many Roman town houses, a much larger bath suite was added to its eastern side. This, however, was where the resemblance to town houses ended. As Vitruvius notes, 'A house in town obviously calls for one form of construction; that into which stream the products of country estates requires another'. Hence at La Cocosa a large working farm was built on to the west side of the villa. However, it was conceived as a self-contained unit and situated away from the owner's luxurious residence, so as not to spoil the carefully nurtured urban illusion.[37]

This kind of layout was not restricted to villas owned by the aristocracy of the larger *coloniae*; peristyle villas with baths and mosaics have been found in most parts of Hispania. The villa Torre Llauder,[38] just outside the Hispano-Roman town of Iluro (Mataró) on the Mediterranean coast, for instance, had an even more traditional layout. The visitor entered the 'urban' part of the villa by way of an *atrium*; at its centre was an *impluvium* surrounded by four exquisite polychrome geometric mosaics. One door led into a large *triclinium*, with a third-century geometric mosaic; two others led into large reception rooms with mosaics of similar quality. In addition, a narrow passage with mosaic floor led into a large square peristyle (28 metres square) with mosaic corridors. By the beginning of the third century AD such residential villas were becoming well established along the east coast of Tarraconensis, Baetica and other parts of Hispania. Examples have been discovered as far apart as Chiprana (near Dehesa de Baños, Zaragoza) in the Ebro valley, Comunión (near Cabriana, Alava) in north-western Tarraconensis, and at Pisoes (near Beja) in southern Lusitania.

One of the most attractive aspects of these country houses is the profusion and variety of mosaics decorating the *triclinia*, *cubicula* and baths. At the large villa of El Puaig (near Moncada), near Valentia, a beautiful coloured mosaic of the nine Muses was installed in one of the *cubicula*. The two beds were placed along two of the four sides of the room, over a white mosaic: the remaining space was divided into nine squares, each of which depicted one of the Muses. Melpomene, Calliope, Erato and the others can all be identified by symbolic attributes. Six kilometres to the west of Marbella (province of Málaga) a peristyle villa was discovered with a mosaic of *c.* AD 100 which is unique in Hispania. It is a long strip (16 by 0.6 metres) depicting an extraordinary variety of household objects, kitchen implements and food in black and white tesserae. Amongst the items illustrated are a pair of boots, a kitchen table covered with ribs of pork, a rabbit, a headless chicken, a fish, clams and a meat knife, an array of drinking cups, a fish-sauce amphora and a portable stove. Dinner guests passing from the peristyle to the two *triclinia* would thus have had a foretaste of the culinary delights to come.[39]

The development of architecture and art in Roman Spain was a long and complicated process, which mirrors the evolution of the Spanish provinces themselves. It began with the settlement of Roman citizens of Italian origin at new and pre-existing towns during the later Republic. Traditional Italian temples, public buildings and richly decorated private houses – with their strictly axial planning – were directly implanted into regions of strong Phoenician, Turdetanian, Celtic, Greek and Iberian traditions. Driving personal ambition in Roman citizens, mixed with patronage and civic pride, ensured the continued renewal and replacement of earlier buildings in the new architectural and artistic styles prevailing in the Roman Mediterranean of the first two centuries AD. *Municipia* and other Hispano-Roman towns followed this example. By the second century AD, therefore, their architects successfully blended new Roman concepts with old techniques. By the end of the century the building of lavish mansions had spilled on to the estates of the landed aristocracy throughout Hispania, transforming their farms into magnificent country homes. This was only part of a fascinating process which over the next 150 years was to transform the character of Roman Spain.

FURTHER READING

Mélida 1925 and B. Taracena *et al.*, *Ars Hispaniae II* (1947), are important general surveys, while J. Puig y Cadafalch, *L'Arquitectura Romanica a Catalunya* (1909), remains a valuable regional study. More recently Balil (1974), collected papers in *Symposion de Ciudades Augusteas. Bimilenario de Zaragoza*, 2 vols (Zaragoza, 1976) and Lostal (1980) have presented new surveys and evidence. Important detailed studies of town centres are provided in Aquilue *et al.* 1984, T. Hauschild, 'Munigua. Ausgrabungen an der Stutzmauer des Forum-1985', *MM* 27 (1986), 325–43, and M. Osuna Ruiz *et al.*, *Valeria Romana I* (Cuenca, 1978).

A. García y Bellido, *Los Hallazgos Cerámicos del Area del Templo Romano de Córdoba* (Madrid, 1970), provides details about the layout and chronology of the temple of the Imperial Cult at Corduba. A. Jiménez, *Arquitectura Forense en la Hispania Romana. Bases para su Estudio* (Zaragoza, 1987), provides a useful survey of Roman fora in Iberia, while theatres are studied by various authors in the Conference volume, *El Teatro Romano en Hispania* (Badajoz, 1982). Marble sculpture from public monuments at Tarraco is studied in depth in Koppel 1985. Early Imperial building techniques are discussed by P. León, 'Notas sobre técnica edilizia en Italica, *AEA* 50–1 (1977–8), 143–64. Domestic architecture is the subject of a number of studies, such as A. Balil, 'Sobre la arquitectura doméstica en Emerita, in *Emerita Augusta. Actas del Bimilenario de Mérida* (Mérida, 1976), and Nieto (1979–80), but has benefited from the example set by the very thorough publication of the Casa de los Delfines at Celsa in Beltrán *et al.* 1984. Mosaics in towns and on early Imperial villas are in the process of gradual publication in fascicules of the *Corpus de Mosaicos Romanos de España* (Madrid). The architecture of early Imperial villas is examined in Fernández Castro (1982). The best synthesis of architectural trends outside the Iberian peninsula is to be found in Boethius, *Etruscan and early Roman architecture* (Harmondsworth, 1978), and J. Ward Perkins, *Roman imperial architecture* (Harmondsworth, 1981).

─ 7 ─

RELIGION
IN ROMAN
SPAIN

T he colour and excitement of popular religious festivals in modern Spain and Portugal are familiar to even the most casual traveller. Ostensibly national saints are venerated, although the roots of many of these festivals may well lie in antiquity. From our modern standpoint it is hard for us to appreciate fully the importance of religious belief to the people of Roman Spain. Most daily activities were conditioned by personal beliefs and regulated by rituals and ceremonies. Indeed, it is impossible to understand Hispano-Roman society fully without looking at its religious practices and trying to gauge people's attitudes to the gods.

The story of Roman religion in Iberia begins with the expulsion of the Carthaginians in 206 BC. Roman gods accompanied those few discharged soldiers that settled in the south and east, together with small communities of Italian merchants. Among them were probably the Capitoline triad, Jupiter, Juno and Minerva.[1]

The earliest Roman temple in Hispania may have been built shortly after the foundation of Italica in 206 BC. Recent excavations have uncovered a building with three chambers (*cellae*), each of which may have housed one of the triad.[2] A long way to the north a simple stone relief of Minerva was built into one of the late third-century BC defensive towers of Tarraco. This is the earliest known Roman religious figure in Hispania and can still be seen.[3]

During the Republic Roman religious belief was based on rigorous observance: it had no emotional heart or set of prescribed beliefs. Instead it was concerned with maintaining the *status quo*, under the watchful gaze of the gods.[4] They had to be appeased, and Roman towns in Hispania came to appoint priests and magistrates to do this according to a strict protocol of divination, prayer and sacrifice. The great formal *capitolium* at Emporiae

Marble roundel (*clipeus*) depicting the head of Jupiter Ammon, from the great Imperial Cult complex at Tarraco (modern Tarragona).

shows how central this had become to Roman thinking by the end of the second century BC.[5] This protocol had fossilised by the early empire but had come to provide Hispano-Romans with a link to their past when confronted with the uncertainties of the future.

The greatest impact of Roman religion was the introduction of new gods in human form. Iberian and Turdetanian religions, by contrast, belonged to a totally different tradition. Their gods were never 'personalised' and rarely worshiped by way of images and statues.[6] Despite this cultural clash, certain Roman gods with no native, Phoenician or Carthaginian predecessors were soon adopted by the élites of major towns in the south and east. They can still be seen on the obverse sides of coins minted by native towns at Roman behest during the last two centuries BC. The bearded head of the Roman sea god Neptune appears on coins from Salacia (modern Alcoçer do Sal), and the helmeted head of the war god Mars on coins from many towns like Onuba (modern Huelva) and Carmo (modern Carmona).[7]

At the same time Phoenician, Carthaginian and Greek deities were rapidly identified with their Roman counterparts. The most famous example is the assimilation of Hercules with Phoenician Melkaart by communities in Hispania Ulterior. Hercules was identified with the Greek Herakles, warding off the evil eye and protecting travellers. His portrait appears on coins struck by towns like Carmo, Carissa (modern Corija) and Abdera (modern Adra).[8] The centre of the cult, however, was the great temple of Hercules-Gaditanus on the island of Sancti-Petri, a short distance from Gades (modern Cádiz). According to tradition, this was of great antiquity and was one of the most important shrines of this god in the ancient world. Two great columns of gold and silver stood in its forecourt, while inside there was a great stone altar to the Greek Herakles and two bronze altars — one dedicated to Melkaart and the other to his companion Reshef.[9] The temple served as an oracle and was consulted by many people, including Hannibal and Julius Caesar. It was looked after by a caste of shaven-headed, celibate priests who excluded women and foreigners from such sacred rites as the annual burning of an image of Hercules-Melkaart. The cult of Hercules in southern Spain is therefore a continuation of the Phoenician cult of the great god Melkaart. The cult of Vulcan in southern Spain masks the continued worship of the Greek god Hephaistos and his Phoenician counterpart, Chusor. Coins from Malaca (modern Málaga) carry portraits of the god wearing a characteristic cylindrical or conical cap.[10] Similarly, at Carmo Aresh is assimilated with Mercury, the Roman god of industry, commerce and war, while at Carbula, Salpensa (modern Facialcasar), Carteia and Obulco, Rešep assumes the identity of Apollo.[11] To the north-east, in Hispania Citerior, the head of Diana appears on a later issue at Emporiae, masking the continued worship of Artemis of Ephesus.[12] To the south-east, at Illici (modern Elche), Juno is assimilated with the Carthaginian Mother-Goddess, Tanit.

During the last two centuries BC, therefore, the major Roman deities in Ulterior and eastern Citerior gradually absorbed their Greek and Semitic counterparts; but this did not prevent new non-Roman deities being introduced to the peninsula. At Emporiae what has been interpreted as a sanctuary to the Graeco-Egyptian god Serapis was built on the southern edge of the Greek town in the late first century BC.[13] Serapis was recognised as a sky-father, a god of healing, a sun-father and a god of the underworld; he also became closely identified with the Egyptian goddess Isis. His sanctuary at Emporiae comprises a single chambered temple at the far end of a long, porticoed precinct. The god himself is usually portrayed as a bearded man with a corn measure on his head.

The wider acceptance of the Roman gods in Hispania took place during the early empire. They were imported during the great wave of Roman colonial settlement at the end of the first century BC, taking root at towns in the south and east. The spread of Roman religion to the less urbanised parts of the peninsula was assisted by Hispani returning home after long service overseas in the *auxilia*, where they had been in close contact with the Roman citizens of the legions. In the north-west Roman religion was restricted to administrative centres like Asturica Augusta (modern Astorga).

By the middle of the first century AD the Capitoline triad was worshipped at major towns in many areas. At Tarraco, for instance, Afrania Tertullina fulfilled a vow to Jupiter, the 'Greatest and Best', by setting up an altar to him.[14] Some towns, like Clunia (modern Coruña del Conde) and Baelo (modern Bolonia), boasted monumental centres (*capitolia*) for the worship of the triad, with sacred precincts, temples, altars and administrative buildings grouped around the forum. The Capitoline triad symbolised the Roman state, and in paying proper respect to them Hispani were seen to be pledging their loyalty to the state. At the same time Jupiter, Juno and Minerva were often adopted as personal gods, or as the patron deity of groups of people. Jupiter, the 'Greatest and Best', was, for instance, the patron deity of a burial association at the mines of Río Tinto, in western Baetica,[15] and the soldiers of the Ala I Gigurorum, an auxiliary cavalry unit in northern Tarraconensis.[16]

The religious centre of Bilbilis (Calatayud), showing the forum, temple platform and adjacent theatre.

At Tarraco, Lucius Caecilius Epitynachanus set up an altar to Juno in memory of his wife Caecilia Januaria.[17] Minerva, as a patron of industry and handicrafts, was adopted by a group of labourers at Barcino.[18] A magnificent white marble head of Minerva was discovered at Tarragona in 1929, showing the goddess with long flowing hair and wearing a Greek helmet.

Most aspects of everyday life in the town and country were personified by gods. Combative occupations were patronised by the war god, Mars. Sulpicius Cilo, a soldier of the VII Gemina legion, dedicated an altar to him at Vivatia (modern Baeza).[19] Hercules was popular in Baetica during the Republic as a thinly disguised version of Melkaart; however, during the early empire he was worshipped widely in central and eastern Hispania in his more Roman capacity as a god of war. A white marble statue from Tarraco shows him as an infant wearing a characteristic lionskin and holding a club. Many of his devotees were freedmen, like Pompeius Docilicus from the region around Uxama (modern Burgo de Osma), and free-born people of low status.[20] One of the oldest war deities, the goddess Bellona, had a very strong following in the vicinity of the small town of Turgallium (modern Trujillo) in eastern Lusitania but, curiously, is otherwise unknown in Hispania.[21] Perhaps she had become identified with a local deity.

Skill and success in the arts, industry and commerce were believed more certain if deference was paid to such gods as Mercury and Apollo. The vow fulfilled by Quintus Garonicus and commemorated on an altar to Apollo at Aquae Calidae (modern Caldes de Malavella),[22] in eastern Tarraconensis, was probably carried out in this belief. Devotion to both gods was also expressed in cult images, like the magnificent white marble statue of Mercury discovered at Italica in 1788. This was carved in the late first century AD and shows the god as a naked youth wearing a long draping garment (chlamys).

The Roman gods of health were also widely venerated. Sick people would spend the night in a temple of Aesculapius, the god of healing, who would appear to them in a dream and recommend a cure. Many satisfied people set up votive altars to him throughout Tarraconensis and Lusitania, including Fabius Isas, the heir of Cattius Ianuarius, a doctor from Pax Iulia.[23] More usually, however, the devotees of Aesculapius were people of lower social status, like Quintus Calpurnius Alypion, a freedman from Valentia.[24] The same is true of devotees of Salus, the Roman god of health.

The rural peoples of Iberia depended above all on the fertility of the soil. Since their landlords and the Roman state made regular and heavy demands on their hard-won produce, veneration of the Roman gods of the countryside was important in ensuring successful harvests. The land itself was protected by deities who occasionally assumed the Roman names of Ceres and Tellus. Ceres was the patron goddess of the association of land-surveyors at Carmo, as well as many rural farming associations (centuriae) in the area. She is represented on a marble statue from Tarraco as a veiled lady seated on a high-backed throne and holding a cornucopia. Tellus, an ancient Italian earth deity related to Ceres, was offered a votive altar by the Roman citizen Caius Sulpicius Flavus in north-western Tarraconensis. Liber Pater, an ancient Italian god of fertility, later came to embody the vine and was identified with Roman Bacchus and Greek Dionysus. He also exercised powers over male fertility. Surviving votive altars to Liber in Hispania were dedicated by both wealthy freedmen and freeborn Roman citizens. One records the god appearing to Caius Alionius Severinus of Caurium in a vision – perhaps a polite reference to an erotic dream.[25] No statues of the god survive, although those of Dionysus probably give us an idea of the god whom Severinus believed he saw in his dream at Caurium. One found near Valentia shows the god as a very effeminate young man standing next to a panther. His face is delicately carved, framed by longish hair and crowned by vine leaves. He wears a *chlamys* and lets wine drip from an overturned cup into the panther's mouth. The dominant wild spirit of the fields was Silvanus. At Italica he was carved in the form of a naked, bearded man wearing an animal skin and holding a selection of seasonal fruits.[26]

The gardens, flowers and vineyards were also personified by powers and deities. The most important of them all was, of course, Venus, who had a double role as the protectress of gardens and the patroness of beauty. Needless to say she was represented as a beautiful half-naked woman in shrines at towns like Egitania, Illici and Malaca. One of the most beautiful sculptures was found at Emerita, where Venus modestly covers herself with light drapery. Another, from the theatre at Italica, makes no such concession to sobriety and boldly asserts her nakedness. Venus' devotees occupied a wide cross-section of society, including Lucius Cordius Symphorus, a doctor from Las Navas de Marqués (Badajoz).[27] Traditionally, Priapus personified the fertility of gardens and vineyards. He was the son of the Greek gods Dionysus and Aphrodite and is sometimes represented on sculptures as an exceptionally well-endowed youth bedecked with grapes and other fruits. Alternatively, he is shown as an enormous phallus with a face and beard, like the marble sculpture from Tarraco. In 1981 a small and intimate sanctuary to Priapus was discovered in the deepest recesses of an extensive subterranean gallery beneath the Roman town of Clunia.[28] The galleries consist of very narrow passages (about one metre in diameter) cut naturally by ground water and running for up to 1,000 metres. The sanctuary was some 600 metres from the entry to the galleries and at a great depth beneath the forum. It was littered with clay phalli and figurines of Priapus, together with graffiti scratched by such local magistrates as the aedile Bergius Seranus, and individuals like Secundia and Aemilius Fitaus. The sanctuary was frequented during the early first century AD and was probably intended to ensure the life-giving powers of ground water in the day-to-day life of the town.

Hunting wild animals played an important role in the social life of the

Statuette of Priapus, in the guise of a bearded phallus, from Tarragona.

élite in Hispania, and veneration of the goddess Diana was believed to be the key to the successful outcome of a foray. A magnificent cult statue from Emerita shows her as a dashing, short-haired woman wearing a short tunic and sandals. She usually carried a bow and was accompanied by a stag. The success of an individual in a hunt was an important measure of his prestige, and divine assistance was rewarded by the dedication of a votive altar or the sacrifice of animals. Diana's cult is spread widely in Hispania, with a temple and association promoting her worship at Saguntum, and other temples at Italica, Arucci (modern Aroche), Segobriga and Legio.[29]

Water was also believed to harbour gods and spirits, and these too had to be appeased. Neptune, the Roman god of the sea, was curiously unpopular; however, powers of the fountains were respected at towns in Baetica and Lusitania, as were nymphs in streams and rivers. These were especially popular in north-western Tarraconensis, claiming amongst their adherents Titus Pomponius Proculus Vitrasius Pollio, the ex–consul and ex-army commander of Hispania Tarraconensis, and people of indigenous origin, like Boelius Rufus from San Juan de Baños (Orense).[30] Indeed, these nymphs may well conceal the survival of native spirits into the Roman period.

None of these gods would have been considered as forces for good or evil so much as presiding powers of whom favours could be asked and who had to be placated. The gods of the underworld, who lorded over a limited and purposeless form of existence after death, were regarded in the same way. The spirits of many people were understood to be claimed by Somnus, the sleep of death. On the other hand, the family of Marcus Acilius Fontanus, a youth from Saguntum, who died suddenly just before joining the army, interpreted the tragedy as an intervention of the Parcae – fates who led spirits into the realm of Pluto and Proserpina, the king and queen of the underworld.[31] A magnificent statue of Proserpina graced the theatre at Emerita, portraying the goddess as a robust woman wearing a long flowing gown. Caius Vettius Silvinus, from Villaviciosa, had every reason to be grateful to the goddess and dedicated a votive altar to her after she intervened in allowing his wife, Eunoida Plautilla, to return from the threshold of death: she had probably suffered from a serious disease.[32] Dis-Pater was the companion of Pluto and Proserpina, brooding in the bowels of the earth and lurking in deep mountain fissures. He had a violent temperament and usually made his presence felt by earthquakes, or spreading pestilence. At Munigua (Castillo de Mulva) Lucius Aelius Fronto attempted to appease Dis-Pater for some unknown catastrophe by erecting to him a large bronze horse on top of an inscribed pedestal in the forum, as well as a special temple or stable.[33]

The Romans clearly believed themselves to live in a world ruled and constrained by powers and deities, who inhabited every corner of the tangible world; but they also felt their lives governed by abstract forces. Fortuna, Victoria and Concordia were amongst the most important. Victoria is easily recognised in sculptures as a young woman in a pleated gown with prominent wings. One of the few examples known from Hispania was carved on to the keystone of a triumphal arch at Malaca (modern Málaga). All three powers were quite commonly invoked in Hispania and closely identified with the Roman state. Abstract forces such as Iuventus ('youth'), Bonus Eventus ('successful outcome'), Abundantia ('prosperity') and Pietas ('devotion') were also venerated. The Tutela was a spirit of conscientiousness

View of the religious sanctuary dominating the heart of the Roman town of Munigua (modern Castillo de Mulva).

and particularly popular amongst slaves and freedmen, who wanted to serve their masters well. A small temple to the Tutela was built in the Roman forum at Emporiae, towards the middle of the first century AD. It was paid for by Caius Aemilius Montanus, a senior magistrate, and housed a statue to the Tutela.[34] To the west the freedman A. Annius Eucharistus set up an altar to the Tutela of his work in granaries at Caesaraugusta (modern Zaragoza). The *genius* was the productive streak and the guiding spirit of an individual, a building, a town or even the Roman state, and ensured the continuity of its existence through time. For instance, there was a *genius* of a market building (*macellum*) at Bracara Augusta (modern Braga) and of the Flavian *municipium* of Arva (Peña de la Sal).[35]

In some ways Roman religion had little spiritual heart. The only personal religious act was an essentially passive one: the supplicant asked the deity

for a favour and, if successful, kept the god happy with a votive offering. As Martial remarked, 'Honour the gods, and you may just survive – against the odds'.[36] The main public religious acts were performed within the towns, since Roman religion had evolved into an urban form of a primitive agricultural religion. Moreover, after the civil wars of the first century BC Augustus reorganised the state religion so that it was now closely tied to the well-being of the empire. In Hispania, therefore, public observance of traditional Roman religion was organised in such a way as to ensure the smooth operation of daily ritual for the good of the state in all major towns.[37]

The great bronze tablets from Urso (modern Osuna) make it clear that in the *coloniae* there were two colleges of priests, with no fewer than three members each. The *pontifices* were the most senior, taking charge of public sacrifices and the formal observance of all deities in the town. *Pontifices* were also responsible for the *sacrae curiae*, and regulated cults in the towns. Marcus Servilius Asper, for instance, was *pontifex* of the *sacrarum curiarum* at Acinipo (modern Ronda la Vieja).[38] The *augures* were more concerned with divination, interpreting the omens for particular events by studying the flight and song of birds and the entrails of sacrificial animals. Both colleges of priests had an essentially passive role and acted as opaque intermediaries between the gods and their fellow citizens. However, they ensured that the traditional formalities of Roman religion were observed, so that the well-being of the Roman state was assured.

The priests were also responsible for the regulation of the religious calendar. Religious observance was based upon festivals throughout the year.[39] Little is known of the calendars followed by Roman towns in Hispania, although the Urso law states that their calendar was set up shortly after the foundation of the *colonia* by the senior magistrates. Surviving calendars, like that from Cuma in Italy, suggest that they might have been closely modelled on the state calendar at Rome. This is probably true of Hispania too. Quintus Marius Balbus of Acinipo concluded an agreement of reciprocal hospitality (*hospitium*) with the town of Lacilbula (modern Grazalema) on 18 October AD 5, the anniversary of the 'Jupiter the Liberator' games at Rome.[40]

Pontifices and *augures* were privileged members of the town aristocracy. Indeed, some, like the *pontifices* Blattius Traianus Pollio and Caius Fabius Pollio at Italica, had first held posts as senior magistrates (duumvirs). They were therefore more akin to administrators than either the priestly castes of the Carthaginian religion or the holy men of Christianity. Once elected, they would probably serve for the rest of their lives, gaining immunity from military service and other public duties for themselves and their children. They were also permitted to sit next to magistrates in specially designated seats at public shows.

Religious associations (*collegia*) played an important role in the worship of the gods among the poorer communities in the towns. They were formally organised and presided over by a *magister*, who regulated worship and ensured care of the shrine or meeting-place belonging to the association. At Nescania (modern Escaña) the *iuvenes Laurenses* college dedicated a temple to their patron god Iuppiter Pantheus Augustus, while at Tarraco the *cultores Minervae* met in a semicircular room (*exedra*) adjacent to their own temple to Minerva.[41]

If traditional Roman religion was intended to ensure the continued well-being of individuals, towns and, ultimately, the empire, then worship of the emperor was a way of transforming religious loyalty into political loyalty. After the end of the civil wars Augustus, in his role as high priest of the Roman state, rapidly identified the traditional Roman gods with members of his ruling family. Religious ceremonies therefore now aimed at expressing and developing loyalty to the state through the medium of the emperor himself. This was because in the complex cultural mosaic of the Roman Empire the emperor and the goddess Roma symbolised unity.[42]

In Hispania this Imperial Cult drew upon both Roman and Iberian traditions. The former had always venerated the spirits of the dead in the privacy of their own homes. The Iberians had traditionally honoured prestigious leaders and generals during the Republic. For instance, a small temple discovered at Cabezo de Alcalá, in the Ebro Valley, appears to have been dedicated to the veneration of Quintus Iunius Hispanus, a Hispano-Roman diplomat who served with Caesar in Gaul, and the goddess Victoria. Bronze effigies of both were discovered in the ruins of the temple. As victor of the Civil War against Marcus Antonius, Augustus enjoyed great prestige in Hispania and throughout the rest of the Roman world.

In 26 BC an altar to the joint worship of Augustus and Rome was built at Tarraco and in 15 BC at Emerita. Neither has survived; however, the former is depicted on coins issued at Tarraco as a large stone block displaying a copy of the ceremonial shield granted to Augustus by the Senate in 27 BC. This was inscribed with his most important political qualities, virtue (*virtus*), justice (*iustitia*), magnanimity (*clementia*) and devotion (*pietas*). The altar was decorated with oak-leaf swags symbolising the civic crown also given to Augustus in 27. At a later date altars were set up in the north-west at Aquae Flaviae (modern Chaves), Bracara Augusta and Noega (modern Gijón).

After his prominent personal success in the Cantabrian Wars and his foundation of new towns in the Spanish provinces, Augustus had become a larger-than-life figure to Hispano-Romans. It was but a short step, therefore, for them to recognise his extraordinary personal prestige by regarding him as a god. Shortly after his death in AD 14 his successor, Tiberius, granted the people of Tarraco permission to build a temple to the deified Augustus. This was located at the forum in the lower town and until the later first century AD may have served as a focus for the Imperial Cult throughout the province of Hispania Tarraconensis too. Another temple was built at Emerita shortly afterwards.

The temple of Augustus at Emerita (modern Mérida), now known as the Temple of Diana.

By AD 25 such loyalty to the emperor had been formalised into a hierarchy of priesthoods serving an organised cult in the towns. At its lowest level worship of the emperor was conducted by low-status individuals, especially rich freed slaves (*liberti*), who formed themselves into priestly colleges presided over by a priest elected annually. The *seviri* and *augustales* (later combined as the *seviri augustales*) flourished at towns throughout Baetica, eastern Tarraconensis and southern Lusitania. The priests officiated at rites and ceremonies to commemorate the emperor's birthdays, dates of accession, military victories, etc., and donated huge sums of money to pay for expensive games, sacrifices and public banquets.

These colleges fostered loyalty to the emperor amongst poorer people in the towns. At Olisippo (modern Lisbon) the *augustales* Caius Arrius Optatus and Caius Iulius Eutyches honoured the deified Augustus by setting up a monumental dedication to him in a public place.[43] This would have been the high point of a special anniversary, witnessed by the poorer townsfolk amidst much pomp and excitement. As the emperor gradually became synonymous with the old Roman gods – the more traditional guardians of the state – the *seviri augustales* set up joint dedications and votive altars, like Mars Augustus and Silvanus Augustus. Other priestly colleges existed in Tarraconensis and in Baetica, but are of less importance.

Throughout the Spanish provinces the élite of individual towns advertised their loyalty to the emperor through exclusive honorary priesthoods. The priests were known as *flamines* and the priestesses as *flaminicae*. The holders of these positions were usually wealthy Roman citizens of Italian descent, from the *coloniae* and *municipia* in southern Lusitania, Baetica and eastern Tarraconensis, like Quintus Iulius Plotus from Olisippo and Marcus Iunius Paternus from Castulo (Cazlona). Priests and priestesses were elected annually by the town council. At Tarraco they presided at ceremonies which focused upon the altar of Augustus and its adjacent temple at the forum in the lower town. The remains of the temple of this town-based cult have yet to be discovered.

The *flamines* and *flaminicae* presided over the celebration of the many imperial anniversaries celebrated each year. Augustus' birthday, his accession to power, the capture of Alexandria in 31 BC and his appointment as high priest of the Roman state were important dates.[44] Later the birthdays and dates of accession of 'good' emperors, like Tiberius, Vespasian, Trajan, Hadrian and Marcus Aurelius, were added. Recent archaeological discoveries at Tarraco provide an insight into how such feast-days were celebrated. The two focal points were the basilica of the lower forum and the theatre, where sculptures of many members of imperial families have been discovered. The *flamen*, dressed in purple robes and wearing a conical cap, would have led a solemn procession from the altar near the basilica to the theatre. It is probable that gold and silver statues of emperors past and present would have accompanied them,[45] rather like the colourful giants (*gigantes del barrio*) which are carried around the narrow streets of modern Tarragona on feast-days. At some stage in the procession a small inscribed bronze bell was rung. The procession would have culminated at the theatre, with plays, shows and public banquets, partly paid for by the *flamen*.

Priests also paid for statues in honour of the emperor, as did Marcus Cornelius Proculus, who was *pontifex Caesarum* ('priest of the Caesars') at Anticaria (modern Antequera) in Baetica and set up a statue to Germanicus in AD 18 or 19. Such open-handedness was not entirely due to personal loyalty to the emperor; it enhanced the prestige of the donors, who were also granted privileges akin to those enjoyed by priests of the traditional Roman religion.

These priesthoods were embedded in the social fabric of the main towns in the more Romanised parts of Hispania. As discussed in Chapter 3, such towns were largely absent from the north-west of the peninsula, and no *flamines* or *flaminicae* are known. However, the area still had to be drawn into the system of the Imperial Cult to ensure the loyalty of local élites. Thus the emperor Vespasian devised a regional Imperial Cult, which slotted into the new system of assize districts (*conventus*).

Regional cult centres were established at the north-western *conventus* capitals of Bracara Augusta, Lucus Augusti (modern Lugo), Asturica Augusta (modern Astorga) and Clunia (Coruña del Conde). The priests (*sacerdotes*)

White marble head of the Emperor Marcus Aurelius (AD 161–80), from the basilica of Tarraco (modern Tarragona).

were men of local origin, like L. Iunius Maro Aemilius Paternus and Memmius Barbarus. Most were ex-magistrates from local towns and presided over meetings of the *conventus* assembly and officiated at ceremonies in the emperor's honour. By virtue of this system the indigenous communities of the area did take part in periodic displays of loyalty to the emperor and state; but the persistence of pre-Roman social traditions meant that the *conventus* cult never really took root.

The *conventus* and municipal cult fitted into the framework of a wider, provincial cult. This drew upon the religious and political loyalty of all the communities in each province, with centres at the three capitals of Corduba,

Emerita and Tarraco. Every year a priest was elected by the assembly of each province, bearing such titles as the *flamen* of Hispania Baetica, the *flamen* of the gods of Rome and Augustus, etc. The provincial priesthood was an important step in public life, and most candidates would have served hitherto as town magistrates, priests of the municipal or, occasionally, as *sacerdotes* of the *conventus* cult. Moreover, on completion of one year's service a provincial *flamen* could pursue a career in the equestrian order.

The duties of a provincial *flamen* were similar to those of a municipal *flamen*, except that they were on a far larger scale. So too were the ceremonies and celebrations. At Tarraco these were all transferred from the forum in the lower town to the huge complex in the upper town during the later first century AD. The delegates to the provincial assembly would have congregated in the great square forum, which covers the middle terrace, amidst much pomp and ceremony: it is possible that they met in a large basilica on its southern side. The *flamen* would preside over meetings, whose business would include letters from the governor, making up embassies to the emperor at Rome, the voting of extravagant epithets to the emperor on special anniversaries, or supervising elections to the flaminate for the following year. The assembly was occasionally treated to an address by the emperor himself, as happened during the reign of the emperor Hadrian. Apparently some Spaniards had been voicing their distaste of military conscription. Any business concluded in the provincial assembly would have been sealed by a sacrifice to the genius of the living emperor and to the spirits (*manes*) of his predecessors in front of the temple of Augustus on the upper terrace. A marble relief found in the town has frozen part of such a scene for posterity. It shows a bull being led to sacrifice by two of the *flamen*'s aides, who were naked to the waist and armed with small axes and other sacrificial implements. Afterwards there would have been banquets and ceremonial games. The climax, however, would have been chariot races in the great circus on the lower terrace, attended by the *flamen* and magistrates and approved vociferously by the great mass of the urban populace.

It would be wrong to think that all religious sentiment in Hispania at this time was bound up in the worship of the emperor and the traditional Roman gods. The religious traditions of the south and east had drawn upon different Greek, Phoenician and Carthaginian roots, so that the ports and larger towns were always susceptible to new, exotic religions. Moreover, provided the devotees of such religions paid loyal obeisance to the emperor and the Roman gods, they were then free to build temples and worship them.

Devotees of the Greek god Nemesis were present in Hispania from the first century AD onwards.[46] Nemesis personified the vengeance of the gods and preyed especially on fortunate people who had forgotten their debt to the gods. A painting discovered beneath the arena of the amphitheatre at Tarraco portrays Nemesis as a short-haired woman in a short tunic holding

A view down the side of the Roman aqueduct at Segovia, showing rows of superimposed arches built from rusticated stone blocks.

Marble relief from Tarragona depicting a sacrificial aide to the provincial high-priest (*flamen*), leading a bull and carrying a sacrificial axe.

a globe and with one leg resting on a wheel. Her followers were people of low social standing, like the slaves Crescens and Eulalus at Tucci (modern Martos), or professional fighters in the arena.

The cult of Caelestis concealed worship of the old Carthaginian goddess Tanit and rapidly became identified with the Roman goddess Juno. Not surprisingly her cult is attested mainly in the old Carthaginian sphere of influence at towns like Malaca and Carthago Nova, as well as at Lucus Augusti, Gerunda (modern Gerona) and Emporiae (Empúries). Indeed, a priest of the cult, Caius Avidius Primulus, is known at Tarraco. Her votive inscriptions are usually to be recognised by the impression of a pair of feet,

One of the entrances to the Roman amphitheatre at Emerita (modern Mérida).

which symbolises the journey undergone by those seeking her protection.[47]

The relatively open attitude of the Roman authorities to these religions also ensured the shadowy survival of earlier pre-Roman cults throughout Hispania. In eastern Spain, for example, Iberian cave sanctuaries like the Cova de Font Major de l'Espluga de Francolí (Tarragona) and the Cova de les Meravelles de Gandía (Valencia) were frequented until the late empire. The god Herotoragus, known at Egara (Terrassa) in the third century AD,[48] is surely a surviving pre-Roman deity. In central Tarraconensis, along the Ebro valley and in Celtiberia, at places like Pardinia, Sofuentes and Bañales (all in Zaragoza), and Eslava and Artàjona (both in Navarra) the pre-Roman bull cult seems to have lost little of its fervour.

However, it was really the Celtic west and north-west of the peninsula where the survival of pre-Roman religions was strongest. These areas had been conquered later than the rest of the peninsula, and neither the traditional Roman gods nor the Imperial Cult had become well established. One of the best-known local gods in southern Lusitania was Endovellicus. A god of healing, similar to the Roman Aesculapius, he had an important sanctuary at San Miguel de Mota, near Evora (modern Ébora). Three marble heads of the god survive, showing him to have a serene bearded face similar to Aesculapius. In this guise Endovellicus appeared to a wide cross-section of people: he would suggest the best cure for their ailment and, if successful, was rewarded by votive altars, silver statues and little shrines. Ataecina was an important Lusitanian goddess of the underworld. One devotee refers to her jointly with Proserpina on an inscription beseeching, ' ... I beg, pray and beseech you by your majesty to revenge the theft that has been committed against me and to punish (with a terrible death) whosoever has borrowed, stolen or made away with the articles listed below: 6 tunics, 2 cloaks, etc'.[49] Ataecina was native to Turobriga (modern Almorchón), but as her popularity increased her devotees were to be found at towns as far apart as Pax Iulia (modern Beja), Segobriga (Cabeza del Griego), Metellinum (modern Medellín) and Emerita. The god Bandua, Bandusus or Bandogus commanded an even wider following, extending from the river Guadiana in southern Lusitania to Lucus Augusti in north-western Tarraconensis. He seems to have been the native equivalent to Fortuna and counted slaves, soldiers and Roman citizens amongst his followers.

In northern Lusitania and north-western Tarraconensis many more Celtic gods survived, unchallenged, into the imperial period. They were rarely represented in human form and, since local religious ceremonies were performed at open-air sanctuaries, were hardly ever housed in temples. Moreover, no one deity had a wide distribution, since many were closely identified with individual clans (*gentilitates* or *centuriae*) or peoples. Votive altars are our greatest source of information, frequently coupling the names of Celtic gods with those of their Roman counterparts. Thus the Roman sky-father Jupiter (or Jove) is often associated with the gods Anderoni, Candiedo and Lacidus on altars found in different parts of modern Galicia and Asturias. At modern Mesquita (Tras-o-Montes), in northern Portugal, Jupiter is the patron god of a community called the *civitas Baniensium*,[50] possibly masking a native divinity. Mars, the god of war, is associated with Coso at Bracara Augusta, and elsewhere with Tilenus and Sagatus. The fertility of the fields in western Celtiberia was ensured by appeasing the mothers (*Matres*). Again, some *Matres* were clearly the patron fertility goddesses to individual clans. Laelius Phainus set up an altar to the *Matres* of the Brigaici clan at Clunia.[51] Mercury was sometimes associated with such deities as Colualis, at Salvatierra de Santiago (Cáceres), in his capacity as a protector of housework. He also shared identity with the Celtic god Lug, who is known widely in Gaul and Britain. At Uxama (modern Burgo de Osma) an association of cobblers put up a votive altar to the Holy Lugoves, and other dedications are known around Lucus Augusti.[52]

One of the few surviving sanctuaries in the north-west is to be found at Panoias (near Vila Real) in northern Lusitania.[53] It comprises three forbidding rock outcrops, which are flat-topped and into which are cut a series of rectangular vats. The senator Cnaeus Calpurnius Rufus dedicated this to the Egyptian god Serapis and a host of local deities, including the *numina Lapitearum*, in the third century AD. Inscriptions cut into rock tell us that animal sacrifices were performed here in three stages. First, the animals were ceremonially killed in a building (now disappeared) which crowned the highest rock. The entrails were then tipped into the larger vats and burnt, while the blood was allowed to run off into the smaller vats.

The Hispano-Roman pantheon of the first two centuries AD therefore comprised an enormous array of deities, some of whom were native and others who were foreign to Iberia. Cultural differences slowly lost definition as the names of Roman gods merged with those of their indigenous counterparts. By worshipping them together their devotees succeeded in winning the co-operation of the gods and pledging loyalty to the emperor and the state. During the second century AD, therefore, 'a man could feel embedded in the closely-knit structure of a world permeated by the care of age-old gods',[54] whether the gods be Iberian, Semitic, Greek, Celtic or Roman in origin.

From the beginning of the first century AD certain quarters of the educated aristocracy of Rome had become disillusioned with the traditional religion. Some people found themselves in a world which was totally lacking in any spiritual or emotional fulfilment. Others, like Lucius Annaeus Seneca the Younger from Corduba, had become alienated by the identification of the old gods with the Imperial Cult, and took refuge in the rather dry doctrines of Stoic philosophy.[55] However, an increasing number were initiated into the emotional mystery religions of Egypt, Greece and Asia Minor. These stand in stark contrast to the official religion, even though they were rapidly incorporated into the Roman pantheon. They offered educated people the emotional excitement of initiation and the revelation of secret mysteries, together with the promise of the defeat of death and spiritual rebirth into

Marble statue of the goddess Cybele, flanked by two lions, discovered at the Roman villa of Els Antigons near Tarragona.

an eternal life. For the poorer onlookers the pomp and ceremony of their festivals were a welcome spectacle.

One of the best-known mystery religions was that of Cybele and Attis. Cybele was but one face of the great Earth Mother, who was known by different names in Cyprus, Greece and Asia Minor. The famous Artemis of

Ephesus, worshipped at the Greek colonies in Iberia, was another of her identities. Cybele personified the great regenerative forces of nature and offered her followers eternal life. In myth she fell in love with an attractive youth called Attis; but as he proved unfaithful, she drove him mad so that he castrated himself and bled to death. However, he rose again, symbolising nature's cycle of autumn and spring, death and resurrection – and, hence, immortal life.[56]

The cult was introduced to Rome in 204 BC and reached Hispania in the early first century AD. By the second century the cult is attested at towns throughout the provinces. Devotees of Cybele and Attis were mostly Roman citizens, like Lucius Tetius Seticnas(?) from modern Garlitos (Badajoz) to whom the Great Mother appeared in a dream.[57] She also appealed to slaves and freedmen. In towns where the cult was sufficiently organised there was a college of eunuch priests (*galli*) who were initiated into the cult by self-castration, or a ritual baptism in bull's blood (*taurobolium*) or ram's blood (*criobolium*). Ritual baptism was also used to initiate new devotees to the cult. The presiding high priest was called the *archigallus*.

One of the few surviving sanctuaries of Cybele and Attis is to be found at the great Roman cemetery of Carmo (modern Carmona) in Baetica.[58] It was a large and roughly square enclosure (11.6 by 13.1 by 10.6 by 12.5 metres) cut deep into the living rock, off which opened niches and small chambers. The most sacred place in the sanctuary was a small room on the north side, partially masked by a larger chamber. It housed the sacred image of Cybele, which was a rounded lump of stone, or *betyl*, and symbolised the earth itself. Periodically this was escorted around the countryside by the *galli* and *archigallus*, 'hawking her along the roads from town to town to the accompaniment of cymbals and castanets', as the Latin writer Apuleius remarks, and followed by barefooted devotees.[59] In this way the fertility of the fields was ensured. The room in front of this small chamber was larger and housed a statue of Attis with crossed legs.

The *taurobolium* took place over a recess in the ground (*fossa sanguinaria*) at the south side of the sanctuary. The bull would have been killed, with its blood flowing into an adjacent ditch. The *archigallus* sprayed the blood on to initiates seated on a bench close by, who then considered themselves reborn into a new life in the service of the Great Mother. At Emerita the baptism of Valeria Avita was celebrated with the dedication of a votive altar by the *archigallus* Publicius and the priest Docyricus Valerianus.[60]

The climax of the year for devotees of Cybele and Attis was the great spring festival between the 15 and 27 March.[61] On the 15th there was a procession of sacred reed-bearers into those towns where the cult was established: the reeds symbolised Attis' birthplace in the river Gallus. The procession culminated in the sacrifice of a bull to ensure the fertility of the fields. There was then a period of mourning for Attis, followed by preparations for the grand celebrations. On 22 March there was a ritual procession with the sacred pine-tree being carried to the temple of Cybele

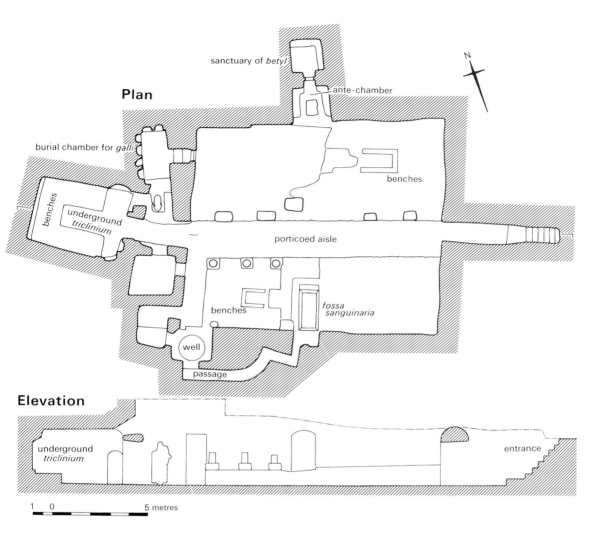

Plan

sanctuary of *betyl*

ante-chamber

N

burial chamber for *galli*

benches

benches

underground
triclinium

porticoed aisle

benches

*fossa
sanguinaria*

well

passage

Elevation

underground
triclinium

entrance

1 0   5 metres

Sanctuary to the goddess
Cybele (tomb of the
elephant) at the cemetery of
Carmo (modern Carmona) in
Baetica.

amidst ritual chants and music. This anticipated Attis' death; at Urso (modern
Osuna) a votive altar was dedicated to one of these trees by Quintus
Avidius Augustinus.[62] The 24th of March was called the day of blood and
was reserved for the more orgiastic rites. It started out with fasting and
mourning, and culminated in self-laceration by the *galli*. Apuleius describes
them as having 'faces daubed with rouge, and their eye sockets painted to
bring out the brightness of their eyes' and wearing 'mitre-shaped birettas,
saffron-coloured chasubles, silk surplices, girdles and yellow shoes'. They
writhed around in paroxysms, biting themselves and cutting their arms with
sharp knives. Some of the priests were then possessed with the 'spirit of
the goddess' and flagellated themselves with long lashes. Finally, the *galli*
smeared the *betyl* with their blood. The 25th of March was the festival of
joy, commemorating Attis' rebirth and the victory of life over death – a

day of sacrifices and celebrations. At Corduba Publicius Valerius Fortunatus underwent a *taurobolium* for the well-being of the empire and celebrated his union with the Great Mother by dedicating an altar on 25 March AD 238.[63]

The festivals were concluded with a symbolic washing of the *betyl* in the river Gallus. At the sanctuary of Carmo the river was symbolised by a well in the western corner of the sanctuary. When archaeologists first discovered the sanctuary, the *betyl* was found at the bottom of the well. To the west was a large underground *triclinium*, slightly misaligned with the rest of the sanctuary. This was deliberately planned to allow the first rays of sunlight on 25 December to strike the back wall of the chamber – a fitting way to celebrate the birth date of Attis. A short distance away was a burial chamber with niches to hold the ashes of the *galli*.

The Egyptian goddess Isis was another face of the Great Mother, again symbolising fertility, death, rebirth and the promise of eternal life.[64] Her cult originated in deepest antiquity, where she symbolised the land awaiting regeneration by the annual floodwaters of the Nile, in turn symbolised by Osiris, her consort. These beliefs evolved in Alexandria and the eastern Mediterranean during the fourth and third centuries BC, and reached Italy in the second century BC. The cult of Isis had established itself in Hispania by the later first century AD, with major centres at Emerita, Valentia and Igabrum (modern Cabra) tended by priests and priestesses, such as Flaminia Pale, the Isiaca of Igabrum. Isis also had devotees at towns throughout Hispania. Some, like Italica and Gades, were in an area historically sympathetic to eastern cults, while the cult was probably spread to towns such as Emporiae, Tarraco and Bracara Augusta by merchants.

The great attraction of the Isis cult to Hispano-Romans was, firstly, its ancient mythological background, and the fact that its philosophical framework was compatible with other mystery religions and that of the state. Secondly, there was the excitement of a gentle, but hard-won, initiation into the mysteries of a loving goddess. Apuleius describes how his protagonist, Lucius, passed through initiation grades involving ritual bathing, fasting, contemplation and, finally, a mystical union in the innermost recesses of the temple of Isis. Lucius refuses to tell us precisely what happened at the critical moment but states allegorically that 'I approached the very gates of death ... yet was permitted to return ... at midnight I saw the sun shining as if it were noon; I entered the presence of the gods of the Underworld and the gods of the Upperworld'.[65] Initiates were thus released from the constraints of their own destiny and reborn into the service of an all-powerful goddess with the promise of eternal life. Fabia Fabiana, a wealthy lady from Acci (modern Guadix), was one of many Hispano-Roman women who underwent this spiritual rebirth. In the mid-second century AD she gratefully dedicated an inscribed statue to Isis as the protectress of young girls and bedecked the goddess's diadem, ear-rings, necklace, clothes and bracelets with a sparkling array of precious stones.[66]

Not surprisingly, the statue has not survived; however, it probably resembled a marble statue from Clunia which shows Isis as a beautiful young woman, veiled, and with a long flowing tunic drawn up with a knot between her breasts.

Poorer people in the towns were unable to afford the expenses of initiation. However, they could participate in the pomp and excitement of cult ceremonies, such as those commemorating the death and resurrection of Osiris. Another important religion was the cult of Mithras. It differed from the cults of Isis and Cybele in that instead of a simple process of initiation and rebirth it offered its devotees the reward of victory over evil. In mythology Mithras vied for supremacy of the sky with the sun, who was the chief representative of the great sky-father (Ahura Mazda). He was successful and then captured Ahura Mazda's bull, imprisoning it in a cave below ground. However, the bull escaped, and when Mithras recaptured it he killed it. Despite the attempts of the dark powers (Ahriman) the blood spread over the world giving life.

The cult of Mithras reached Hispania during the second century AD, flourishing at many towns and sometimes at villas too. Discoveries in Britain and Italy have revealed that Mithraic ceremonies took place in sunken rooms (*spelaea*), specially designed to resemble the cave in which Mithras imprisoned Ahura Mazda's bull. At Igabrum excavations uncovered a magnificent marble sculpture of Mithras (93 by 96 cm), which originally adorned the second-century AD *spelaeum* there. It shows the god jerking back the bull's head with his left hand and plunging a dagger into its chest with his right hand. The god is dressed in long Persian trousers, a tunic and *chlamys*, and a characteristic Phrygian cap: his head is turned towards the sun, while a snake and a dog drink the bull's blood.[67]

Devotees of Mithras had a regular routine of intimate worship centring upon gradual initiation into the mystery. They formed themselves into a community divided into seven grades. Progress from one to the other was marked by demanding endurance tests, such as fasting, ordeals of heat and cold, scourging and branding. Devotees wore different costumes to signify their relative positions in the hierarchy. The very highest position was the father (*pater*), who acted as the high priest of the community. The wealthy Caius Accius Hedychus was the *pater* of a Mithraic community at Emerita and commissioned an array of statues of deities to adorn their *spelaeum*. The devotees themselves came from all walks of life, such as Lucius Petreius Victor, a garlic merchant from the vicinity of Iluro, and members of a funerary association at Pax Iulia; women, however, were barred from the cult here as elsewhere.[68] Mysteries revealed at initiation suggested that the soul descended to earth from heaven, passing the planets and picking up tainted qualities from each. Once on earth it was imprisoned in the human body, and throughout his life the individual tried to rid himself of spiritual impurities. At this point initiation into the mysteries provided great assistance and an understanding of the purpose of life. At death the soul left the body and if bad qualities had come to outweigh the good the soul was then dragged into the underworld by demons. If the opposite was true, the soul slowly shed its impurities and eventually reached paradise where Mithras received it into eternal life.

Lesser known mystery religions have also been attested. At Bergidum (modern Villafranca del Vierzo) in north-western Tarraconenesis Aemilius Cilimedus, a centurion of the VII Gemina legion, set up a votive altar to Iupiter Dolichenus on 12 February AD 224.[69] Dolichenus was the sky-father closely associated with Syria and Asia Minor and had become identified with the Roman Jupiter. At Emporiae fragments of a silvered bronze triptych representing the god Sabazios was discovered in one of the early imperial cemeteries.[70] Sabazios originated in Phrygia (western Turkey), and the complicated imagery of the plaques reflects his close association with Greek Dionysus, Cybele and Attis, and Helios the sun-god. To the south, at Corduba, a remarkable altar was discovered in 1921. It was dedicated in the early third century AD by a group of people, possibly merchants, to the Nabataean earth-mother Allath, a Syrian earth-mother Kypris, and the Syrian gods Yari and Nazaia. It also mentions the Syrian sun-god Elagabal, whose stone image had been brought to Rome by the emperor Elagabalus some years before.[71]

The emotional and spiritual character of the mystery religions was an attractive alternative to the passive religion of Rome and emperor worship. Each recognised the existence of an all-pervading god, advocated ascetic purity and, after considerable spiritual trials, rewarded their devotees with eternal life. They also satisfied Rome by identifying themselves with deities of the state, thus allowing their devotees to perform the obligatory gestures of loyalty. However, there were also drawbacks: despite the promise of eternal life, followers of Mithras, Cybele and Isis had to accept the concept of a remote and unreal deity. There was still a barrier between man and his god. Moreover, the cost of initiation into mystery religions and the exclusion of women from certain cults alienated many would-be followers.

Many of these qualms were allayed by the other great mystery religion, Christianity, which had emerged in Judaea (Palestine) in the early first century AD. It was presented as a religion for men and women of all classes, races and backgrounds and effectively 'democratised' mystery religions. Christians were initiated through baptism in water and met every week in small discussion groups, where they shared bread and wine. This symbolised the body and blood of Jesus Christ and the power of his life. The 'mystery' in Christianity was the guarantee of eternal life after death in the company of God. However, it differed from other mystery religions in that Christ actually claimed that he was God incarnate upon this earth. Thus the barrier between man and God was irrevocably torn, and the Christians enjoyed an intimacy and immediacy which the other mystery religions lacked.

By the later second century AD Christian communities flourished in many parts of the empire. As yet the communities were disunited and many

White marble statuette of the fertility goddess Ceres, from Tarragona.

preached their own versions of the gospels. Christianity probably reached Hispania in much the same way as the other mystery religions, and may also have been spread by soldiers of the VII Gemina legion and Spanish auxiliary units returning from service in Mauretania (modern Morocco).[72] Jewish communities in Spanish towns doubtless also played their part.

Christians spent their lives in preparation for life after death, effectively withdrawing themselves from everyday life. Moreover, they refused to compromise their beliefs either by praying to the traditional gods or paying homage to the emperor. They were also utterly intolerant of non-believers, whom they considered to be condemned to eternal damnation after death. During the third century, when the western empire was racked by civil wars and separatist movements, the emperors considered such views divisive and began concerted persecutions. However, Christian communities were now well organised, with a network of bishoprics throughout the western provinces, under the authority of the Pope at Rome, and served by a hierarchy of priests and deacons. By AD 254 there were substantial Christian communities at Emerita, Asturica Augusta and Legio closely linked to others at Carthage and the Pope at Rome.[73] Christian communities were therefore sufficiently well organised to resist persecution. Indeed, they did not have long to wait: in AD 259 Bishop Fructuosus of Tarraco and his deacons Augurius and Eulogius were burnt to death in the amphitheatre for refusing to recant their beliefs. Unlike the followers of many contemporary religions, the Christians were so convinced of their faith and the promise of eternal life that they were often prepared to die for it.

Between the second century BC and the middle third century AD religious beliefs in Hispania had undergone major changes. In the early years the Romans had gradually introduced an array of gods that were totally alien to local communities in Iberia. The greatest impact of this was the way in which the Romans worshipped gods in human form and enshrined them in temples. In terms of personal religious outlook, however, the effect of Roman religion was more apparent than real. Gods like Hercules, Mars and Jupiter rapidly merged with their local counterparts, ensuring the continuity of centuries of native belief beneath a Roman mask. In the early empire these Hispano-Roman gods permeated every corner of daily life, with many days of the year taken up with colourful festivities. Yet this was a religion presided over by remote and passive gods. Simply by being there they guaranteed the well-being of the empire. Emperor worship enhanced this by successfully diverting the energies of devotees to ensure political stability. The mystery religions allowed the Hispano-Romans some spiritual excitement and indulgence; but it was Christianity which really broke the mould, a process that was to have far-reaching consequences for the religious, administrative, cultural and social life of Hispania.

FURTHER READING

Good general introductions to Roman religion are provided in Ogilvie 1969, Ferguson 1970 and R. MacMullen, *Paganism in the Roman Empire* (New Haven, 1982). By contrast, M. Beard and M. Crawford, *Rome in the Late Republic* (London, 1985), examine the different approaches open to students of Roman religion and the difficulties of interpreting its outward characteristics from a modern viewpoint (Chapter 3). There is no comprehensive synthesis of Roman religion in Spain and Portugal. A useful source of archaeological discoveries and historical references is to be found in Mangas 1982, while the conference volume *La Religión Romana en Hispania* (Madrid, 1982) contains studies on individual deities.

The persistence of native religions in the north-west and west of the Iberian peninsula is documented in Mangas 1982, J. M. Blázquez, *Religiones Primitivas de Hispania I: Fuentes Literarias y Epigráficas* (Madrid, 1962), and discussed in their regional context in Tranoy 1981. F. Fernández-Gómez, 'El Santuario de Postoloboso Candeleda, Ávila', *NAH-Arqueología* 2 (1973), provides a detailed study of an indigenous god, Vaelius, in the context of a sanctuary frequented from pre-Roman to medieval times. The primary source for the Imperial Cult in Iberia remains Etienne 1958, while K. Hopkins, 'Divine Emperors', in *Conquerors and Slaves* (1978), provides an interpretative framework for the Cult in the Roman Empire. García y Bellido 1967 is a useful sourcebook for Eastern and mystery religions, to be supplemented by such detailed studies as M. Vermaseren, *Mithras the secret god* (London, 1963), and *Cybele and Attis. The Myth and the Cult* (London, 1977), and R. Witt, *Isis in the Graeco-Roman World* (London, 1971). Christianity in Iberia is discussed in Blázquez 1982b and in 'The possible African origin of Iberian Christianity', *Classical Folia* 23 (1969), while a broad analysis is provided by R. MacMullen, *Christianizing the Roman Empire AD 100–400* (1984).

HISPANIA DURING THE LATE EMPIRE

Anyone visiting the heart of modern Barcelona will be impressed at once by the massive town walls and towers of late Roman Barcino, which still shut off the medieval town from the modern city. Built according to the best architectural canons of the day, they represent Rome's attempts to assert its authority in the Spanish provinces in the third and fourth centuries AD. The second major monument to catch the eye is the great Gothic cathedral of Santa Eulalia, which dominates the medieval town. This is built above an earlier Christian church and signifies the triumph of Christianity over paganism. The restatement of Roman authority and the triumph of Christianity are of key importance in understanding the late empire in Hispania and, by implication, early medieval Spain and Portugal.

The social, political, religious and artistic life of the first two centuries AD was radically different from that of the third and, especially, the fourth centuries AD. What processes of change were at work to explain this? Does it represent the gradual decline of the provinces or the achievement of a new maturity? A summary of the main characteristics of the early Imperial provinces helps to answer these questions. Tarraconensis, Baetica and Lusitania incorporated peoples with very different cultural traditions and were governed by a network of towns. The Romans delegated the day-to-day business of government to the local élites, who also fostered and developed towns through a mixture of strong civic pride and social competition. These 'egregious nuclei of self-respect' were also centres of the state religion and Imperial Cult, observance of which helped to ensure the cohesion of the provinces.

Flaws in this system developed towards the end of the second century AD necessitating major structural changes in the fourth century. For instance, the relatively small Roman governing bureaucracy found it difficult to cover the huge and culturally different areas within their jurisdiction. This was especially true in Tarraconensis, and is implicit in the creation of the *conventus* system in the later first century AD. It may also explain the abandonment of such towns as Celsa (near Velilla del Ebro), Blandae (modern Blanes) and Lacipo (near Casares) in Tarraconensis and Baetica in the early first century AD. An even greater problem was the process of Romanisation itself. The continual absorption of local aristocratic families into the equestrian and senatorial orders during the first two centuries AD gradually undermined the Roman urban system in Hispania. A career based at Rome effectively removed the participation and financial contributions of individuals from local town life. The financial burden on the remaining families who erected new monuments and made new bequests, as well as maintaining earlier ones, became heavier.

Some élite families were therefore threatened with the spectre of impoverishment, and town life began to lose its attractions. Others became very wealthy and came to control increasingly large shares of land and other property resources. Finally, in the spiritual sphere, Christianity began to emerge as an uncompromising opponent of the state religion, introducing a divisive element into provincial life.

The third century

Until the late second century the administration of Hispania was a fairly tranquil affair and almost certainly profitable to the Roman state. However, this calm was shattered in the years AD 171–3 by an invasion of Baetica by Moorish tribesmen (Mauri).[1] They had swept up through Mauretania Tingitania and no doubt caused widespread disruption. Between the years 177 and 210 the Mauri and Costobocci invaded again, establishing a foothold in the vicinity of Malaca (modern Málaga) and then laid siege to Singilia Barba (modern El Castillón). The situation was soon retrieved by the timely intervention of C. Vallius Maximianus, the procurator of Mauretania Tingitana, who temporarily assumed military jurisdiction over Baetica. An inscription set up to Vallius by a grateful population at Italica (modern Santiponce) suggests that the Mauri may have attempted a clean sweep of the Guadalquivir valley and that there was quite serious disruption to communications and the sense of security in the area. There were also disturbances in north-eastern Tarraconensis, when a large group of army deserters led by Maternus swept into the province from Gaul. This time the threat to peace and stability was probably countered by a detachment of soldiers from the VII Gemina legion stationed at Emporiae (Empúries).[2]

These events were a harbinger of the political instability and wars which plagued some parts of the empire during the third century AD. Indeed, the tone of the next eighty years was set by the African emperor Septimius Severus, when he grossly debased the silver coinage so that he could pay his soldiers attractively high salaries.[3] The silver denarius had enjoyed a fixed relationship to the gold coin (*aureus*) and was the linchpin of the early

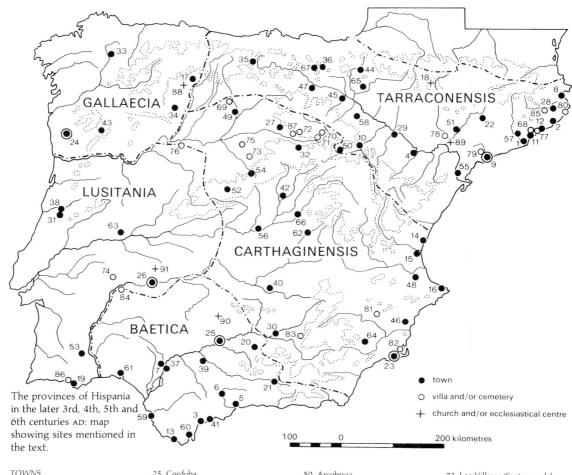

GALLAECIA

TARRACONENSIS

LUSITANIA

CARTHAGINENSIS

BAETICA

The provinces of Hispania
in the later 3rd, 4th, 5th and
6th centuries AD: map
showing sites mentioned in
the text.

● town
○ villa and/or cemetery
+ church and/or ecclesiastical centre

100   0   200 kilometres

TOWNS		
1 Barcino	25 Corduba	50 Arcobriga	72 Los Villares (Santervas del
2 Blandae	26 Emerita	51 Ilerda	Burgo)
3 Lacipo	27 Clunia	52 Abela	73 Santa María (Aguilafuente)
4 Celsa	28 Gerunda	53 Myrtilis	74 Torre de Palma (Monforte)
5 Malaca	29 Caesaraugusta	54 Segovia	75 San Miguel de Arroyo
6 Singilia Barba	30 Castulo	55 Dertosa	(Valladolid)
7 Italica	31 Conimbriga	56 Toletum	76 Fuentespreadas (Zamora)
8 Emporiae	32 Termes	57 Egara	77 Can Llauder (Mataró)
9 Tarraco	33 Lucus Augusti	58 Turiaso	78 Villafortunatus (Fraga)
10 Bilbilis	34 Paetaonium	59 Gades	79 Centcelles (Constantí)
11 Baetulo	35 Veleia	60 Carteia	80 Els Ametllers (Tossa de Mar)
12 Iluro	36 Veleia	61 Onuba	81 Las Cipresas (Jumilla)
13 Baelo	37 Hispalis	62 Segobriga	82 Los Alcazares (Murcia)
14 Saguntum	38 Aeminium	63 Egitania	83 Brunel (Quesada)
15 Valentia	39 Astigi	64 Bergastri	84 Dehesa de la Cocosa (Badajoz)
16 Dianium	40 Oretum	65 Ologicus	85 Vilauba (Camos)
17 Legio	41 Silniana	66 Reccopolis	86 Milreu (Estoi)
18 Asan (monasterio)	42 Complutum	67 Victoriacum	87 Baños de Valdearados (Santa
19 Ossonuba	43 Aquae Flaviae	*Villas and/or cemeteries*	Cruz)
20 Tucci	44 Pompaelo	68 Sentroma (Tiana)	*Churches and/or ecclesiastical centres*
21 Illiberis	45 Calagurris	69 Olmeda (Pedrosa de la Vega)	88 Marialba (Leon)
22 Iesso	46 Illici	70 Dehesa de Soria (Cuevas de	89 Bobala (Seros)
23 Carthago Nova	47 Tritium Magallum	Soria)	90 El Germo (Córdoba)
24 Bracara-Augusta	48 Saitabis	71 Los Quintanares (Rioseco de	91 Casa Herrera (Mérida)
	49 Pallantia	Soria)	

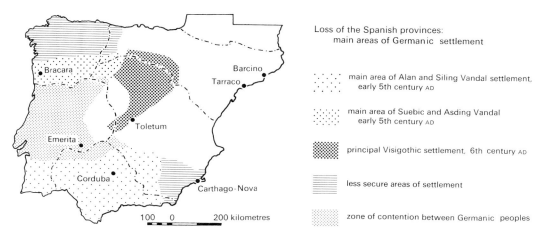

Loss of the Spanish provinces:
main areas of Germanic settlement

main area of Alan and Siling Vandal settlement,
early 5th century AD

main area of Suebic and Asding Vandal
early 5th century AD

principal Visigothic settlement, 6th century AD

less secure areas of settlement

zone of contention between Germanic peoples

imperial monetary system. Spiralling military bills led later emperors to follow suit. This engendered a lack of confidence in the coinage; but it also made a nonsense of monetary endowments by the urban élites and made the payment of large sums of money for new public buildings increasingly unattractive. Indeed, the inscriptions which had so blatantly recorded these great gestures disappear from the archaeological record towards the end of the second century.[4] This marks a change in the aspirations of the Roman municipal aristocracy. Henceforth wealthy private citizens began to divert money into private projects on their villa estates. The comfortable country houses discussed in Chapter 6 were the first fruits of this trend.

The third century therefore saw the breaking down of the strong civic pride and community spirit which had fostered the Hispano-Romano towns of the early empire. Deprived of this patronage, towns like Tarraco ceased to develop and expand. Excavations in the enormous suburban area between the modern bullring and the river Francolí have shown that several great early imperial mansions like the Casa del Mar and those discovered beneath the Carrer Alguer near the tobacco factory were abandoned towards the late third century. Before long they had been demolished and the open area used as a huge cemetery. To the west the religious complex at Bilbilis (Cerro de la Bámbola, near Calatayud) decayed during the third century, and the theatre at Malaca was abandoned.

At the same time there are signs that the Roman authorities were working towards certain changes of emphasis in the administrative framework of the provinces. For example, there was an attempt to separate the *conventus Lucensis, Bracaraugustanus* and *Asturum* from the province of Tarraconensis during the reign of the emperor Caracalla (AD 211–17). An inscription from Legio (modern León) tells us that they were formed into the 'Antonine New Province' of Hispania Citerior.[5] This was probably an attempt to tighten control over the gold-mines in the area. In any event the experiment seems to have been aborted shortly afterwards. A rather more radical change was the slow decline of several towns that had been of prime regional administrative importance during the early empire. Excavations in public buildings and private houses at Baetulo (modern Badalona) and Iluro (modern Mataró) have shown towns effectively abandoned by the later third century. The evidence is even clearer at Emporiae, whose harbour began to silt up in the early imperial period. As early as the late first century AD the two wings of the great two-storey portico (*cryptoporticus*) enclosing the *capitolium* at the north end of the forum complex collapsed and were demolished. Two small temples were then built at either end, facing on to the forum and shutting off the ruins from the public gaze. During the second century the two palatial mansions overlooking the Greek port ('neapolis') were abandoned, while in the third century the forum square itself fell into disuse. Recent excavations have uncovered a stretch of the portico still in the position where it eventually collapsed.[6] Late imperial occupation focused on a small community on the 'palaiapolis' and in the 'neapolis'. In regional terms the administrative role of Emporiae was absorbed by Gerunda (Gerona), while that of Iluro and Baetulo were absorbed by Barcino. Gerunda and Barcino became more important regional centres, although primacy fell to Barcino as the only port between Narbo (modern Narbonne) in Gallia Narbonensis and Tarraco (modern Tarragona). It is probable that similar changes were taking place along the coast of Baetica. At Baelo (modern Bolonia), for instance, civic planning broke down and public buildings were abandoned during the second and third centuries AD.[7]

During the later second and third centuries, therefore, administrative control of coastal communities in Tarraconensis and Baetica was gradually centralised. At the same time there was a visible contraction in Hispania's role as an exporter of foodstuffs. Wine produced on estates in the hinterland of ports like Emporiae, Baetulo, Iluro, Barcino, Tarraco, Saguntum, Valentia and Dianium was no longer exported but was presumably retained for domestic consumption in the areas of production. This is to be explained partly by the growth in demand by larger populations on country estates and partly by the abandonment of ports as convenient outlets for export. The Baetican fish industry suffered a similar transformation with both *garum* factories being abandoned and transport amphorae ceasing to be manufactured, perhaps due to increased competition from Africa. Similarly, in Baetica and northern Tarraconensis the production of *terra sigillata hispanica* seems to have contracted in the course of the third century.

By contrast the production of Baetican olive oil on the large estates in the Guadalquivir valley continued unchecked throughout the third century. However, there was an important shift in the direction of export. In the first two centuries AD the principal markets had been the city of Rome and legionary camps along the British, Rhine and Danube frontiers. By the reign of Gallienus export to Rome had dwindled sharply – again due to African competition – and Monte Testaccio ceased to be used as the main dump of Dressel 20 amphorae imported to the city. Instead, olive oil was exported in smaller amphorae (Dressel 23), mainly to the northern frontiers.[8]

Detail of a fish from a 3rd-century AD mosaic at the Casa del Anfiteatro at Emerita (modern Mérida).

Private mansion and street of late Roman date at the Diocesan capital of Emerita (modern Mérida).

It is at this point that Hispania briefly reappeared in the historical record, with events which tell us more about the political instability of the empire than they do about internal developments in any of the provinces. For a short period between AD 258 and 270 Hispania left the fold of the Roman Empire together with the provinces of Gaul, Britain and Germany. This move was led by Latinius Postumus (AD 259–68), a disgruntled general on the Rhine frontier, who was reacting against the administrative and military incompetence of the emperor Gallienus.[9] His leadership, however, was not effective enough to prevent groups of barbarians from breaching the Rhine frontier and crossing into Gaul. By 262 a body of Frankish tribesmen crossed into north-eastern Tarraconensis from southern Narbonensis. Their path and numbers remain unclear, although the writer Aurelius Victor tells us that they sacked Tarraco and, eventually, crossed over to North Africa by sea. Their direct impact was probably quite limited; however, the disruption and the psychological shock caused by this invasion were clearly profound. Over 150 years later the Hispano-Roman writer Orosius was still able to write vividly about it.[10] There is no recorded response by the VII Gemina legion stationed at Legio (modern León) in the north-west, probably because its role was confined to safeguarding gold production. There were further disturbances in AD 297, when it was recorded that Frankish tribesmen attacked the shores of Hispania, Italy and Africa. The emperor Maximian (AD 285–305) managed to eradicate this piracy and after suppressing tribal revolts in Mauretania Tingitana entered Carthage in triumph in AD 298.[11]

Prior to AD 171–3 the provinces of Tarraconensis and Baetica had enjoyed nearly 200 years of virtually continuous peace. By contrast the many civil wars and political changes in the course of the third century and the events of AD 171–3, 177–210, 262 and 297 must have caused considerable apprehension in the provinces and a loss of confidence by the élite in the emperor and the imperial system. This was exacerbated by the continued debasement of the silver coinage by successive emperors. By the 260s the intrinsic value of silver coinage (*antoniniani*) issued from the central mint at Rome was virtually nil, so that it ceased to be a viable unit of accounting

The *cavea* and 2nd-century AD stage-building (*scaenae frons*) of the Roman theatre at Emerita (modern Mérida).

and exchange, and complicated the task of revenue collection. As the fixed relationship between gold, silver and copper disappeared, it became harder to calculate levels of taxation, so the state's income suffered. In Hispania the period between c. AD 253 and c. AD 285 was marked by an unprecedented wave of hoarding. As 'silver' coins were continually debased, people withdrew earlier and better-quality issues from circulation and buried them in secret places. As the intrinsic value of the newer issues was progressively lower than that of the older coins, the value of the latter grew through time. Many people, however, did not retrieve their lost savings. Their hoarded coins have been found along the Atlantic coast of Lusitania and north-western Tarraconensis as well as in the vicinity of north-eastern Baetica and south-western Tarraconensis. The hoards vary in size from 29,860 *antoniniani* deposited in AD 200/268 and discovered at La Serrania de Ronda near Acinipo (modern Ronda la Vieja) to small lots like one of thirty-one coins from Bares (La Coruña) deposited in AD 268/270.[12]

Given the collapse of the currency and the loss of confidence in the imperial system, it is not surprising to discover that the Imperial Cult, the most vocal expression of provincial unity, began to disappear in the course of the third century too. Inscriptions commemorating the benefactions of *severi augustales* and *flamines* cease to be set up in public places; instead, town councils, like those of Ossonuba (modern Faro), Valentia, Tucci (modern Martos), Illiberis (modern Granada) and Iesso (modern Guissona), took over the practice of setting up commemorative statues to the *numen* of the emperor. However, even this practice died out by the 280s AD. Moreover, the constant challenges of rival emperors and usurpers, civil wars and the sheer military and political incompetence of successive emperors further undermined the emperor's prestige in the eyes of his subjects.

Between AD 217 and 284 an unprecedented number of emperors were recognised by the Roman Senate, and in addition many separatists and usurpers. This was in sharp contrast to the slow succession of the aristocratic Julio-Claudian, Flavian, Antonine and Severan dynasties of the first two centuries AD. The emperor was no longer a larger-than-life figure of exceptional ability and prestige, but had degenerated into something much more human and fallible.

Later emperors, like Gallienus, Claudius II (AD 268–70), Aurelian (270–5) and Probus (276–82), were hard and unsophisticated military men, who fought to maintain the unity of the empire above all else. However, they had lost their position as an almost divine focus of loyalty and unity. This hastened the breakdown of the Imperial Cult and the decentralisation of the Spanish provinces.

The later third and fourth centuries AD

In AD 284 Valerianus Diocletianus was proclaimed emperor by the army and for twenty-one years ruled the empire by a system of co-emperors before retiring in AD 305. His great achievement was to consolidate the administrative and fiscal structure of the empire which had suffered so greatly during preceding decades. Many of his changes were based upon the work of earlier emperors, like Gallienus and Aurelian, and were only completed by his illustrious successor Constantine I (AD 306–37).

Part of Diocletian's success was to recognise the great regionalism of the provinces and that with the changes of the third century provincial government had become far more complex. At his instigation provincial boundaries throughout the empire were therefore redefined. The forty-eight provinces of the early empire were subdivided into 104 and grouped together in larger regional blocks called dioceses. In Hispania both Baetica and Lusitania were left untouched with their capitals still at Corduba and Emerita. However, in AD 298 Tarraconensis was subdivided into a lesser Tarraconensis (roughly corresponding to the *conventus Tarraconensis, Caesaraugustanus* and *Cluniensis*), with its capital at Tarraco, Carthaginensis (roughly, the *conventus Carthaginensis*) with its capital at Carthago Nova, and Gallaecia (roughly the *conventus Bracaraugustanus, Lucensis* and *Asturum*), with its capital at Bracara Augusta (modern Braga).[13]

The smaller provinces of Gallaecia, Tarraconensis and Carthaginensis obviated the early imperial *conventus* divisions, which disappeared during the third and fourth centuries AD. The new provincial capitals of Bracara Augusta and Carthago Nova, therefore, gained added status at the expense of other *conventus* capitals, like Clunia. These smaller provinces, together with Baetica and Lusitania, clearly hinged upon a more centralised system of regional control than that of the early empire. Consequently, the administrative role of at least thirty major towns in all five provinces was redefined by a reconstruction of their walls. This was a blatant restatement of Roman authority in Hispania, in keeping with the 'military' character of the age. In the more important centres the re-enclosed areas were much the same as those of the early empire. At Gerunda the town walls were rebuilt between AD 290 and 300. They run along the lines of the late Republican circuit, which can still be traced over an area of six hectares.[14] The circuit is pierced by at least two gates, which are partially preserved at the Porta Rufina and the Portal de les Gàllies. The walls of Barcino were probably completed between AD 270 and 310 and were built directly in front of the old Augustan walls.[15] They enclosed an area of about twelve hectares and incorporated an elaborate system of at least seventy-two towers and four major gateways. The best stretch of wall and its towers are to be seen in the Plaza Nueva and the Avenida de la Catedral, on the northern side of the town. The lower section is built from large ashlar blocks, frequently using old tombstones, altars and architectural fragments, while the upper section is built from small bricks and concrete. The magnificent north gate of the town (Puerta del Angel) still stands, consisting of two great semicircular towers flanking a narrow entrance.

Town walls of a similar scale and grandeur are still to be seen at

Towers and gateway of the early fourth-century AD walls of Barcino, in the front of Barcelona Cathedral.

Caesaraugusta (modern Zaragoza) and Castulo (Cazlona). In the north-west Bracara Augusta, Asturica Augusta and Lucus Augusti were also walled. Indeed, it is still possible to follow the walls of Lucus Augusti in the centre of modern Lugo.[16] One of the best-preserved stretches is between the Puerta del Obispo Odoario and the Puerta de Santiago, where one can see alternating semicircular and square towers built from the characteristic ashlar masonry and slate slabs.

In other late Roman walled towns the enclosed area appears to be very small and the walls themselves are laid out with little regard for private houses or other buildings in their path. At Conimbriga (modern Codeixa a Velha) the late Roman wall cuts right through two of the great palatial mansions on the east side of the town, while the east gate effectively demolished a third adjacent mansion. Only short stretches of the late Roman wall at the rocky plateau town of Termes (modern Tiermes) have been discovered; but here again excavations have shown that it cut across the line of earlier buildings and that it was built from large blocks of re-used masonry.[17] Finally, in Carthago Nova (modern Cartagena) the discovery of an enormous semicircular bastion and a triple defensive wall in the south-western corner of the town (La Calle Nueva) suggests that only a limited area was enclosed.[18]

In the early fourth century, therefore, each of the five provinces of Hispania was closely supervised by a series of fortified administrative centres and co-ordinated by a governor based at the provincial capital. In the earlier fourth century all the provinces were administered by an equestrian governor (*praeses*), although they were replaced at a later date by high-ranking senators (*consulares*) in the provinces of Baetica, Lusitania and Gallaecia.[19] Initially, provincial governors ensured the prompt collection of taxes. The reluctance of the municipal aristocracy to carry out such work meant that this assumed a special significance. The governor ensured the upkeep of the imperial postal system and essential public buildings and heard law cases. He was assisted by a staff of some fifty to 100 officials.

The five provinces of Hispania and Mauretania Tingitana formed the 'Dioceses of the Spains'. This large regional division was in the charge of a very important official called the *vicarius*, who was appointed as an intermediary between the lower-ranking provincial governors and the chief imperial minister of the western empire – the Praetorian Prefect of the Gauls, based at Arelate (modern Arles) in Narbonensis. Quintus Aeclanius Hermias was one of the first *vicarii* in the Diocesis of the Spains. He was based at Emerita (modern Mérida), the capital of the dioceses, and co-ordinated the collection and transport of tax from all six provinces, acted as an appeal judge, and generally supervised all civil affairs. This work clearly required an extensive staff (300 men) including secret police, legal registrars and officials for state supplies (*annona*). The Count of the Spains was an official who, until AD 340, assisted the *vicarius* and carried out specific tasks on the emperor's behalf. Other officials in the dioceses included an appointee to deal with imperial property and a delegate of the financial minister to oversee economic matters.

All these measures went some way towards making the provinces of Hispania more accountable to the imperial administration. Moreover, the profitability of the Spanish provinces was enhanced by an overhaul of the state fiscal system by Diocletian and Constantine. Diocletian tried to rebuild the Roman monetary system by issuing a new but limited gold and silver coinage, and a large new silvered copper coin (*follis*). Constantine increased the volume of the gold coinage and at the same time introduced smaller and lighter *folles*. The minting and issue of coinage were now directly tied to the payment of tax, although taxes were now based upon assessments in kind rather than in terms of monetary value. The productivity of the land was calculated in terms of agricultural units (*iuga*), while all the men, women and animals on estates were assessed by other units (*capita*). This system came to be known as *capitatio* and *iugatio*, and dues were paid to the praetorian prefect of the Gauls. Taxes could also be paid in kind. The great Theodosian Law Code records a letter from the emperor Constantius II (AD 337–61) to Egnatius Faustinus, the *praeses* of Baetica, in AD 337. It complains that the provincials in Baetica frequently 'default of payment of tribute or on the (annual) account of payments due of clothing, gold or silver'.[20] Baetican textiles were therefore considered an adequate substitute for gold or silver. In another letter, this time issued to Constantine from Castulo in AD 323,[21] clothing and horses are mentioned as regular taxes. Otherwise a few indirect taxes survived from the early empire, while Constantine introduced a special tax on traders and craftsmen (*collatio lustralis*).

The only sphere of official life to remain untouched in Hispania was the army. In line with more heavily garrisoned provinces, the VII Gemina legion and an assortment of auxiliary cohorts at Paetaonium (modern Rosinos de Vidriales), Cohors Gallica, Lucus Augusti (modern Lugo), Iuliobriga (modern El Retortillo) and Veleia (modern Iruña) were to all intents and purposes stationary troops and were similar to the poor-quality frontier troops (*limitanei*) of other provinces. The defences of Legio, however, were completely rebuilt,[22] and it seems that the army's main task remained the supervision of the gold-mines within the province of Gallaecia. Unlike other provinces in the empire, Hispania did not have mobile field armies (*comitatenses*) until the fifth century. All these changes were the result of deliberate planning and experiment by the Roman authorities over some twenty to thirty years after the difficulties of the third century. The Romans had successfully redefined their authority in the Spanish provinces.

Constantine's adoption of Christianity as his own personal religion was, however, to have more lasting consequences. By the early fourth century AD Christian communities in Hispania were flourishing. In 305 a church council at Illiberis was attended by bishops from towns in all the Spanish provinces. The council voiced its condemnation of pagan processions, the

Late Roman mosaic from Barcino (modern Barcelona), showing a chariot race, possibly at the Circus Maximus, Rome.

act of making sacrifices at *capitolia* and its disapproval of the more obscene public spectacles. Its Acts also inform us about violent struggles between Christians and pagans. Such opinions were considered divisive, and between 303 and 312 the emperors Diocletian and Galerius began major persecutions against the Christians. Saint Felix was martyred at Gerunda (modern Gerona) and Saint Cucufatus at Barcino, while Saints Justa and Rufina were put to death at Hispalis for desecrating a pagan procession.[23]

All this changed after the conversion of Constantine in AD 312. Effectively enlisting the help of the Christian God in his task of governing the empire, Constantine henceforth took a prominent role in church affairs, convening major church councils on matters of doctrine at Rome, Arelate, Nicaea (modern Iznik, northern Turkey) and Caesaraea (Palestine). In this he was assisted by his religious adviser, Bishop Ossius of Corduba. On the one hand, Constantine's adoption of Christianity permitted the Church to worship freely and openly. On the other, his personal arbitration in religious affairs, the return of confiscated property and the showering of gifts and legal immunities meant that its power in political and administrative affairs grew very rapidly.

With all these administrative and religious changes the character of fourth-century Hispania differed radically from that of the early empire. The most obvious place to look for signs of this new order is in the towns. There was only limited restoration of earlier Roman monuments or construction of new secular buildings. Moreover, they were mostly paid for by officials rather than by private citizens.

At Tarraco an inscription records that T. Iulius Valens, the *praeses* of Hispania Citerior (Tarraconensis), ordered the construction of the 'Jovian' colonnade of a basilica at the request of the reigning emperors Diocletian and Maximian, in AD 286–93.[24] Similarly, the *praeses* Marcus Aurelius

Vincentius was responsible for the rebuilding of the baths of Montanus, an event commemorated on an inscription by the financial controller of Tarraco, Messius Marianus.[25] Other official activity comes in the form of statues dedicated to the *numina* of individual emperors. Their pedestals testify to the work of governors like Badius Macrinus, Valerius Iulianus and Septimus Acindynus in setting up statues to the majesty of the Christian emperors Constantine, Crispus and Constantius II.[26]

Official building works are recorded in other provinces too. At Oretum (modern Granátula) in Carthaginensis, for example, the *praeses* Tiberianus built a granary in AD 387.[27] Similarly, at the Diocesan capital of Emerita, in Lusitania, the Count of the Spains Tiberius Flavius Laetus ordered the restoration of a colonnade and some other monuments at the circus in AD 337–40.[28] He was assisted in this by the *praeses* Iulius Saturninus. Provincial governors and town councils also dedicated statues to fourth-century emperors here and at Aeminium (Coimbra), in Lusitania, and Corduba, Hispalis and Astigi, in Baetica.[29]

This building activity is a far cry from the heady days of the early empire. The names of status-seeking individual benefactors are completely absent. Moreover, it took place against a background of the slow decay of earlier public buildings. At Tarraco a fire destroyed the great basilica at the lower forum during the 350s or 360s, and it is significant that there was no attempt to rebuild it.[30] Civic pride and funds were sufficiently low for the once proud symbol of Tarraco's judicial, religious and administrative life to be abandoned as a pile of rubble at the centre of the town. Not long afterwards this site and commercial buildings on either side of an adjacent road were used as a burial-ground. The great theatre of Tarraco was also abandoned at about this time. In Hispania Carthaginensis the fourth century witnessed a gradual reduction in the inhabited area within the walls of Valentia so that civic life now focused on a small community around the present cathedral, the site of the Roman forum. Inland at Termes (modern Tiermes) one of the town's principal aqueducts fell into disuse in the early fourth century. In Baetica makeshift shelters were built between the pilasters on the old covered pavements at the site of the abandoned new town of Italica. They were the work of poor townsmen reusing old masonry and frequently incorporated small hearths. Meanwhile in the old town near by the theatre had been flooded by the Guadalquivir in the mid-fourth century and had filled up with fine alluvial mud. There was no attempt at rehabilitation and the building was abandoned.[31]

At Baelo the construction of a small bath-building to the west of the forum is evidence of a degree of centralised control in the town. However, at the same time random buildings of poor quality made a mockery of traditional Roman municipal planning. The main east-west street (*decumanus*) was allowed to silt up and during the later fourth century was covered over by a small, shoddy stone building. The theatre was abandoned, filled with dumped rubbish and then used as a cemetery. Some of the inhabitants themselves were discovered in a small cemetery outside the east gate, buried in coffins made from reused masonry.

Although the monumental centres slowly decayed, the towns themselves still served as administrative centres frequented by imperial officials and those town councillors who had not managed to evade their duties. Their large and often luxurious private dwellings were still built from time to time alongside abandoned public buildings. At Emerita, for instance, an imposing second-century *domus* to the south of the theatre was enlarged during the fourth century. One of its features was a range of richly decorated rooms dominated by a great apsidal dining-room (*oecus*). The walls were decorated with coloured paintings in the form of a mock architectural scheme. A series of rectangular panels were subdivided by imitation columns and low, narrow, windows. Two men and two women were painted on the panels, standing at about 1.3 m high and wearing white tunics with the red bands, white lines and decorated patches typical of the period.[32]

Steps leading into the sunken corridor in the late Roman building complex at Castulo (Cazlona).

Another wealthy establishment was discovered near the railway station in 1910. It was decorated by a crude but charming floor mosaic, designed by the workshop of Annius Ponus. The theme is unabashedly pagan and depicts Bacchus taking Ariadne as his bride on the island of Naxos in the Aegean. He is assisted by Pan, who deftly removes Ariadne's clothing while Theseus, dressed in a toga, looks on unawares.

During the fourth century Corduba remained the provincial capital of Baetica and boasted rich residences in different parts of the town. For instance, at the Bodega de la Compañia a magnificent mosaic (3.72 by 2.90 metres) of the four seasons decorated the floor of a dining-room (*triclinium*). Each of the four seasons faced the spectator, wearing long white – or in the case of summer, red – tunics decorated with long shoulder strips and patches on the knees and shoulders. Summer clutches an armful of grapes, Spring holds a flower, and Autumn wields a scythe. The two surviving faces bear serene expressions, although the eyes are somewhat sad. Another pagan theme adorned a mosaic floor found beneath the Avenida del Generalísimo, at the centre of the Roman town. The central tableau shows Cupid and Psyche embracing and kissing, against an intricate series of interlocking circles. A mosaic from Astigi (modern Écija) portrays an even more blatantly pagan theme. The famous 'Torture of Dirce' is illustrated in dull white, grey and brown colours, and shows an attractive and semi-naked Dirce tied to a bounding bull, which is led by one youth and pursued by another with a stout cane.[33]

Until recently little was known about the town of Complutum (modern Alcalá de Henares) in central Carthaginensis, except for the fact that between the late first century BC and the late first century AD it covered the top of a great flat hill on the outskirts of modern Madrid. Recent excavations, however, have shown that in the late first century the town was refounded in the plain below and that during the third, fourth and fifth centuries AD it developed into a rich residential urban centre.[34] Public buildings remain to be discovered; however, the mosaics from the private houses are among the richest in the Iberian peninsula. The best of these were found in the house of Bacchus, in a magnificent apsed *triclinium* to the west of the peristyle (12 by 9 metres). Here the main panel in the central tableau shows a drunken Bacchus being supported by a bare-torsoed satyr on one side and a corpulent Silenus on the other. Bacchus lolls unsteadily, trying to focus on the spectator, with his head weighed down by an elaborate head-dress of grapes and leaves, while an empty wine cup dangles from his hand. In the far left of the panel an approving maenad dances in tune with some orgiastic beat. In a panel on each side of this scene a large chalice of wine is jealously guarded by two leaping leopards; beneath the Bacchus scene three youths with linked hands tread the grapes in a long vat and are kept supplied by two other youths. Adjacent to the central tableau is a small panel depicting the heads of the four seasons – important totems for a good harvest.

This mosaic was laid during the later fourth century, and its blatantly pagan scenes would have shocked the sensibilities of contemporary Christians like St Paulinus of Nola and his Spanish wife Therasia, who probably owned country estates in the area. The mosaic at the house of Leda, a short distance to the west, would have provoked outright condemnation. The central panel shows the pagan god Jupiter in the form of a white swan pulling away Leda's tunic with his beak. Needless to say, Leda looks upset, and her face reveals strong misgivings.

By contrast the partially excavated mansion at the centre of Castulo (Cazlona) in southern Carthaginensis appears more functional with no mosaics. On its eastern side was a suite of baths, boasting at least two warm rooms with a hypocaust floor and a cold plunge bath. This was linked with the western part of the house by a remarkable vaulted passageway

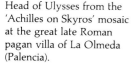

Head of Ulysses from the 'Achilles on Skyros' mosaic at the great late Roman pagan villa of La Olmeda (Palencia).

built from large stone blocks. From here steps led into an open patio surrounded by a portico. The buildings incorporated reused blocks and tombstones, like public buildings in other parts of Hispania, suggesting that their purpose might have been official.[35]

The province of Tarraconensis is considerably poorer in rich residences during the fourth century than it had been under the early empire. Indeed, one of the few mansions with a mosaic floor was discovered beneath the Calle de la Condesa Sobaradiel in the south-west corner of Barcino. Building works in 1840 revealed a room with a hypocaust covered by a large mosaic (5.3 square metres) and decorated with painted wall plaster. A chariot race was vividly depicted showing horses galloping around an oblong central barrier. It has been suggested that this was meant to represent the Circus Maximus at Rome. Another building found a short distance to the north (Passatje del Credit) boasted a very fine mosaic floor, with a central panel depicting the Three Graces.[36]

By the side of these wealthy mansions excavations have occasionally brought to light rather more modest buildings of an indeterminate character. At Dianium (modern Denia) in Carthaginensis work at the L' Hort de Morand has revealed a row of simple structures built on either side of a metalled road near the site of the forum. They were built from stone and mortar — often reusing earlier pieces — with earth floors. One house was abandoned towards the middle of the fourth century, and the area as a whole had been converted into a cemetery by the fifth century AD. Similarly, at Pompaelo (modern Pamplona), in Tarraconensis, excavations uncovered crude buildings built from reused masonry and, occasionally, simple geometric mosaic floors. These too were abandoned during the fifth century AD.[37]

The fourth century also saw the appearance of ecclesiastical buildings as an important new focus in town life. Fourth-century bishoprics are known to have existed in all the Spanish provinces, except for Gallaecia. Indeed, their bishops attended the great church councils of Caesaraugusta in 380 and Toletum in 400. Literary and archaeological evidence show that church buildings began to dominate the centres of major Hispano-Roman towns as they became ever more closely identified with the state.

The late Roman Spanish poet Prudentius, for example, describes the *Martyrium* of Saint Eulalia at Emerita: 'overhead the gleaming roof flashes light from its gilded panels and shaped stones diversify the floor [mosaics] so that it seems like a rose-covered meadow blushing with varied blooms'.[38] In Hispalis the 'Holy Hispalensian church of Jerusalem' is to be located beneath the modern cathedral. Excavations have uncovered a square baptistry and adjacent building of late fourth-century date at the Patio de las Banderas in the Alcázar, outside the walls of the *colonia*. Work at El Pradillo immediately to the north of Italica in 1903 revealed what appeared to be a large (14.5 by 5.6 metres) church with a nave and two aisles and terminating in a semicircular apse. This small *martyrium* was surrounded by the graves of over 100 faithful. One of them was covered by a mosaic lid showing a seated girl called Antonia Vetia, who died aged eleven years and eight months.[39]

Prudentius tells us that in his home town of Calagurris (modern Calahorra), in Hispania Carthaginensis, there was a *martyrium* to the Saints Emeterius and Caledonius. At Clunia (modern Coruña del Conde) a small cemetery focused on a Christian church built within the ruins of a large house on the north-eastern side of the forum. One of the greatest early Christian monuments in Hispania is the sprawling early Christian cemetery at Tarraco. This developed between the end of the third and the seventh centuries AD and is still to be seen on the left bank of the river Francolí, to the west of the town. It held about 2050 burials and covered the sites of early imperial suburban mansions.[40] Poorer people were buried in ditches and makeshift coffins of roof tiles and broken amphorae, while the élite found eternal rest in imported marble sarcophagi, or sarcophagi cut from local limestone and placed within large concrete mausolea. One local sarcophagus carried the remains of Leucadius, an important military official in the town. He was also a Christian, and in one of the panels a togate apostle is depicted receiving the word of God. This was a parchment inscribed with the Christian chi-rho symbol and delivered to him by a hand reaching out of the sky. Optimus' tomb, by contrast, was decorated with a colourful mosaic, which shows him as a bearded man wearing a toga, holding a scroll in one hand and blessing the onlooker with the other. In the mid-fifth century a large church was built on the south side of the cemetery. This was the reconstruction of an earlier church on the same site, and the burials in the cemetery were clustered as close to it as possible to be assured of spiritual protection in the next world. At Barcino a church was built within the walls of the *colonia*, beneath the present cathedral of Santa Eulalia. Again its layout was obscured by a fifth-century church. At Gerunda the church of Saint Felix is located beneath its more modern successor, immediately outside the town walls.

During the fourth century, therefore, Hispano-Roman towns gradually ceased to be the proud centres of political, administrative, religious and social life that they had been during the early empire. With the disappearance of socially competitive families from most towns, the main driving force for the construction, embellishment and renovation of buildings was removed and town centres decayed. The few new or restored public buildings were funded on the initiative of the provincial governor or, occasionally, the town councils. Wealthy residences were still built, although they are rarer than before and probably belonged to those bureaucrats intent on keeping a tight rein on provincial administration. The decline of secular public buildings was matched with the first appearance of churches and other ecclesiastical buildings, marking an important step in the transition of Hispano-Roman towns into the small fortified ecclesiastical centres of early medieval Spain.

One important aspect of this transformation was the decline of towns as the agricultural markets for the surrounding country. This is most apparent along the coast of Tarraconensis and Carthaginensis, where the ports of Barcino, Tarraco, Saguntum, Valentia, Illici and Carthago Nova ceased to act as centres of export and became, instead, net importers. Between the later second and the middle fifth centuries olive oil and *garum* imports from Africa Proconsularis and Byzacena, and to a lesser extent Tripolitania, more than doubled in volume at these ports. The produce was packed in cylindrical amphorae, known to archaeologists as the Africana I, Africana II, Tripolitana III and Keay xxv, which are correspondingly rare at villas. This is symptomatic of a breakdown in the economic interdependence between towns and country estates. As the urban population shrank, the centres of villa estates blossomed, and whatever agricultural surplus remained after taxation would have been directly exchanged with other estates, bypassing the towns. However, the towns supported an important bureaucratic staff and were obliged to import certain foods, like olive oil, from North Africa.[41] Cargoes of African oil amphorae bound for the east coast of Spain invariably carried very fine-quality orange-slipped pottery known as African Red Slip. A wide variety of plates, bowls and dishes frequently decorated with attractive stamped motifs and figures was therefore common at ports, and also managed to reach inland towns like Conimbriga (Condeixa a Velha) and estate centres.

Little is known about exports from coastal Carthaginensis and Tarraconensis. The discovery of a large maritime villa at the citadel of Roses, on the site of Greek Rhode, however, provides clues. Large preparation vats have been uncovered, showing that the villa specialised in manufacturing fish sauce from tunny fish, which may have been exported. This recalls Ausonius' praise of fish sauce from the region of Barcino.[42] Similarly, further south, in the vicinity of Carthago Nova, kilns producing small *garum* amphorae during the later fourth and fifth centuries have been discovered. In Baetica estates along the Guadalquivir were still producing olive oil, which at that time was packed in small pear-shaped amphorae called the Dressel 23. The provincial reorganisation by Diocletian meant that the Spanish provinces came under the authority of the Praetorian Prefect of the Gauls, so that Baetican oil now supplied the army and officials in his jurisdiction. The amphorae are therefore found at military sites along the German frontier and to a lesser extent towns along the Mediterranean coasts of Spain and Gaul. At the same time Rome's needs were now met by olive oil produced in Africa, which was in the praetorian prefecture of Italy.

In northern Carthaginensis, western Lusitania and western Tarraconensis the fourth and earlier fifth centuries saw a resumption of fine pottery manufacture. Production was located at Tritium Magallum (at Najera, near modern Tricio), Clunia and Termes, as it had been under the early empire, as well as at other unidentified sites.[43] Plain bowls, plates, large platters and occasional closed forms were popular. However, the most favoured products are the bowls with characteristic moulded circles and lunette motifs. This late *terra sigillata hispanica* was distributed widely in central Spain and is found at a large number of villas, as well as major towns like Conimbriga, Emerita, Pompaelo, Clunia and Asturica Augusta. By contrast it is extremely rare in Baetica and along the east coast of Spain where African imports dominated the market.

There was clearly a vigorous exchange of goods along the Mediterranean coast, as well as in the interior of the Spanish provinces. However, its character had changed: it had ceased to be fully commercial and left little room for the entrepreneurial activities of the wealthy merchants and shippers of the early empire. Many were now tied to the service of the state, receiving special privileges and immunities provided they ensured a constant supply of essential commodities, like grain and olive oil. Two laws in the great Theodosian Code refer to Spanish merchants and shippers in the service of the state during the first half of the fourth century AD. They were bringing fiscal cargoes from ports in Hispania to Rome. Similarly, special agents of the Church were responsible for the transfer of commodities between its estates, or selling any surplus to other 'tied-traders'. Surplus agricultural products from the estates of the wealthier landowners also moved independently of the towns. They were frequently used to meet social obligations to other landowners. They employed tied agents to carry this out and frequently used their own ships to move it.[44]

The decline of public buildings in towns during the fourth century is matched by an unparalleled development of residential buildings on the estates of wealthy landowners. This is because active service on local town councils had become a compulsory duty which the wealthier members of society sought to avoid at all costs. Not only was it expensive but it was also a major obstacle to a glittering political career in the equestrian or senatorial orders at Rome. Membership of either order conferred immunity from municipal duties and in the case of the senatorial order was a hereditary privilege. Another avenue of escape was to serve in the *comitiva*, a series of important government posts in the military and civil spheres, founded by Constantine. Whatever their motives, many Hispani gained entry to these prestigious positions in the earlier fourth century, gaining immunity for themselves and their heirs. The Christian Acilius Severus was appointed consul in AD 323, while Paulus 'The Chain' was state secretary in AD 353–61.[45] Less exalted *decuriones* gained immunity by being ordained priests, or by admission to different ranks of the army and the praetorian prefectures. Once immunity was gained, individuals pursued a prestigious and lucrative career away from their towns, amassing sufficient wealth to build up their estates and indulge in a secluded life (*otium*) on ever more luxurious estate centres. The latter soon took on the appearance of small towns, with the owners' patronage attracting large numbers of tied peasants (*coloni*), gardeners and farm managers, as well as craftsmen, architects and labourers from the towns. This 'pull' on the towns was sufficiently serious in Hispania and Gaul for the emperor Honorius to write the following letter to the Praetorian Prefect of the Gauls in AD 400: 'The municipalities have been stripped of their skilled workmen and have lost the glory with which they were once resplendent since, indeed, very many members of the guilds (*collegia*) have deserted the service of the cities and are following the country life by betaking themselves to secret and out of the way places'.[46]

Western Tarraconensis, northern Carthaginensis and western Lusitania are the areas *par excellence* for these 'secret places'. The great villa of Olmeda, in the vicinity of Pallantia (modern Palencia), is especially renowned for its artistic embellishments. This remarkable estate centre is still visible a very short distance to the east of Pedrosa de la Vega and was built towards the end of the fourth century AD.[47] The 'urban' part of the villa was laid out like a town house, with a main north-south axis running through a central peristyle and *triclinium* on the northern side. The building was flanked by two pairs of great towers, one on its north and the other on its south side, giving it a fortified appearance. The north side of the peristyle opened into a huge apsidal room at either end. The peristyle enclosed a large garden (about 23 by 29 metres) and was flanked on three sides by luxurious rooms, many of which are decorated with absolutely outstanding mosaics (172 square metres). The very best of these are to be found in the great ceremonial dining-room (*oecus*) on the south-east side of the villa. Upon entering the *oecus* one is greeted by a large coloured mosaic depicting one of the great animal hunts, so beloved of the Hispano-Roman aristocracy. Seven separate episodes are illustrated. In one a huntsman has fallen on to his knees and defends himself from a snarling tiger with an upraised shield; immediately above, another huntsman, clutching a spear, follows behind a hunting dog. At the centre of the mosaic huntsmen on horseback are spearing tigers which have successfully unseated another horseman and sunk their bloodied fangs into the flanks of one of the horses. In the bottom right-hand corner a boar is cornered by hunting dogs and a hunter gripping a pike. The artist has used colour to great and subtle effect and provides us with precious information about contemporary dress: all the huntsmen wear decorated tunics of different colours and long trousers. In the main part of the *oecus* a wide (87 cm) mosaic border runs around all four sides of the room. It is relieved by eighteen individualised portrait busts (only fifteen remain) of men and women within elliptical frames. Each portrait is delicately executed in subtle pinks, oranges, blues and browns and probably represents a friend of the owner of the villa, or members of his family. In each corner of the mosaic one of the four seasons is depicted as a veiled lady. The centre of the *oecus* mosaic is dominated by a beautifully conceived tableau representing the Greek hero Achilles on the island of Skyros.

By contrast there is the great estate centre of Foz de Lumbier (Liedena), near Pompaelo.[48] Here a substantial later second-century AD villa was transformed into an enormous complex of some 135 rooms during the fourth century. Its most impressive feature was its very extensive agri-

Comparative plans of late
Hispano-Roman villas:
Olmeda, Pedrosa de la Vega
(*top*); La Dehesa de la Cocosa
(*middle*); Villafortunatus
(*bottom*).

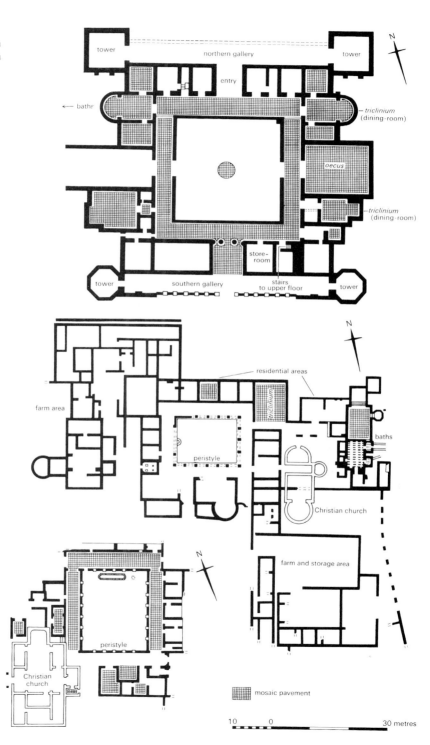

cultural buildings. On the northern side of the earlier peristyle an enormous granary with a raised nave and two aisles was built. This must have stored grain produced on the estate. On the south side of the villa was a special room for the pressing of olives or grapes, together with a range of storerooms. Finally, the south-eastern side of the complex was dominated by forty small rooms laid out in two parallel ranges. These probably housed *coloni* and farm labourers. At the south-western end were two huge barns, which probably served as stables or shelters for livestock.

The large, rich, residential estate centres near Uxama (modern Osma) and Termes (modern Tiermes) stand in stark contrast with the decay of the towns themselves. The three great fourth-century villas of La Dehesa de Soria (near Cuevas de Soria), Los Quintanares (near Rioseco de Soria) and Los Villares (near Santervas del Burgo) have been regarded as textbook examples of late villas for many years. Los Villares is the most unusual of the three. It consisted of a huge (43.5 by 19 metres) rectangular peristyle bordered by large rooms. On the south side was a very grandiose bath block with one great circular *laconicum* relieved by four niches and a *frigidarium* with four separate plunge pools. The *laconicum* floor was decorated with a large mosaic, in the centre of which was a rather crude portrait of the pagan goddess Abundantia. The great villa of Quintanares boasted a more refined portrait of her in the architecturally innovative building on the north side. She stares out at the spectator from a hexagonal panel with a calm but simple expression, typical of the age. She holds a horn of plenty full to the brim with fresh grapes and other fruits, and wears her customary crown and an intricately decorated white tunic. By contrast the mosaicist at La Dehesa de Soria was a master of abstract patterns. The main block of the villa (80 by 60 metres) is ordered axially around a peristyle which was decorated by four different strips of mosaic. Elsewhere in the villa twenty-five rooms were decorated by mosaics in an amazing display of carefully balanced geometrical shapes and rich colours. The most dazzling are to be found on the north side of the peristyle filling at least six major apsidal rooms, as well as an enormous central *triclinium*.[49]

These immensely rich sites are just a sample of estate centres in north-central Spain. On the basis of these and other villas – like that at Santamaría (Aguilafuente) near Segovia – it is easy to understand why many scholars have been led to believe that this part of the Iberian peninsula was the heartland and power base of the Hispano-Roman aristocracy of the late empire. Indeed, many estate-owners were sufficiently powerful to support private armies. At Olmeda, for instance, a cemetery holding some 100 people was discovered 200 metres to the north-west of the villa. This is probably the cemetery of a small armed force raised by the owner, for military equipment was found both here and at the villa. It included elaborate chip-carved bronze bridle terminals and a series of magnificent hanging bronze cauldrons. Similar cemeteries have been discovered at late Roman villas like that near Simancas and at San Miguel de Arroyo (both Valladolid) and also appear at isolated points in the countryside, like Fuentespreadas (Zamora) and Suella Cabras (Soria), and occasionally in such towns as Arcobriga (Monreal de Ariza) in the Jalón valley. The main concentration of these cemeteries, however, is in the upper Duero valley in Carthaginensis.[50]

Patterns of late Roman rural settlement in north-central Spain provide clear evidence of a deep-seated change throughout Hispania. In central Tarraconensis, for example, one should point out the very important Villa-fortunatus which can still be visited some five kilometres from Fraga (Huesca).[51] This was dominated by a large peristyle (20.5 by 17 metres) which was surrounded by an assortment of dining-rooms and bedrooms with colourful geometric mosaic floors. The south range of this portico opened on to a *tablinum* with a rather unusual mosaic floor. This was quite large (5.85 by 4.7 metres) and, towards the middle of the far end, bears the name of the villa owner, Fortunatus, in a tessera inscription. It also tells us that he was a Christian, since the chi-rho symbol is placed at the centre of his name. The mosaic itself is also redolent of Christian symbolism, with peacocks, doves and other animals striving for space, together with pagan-style cupids. The heretic Hispano-Roman Christian, Priscillian, is known to have held devotional meetings with his followers in villas, which would not have been dissimilar to this one. During the sixth century AD the south-west corner of the villa was taken up by a large church (26 by 14 metres).

One of the most important Romano-Christian sites in the western Mediterranean is to be found at Centcelles, a few kilometres to the east of Constantí, near Tarraco.[52] In the first half of the fourth century a large villa was demolished to make way for a much larger complex. The central area consists of a long range of rooms dominated by two huge domes. These were designed as mausolea for some immensely rich family, and large niches for sarcophagi were cut back into walls beneath the domes. Fortunately, one of these domes still stands, and its mosaic decoration greets the visitor with a dazzling display of late Roman secular and Christian themes. These are attested in three concentric rings which fill the vault of the dome and focus upon a central medallion. The outer ring depicts a great hunt setting out from a country villa and consisting of huntsmen on horseback pursuing stags. Other men have hunting dogs on leashes. At some stage a huge net is used in an attempt to catch their prey. The whole hunt is presided over by a clean-shaven and serious-looking man, surrounded by a group of friends or advisers. This may be a portrait of the owner. The next frieze is divided up into sixteen panels by elaborate columns, each one depicting a scene from the Old and New Testaments. One, for instance, shows the three children of Babylon burning in the fiery furnace: their hands are upraised and they wear Phrygian caps. In another scene Jonah is falling into the sea from a fishing boat and is about to be eaten by a whale. The Good Shepherd is also shown, bearing the lost sheep on his shoulders. Much of the rest of the next frieze is missing, but in one important panel a man dressed in very rich ceremonial costume is seated on a high-backed chair

Scene from the great dome mosaic at the early Christian complex at Centcelles, showing a huntsman pursuing stags towards a large net.

and attended by people wearing colourful garments. The regal character of this scene is one of several reasons why many scholars have identified the mausoleum with the emperor Constans. An elaborate crypt was discovered beneath the centre of the floor, and it is suggested that after being defeated and killed by the usurper Magnentius at Illiberis (modern Elne) in southern Narbonensis in 351 Constans was buried here. To the west of the mausoleum was an elaborate bath suite which was expanded to accommodate a major extension later in the fourth century.

Not all the landed aristocracy in this part of Tarraconensis were necessarily Christians. In one very rare case Vitalis, the owner of a large maritime villa between Emporiae and Blandae (Els Ametllers, at modern Tossa de Mar), had his name and portrait preserved on a mosaic at the entrance to the public rooms. The inscription reads *Salvo Vitale/Felix Turissa*, suggesting that the happiness of the population on the Turissa estate was guaranteed only by the health and well-being of Vitalis. This neatly epitomises the dependent relationship of the estate workers on their owners during late antiquity.[53]

Large villas have been found in other provinces of Hispania as well. Los Alcazares near Carthago Nova and Las Cipresas in the vicinity of Jumilla are good examples. One of the best, however, is the great complex at Bruñel, near Quesada (Jaén). A standard villa with a central peristyle was built here during the earlier fourth century AD, and during the fourth century the complex passed to another owner who levelled this sector and replaced it with a more grandiose structure. A large rectangular hall (50 metres long) with two facing apses was built on top of the earlier peristyle. This abutted a new peristyle to the south (34 by 23 metres), which was surrounded by larger rooms than those of the earlier building.

The territory of the diocesan capital of Emerita was also peppered with the estate centres of the Hispano-Roman aristocracy. The grandest of these, La Dehesa de la Cocosa (Badajoz), sprawls over ten hectares to the south-west of the town. All the customary features are represented: a peristyle, two bath blocks, dining-rooms, olive presses, work-rooms and several large unidentified halls. A small chapel was built between the 'urban' block of the villa and the larger bath suite, showing that as at Centcelles the owner at one time was a Christian. There was a similar adaptation at the villa of Milreu (Estoi) in the vicinity of ancient Ossonuba (modern Faro). This was a large and very important villa which developed during the third century AD, boasting a central peristyle, large bath suite and a maze of lesser rooms. In the mid-fourth century AD an enormous temple was built to the south of this complex. Shortly afterwards it was equipped with its own baptismal font and rededicated for use as a Christian church. This conversion is hardly surprising, since near-by Ossonuba was a bishopric with a significant Christian community from at least AD 305.[54]

These great villas were the residential and administrative centres of major estates belonging to Roman senators and the richest members of the Hispano-Roman aristocracy. However, it would be wrong to think in terms of large consolidated estates stretching for miles across the landscape. In fact, most of them were comprised of smaller properties in different parts of a province, or provinces, under centralised management. Excavations have uncovered a multitude of other, smaller and less pretentious villas which were either the centres of these 'constituent' estates or were owned by lesser members of the aristocracy. Vilauba (Camós) in the hinterland of Gerunda (modern Gerona), for instance, clearly conformed to the layout of a peristyle villa, while its buildings were much more modest and the floors made of pink concrete. Moreover, the working area of the farm was more extensive than the 'urban' part. The villas of Can Sans (near Llavaneres, Barcelona) near Iluro (modern Mataró), La Hacienda de Manguarra y San José (near Cartama, Málaga) near Malaca, and that of Santa Colomba de Somoza (near Maragatera, León) in Gallaecia are other examples.

The size of estates must have varied considerably: many, no doubt, were in the region of some 300 square kilometres, while some of the very largest would have covered several thousand square kilometres. Many land-owners, like Vitalis and Fortunatus, were probably of local origin. Similarly, Nummius Aemilianus Dexter probably owned extensive estates in Tarraconensis. Dexter was the son of the evangelical bishop of Barcino, Pacatianus, and was sufficiently wealthy to secure appointment to the post of Praetorian Prefect of Italy in AD 395. The heiress Egeria from north-western Spain was rich enough to indulge in a long pilgrimage to the Holy Land and Egypt in AD 381–4. On the other hand, wealthy senators outside Hispania also owned property in the peninsula. Saint Paulinus from Burdigala (modern Bordeaux) is one example. In the 380s he chose to leave Gaul and live on his Spanish estates. However, in his later years he had a personal religious crisis and, on becoming an extreme ascetic Christian, began to sell his properties. The distinguished Roman noblewoman Melania the Younger chose to abandon her heritage and sell off her many estates in southern Italy, Africa, Numidia and Mauretania; those in Hispania, however, were rendered unsaleable by the barbarian invasions of the early fifth century.[55] The largest landholder in Hispania was, of course, the emperor whose predecessors had accumulated estates over some 300 years. They were administered by a special department of state, called the Ratio Privata.

What do we know about the attitudes of the Hispano-Roman aristocrats themselves? The mosaics from the estate centres discussed above show many aristocrats to have benefited from an education which was very much in the Classical tradition. Schools still existed in major towns. Ausonius, for instance, mentions a certain Dynamius, a professor of rhetoric from Burdigala, who had come to practise at Ilerda (modern Lleida). Other teachers would have been employed on the large estates. The late Roman educational system in Hispania produced some of the very finest writers and poets of the late antique world. Aurelius Prudentius Clemens, for example, was born at Calagurris (modern Calahorra) in AD 348 and produced several major works, including the famous 'Crowns of Martyrdom'. In this he proudly extols the inestimable virtues of the martyrs from towns like Tarraco, Emerita and Caesaraugusta. He describes their glorious exploits as 'heroes of the persecutions' and the guardians of the towns. He also lashes the pagans, and condemns their ill-fated gods with such invective as 'You who fashion yourselves divine persons out of absurd monstrosities'.[56]

In the early fourth century Christianity was still the religion of the lower classes in major Hispano-Roman towns. The conversion of the pagan temple into a church at Milreu-Estoi shows that it soon won adherents in positions of power and influence, while the mosaics at Centcelles and Villafortunatus reflect its penetration amongst the aristocracy in the course of the fourth century. Literary sources tell us that Hispano-Roman Christianity was particularly vibrant, although at the same time often evangelical and intolerant of pagans and heretics. One has only to glance at the career of the Spaniard Maternus Cynegius who served as Praetorian Prefect in the eastern empire between AD 384 and 388.[57] He was a virulent anti-pagan responsible for the destruction of temples in eastern towns like Apamea, in Syria, and encouraging 'Men dressed in black [monks] and who eat more than elephants' to demolish the great temple of Marnas at Gaza. The career of Priscillian is also important. He was a local grandee from Abela (modern Ávila), in western Lusitania, who preached an eccentric version of the Christian faith and rapidly gained a wide following amongst his peers in Hispania and southern Gaul. In many ways his personal crusade masked an attempt by ascetic Christians to wrest control of Spanish bishoprics from their Catholic incumbents. He was not recognised by the Pope Damasus and was eventually executed by the emperor Magnus Maximus (AD 383–8) in AD 385. In Gallaecia he was recognised as a martyr and became the focus of a major popular religious movement, called 'priscillianism' which persisted until the sixth century AD.[58]

Despite all this Christian fervour, paganism in the later fourth century

Detail of an early Christian sarcophagus built into the cathedral at Tarragona, showing New Testament scenes.

was still strong, as indeed it was amongst the senatorial nobility in Gaul and Italy. The predominantly pagan and Classical subject-matter of mosaics in towns throughout the peninsula shows that officials and certain members of local aristocracies were still pagans, even if the empire was officially Christian. Similarly, a study of villa mosaics shows that members of the ruralised aristocracy were also pagans. In AD 399 the joint emperors Honorius and Arcadius sent a letter to Macrobius, *vicarius* of the Spanish dioceses, stating that 'We forbid sacrifices, so it is our will that the ornaments of public works (that is, of temples and other pagan buildings) shall be preserved. If any persons should attempt to destroy such works, he shall not have the right to flatter himself as relying on any authority . . .'.[59] Clearly pagan obstinacy and Christian intolerance led to conflict in the towns, and the despoliation of whichever pagan temples had not collapsed through neglect.

Nevertheless, it was Christian zeal which triumphed. Indeed, Hispania's major contribution to the political and military life of the late empire was the great Christian emperor Theodosius I (AD 379–95).[60] He was born at Cauca (modern Coca) in north-western Carthaginensis, the son of one of the emperor Valentinian I's (AD 364–75) most successful generals. By 374 he had been appointed *dux* of the province of Moesia Prima (eastern Yugoslavia) on the Danube and defeated invading Sarmatian tribesmen. However, in AD 375 Valentinian was succeeded by the emperor Gratian

(AD 375–83), and Theodosius retired to his estates in Hispania: he probably lived in a villa similar to that at Santamaría (near Aguilafuente) or Olmeda (near Pedrosa de la Vega). On the death of Gratian control of the western empire passed into the hands of the puppet-emperor Valentinian II, while Theodosius was appointed emperor of the east. His accession had depended upon the patronage of wealthy senatorial families, like the Syagrii from Gaul, and the active support of the army.

Theodosius' reign drew a tightly knit group of Spanish aristocrats like Nummius Aemilianus Dexter and Maternus Cynegius into the limelight of political life at Constantinople (modern Istanbul), capital of the eastern empire. Images of Theodosius and some of his family and supporters have been preserved for posterity on the freize of the obelisk of Theodosius in the great circus at Constantinople. Throughout his reign Theodosius struggled to maintain the unity of the empire – in both the political and religious sense. On two separate occasions he defeated usurpers who attempted to wrest control of the western empire from Valentinian II – first his fellow Spaniard Magnus Maximus (AD 383) and then Eugenius (AD 392–4). In the religious sphere he attempted to impose a rigid Catholic orthodoxy on heretic Christians and pagans alike. In AD 391 this culminated in the *coup de grâce* against paganism when he banned all pagan sacrifices upon pain of a very expensive fine and closed all pagan temples.

On the occasion of celebrating ten years of his rule, in AD 389, Theodosius gave a magnificent silver dish (*missorium*) to the *vicarius* of the Spanish dioceses.[61] Found near Almendralejo (Badajoz) and now in the Real Academia de la Historia at Madrid, this masterpiece of the silversmiths' art has a double significance. The legend around its edge proudly proclaims 'Our Lord Theodosius, perpetual Augustus, on the most happy day of the tenth anniversary'. Below, Theodosius is portrayed sitting on his throne, larger than life, flanked by his personal bodyguards. This reflects the strength of the Spanish achievement during the late empire – namely, that a Christian emperor dominated both west and east, temporarily providing the unity that the empire was so rapidly losing. Theodosius' success, however, barely outlived him. On either side of him sit his incompetent sons Arcadius and Honorius. Both were destined to become emperors – the latter from AD 393–425 and the former from AD 383–408. Under their rule and that of their offspring the western empire finally split from the eastern provinces and rapidly disintegrated.

During the later third and fourth centuries AD the seeds of change sown during the uncertainties of the earlier third century had borne fruit. There was a restatement of imperial authority in Hispania, in an attempt to prevent the inherent regionalism of the peninsula from weakening Rome's control. Tarraconensis was split into smaller provinces, and administrative centres were redefined. However, the spark had gone out of municipal life, and the towns gradually ceased to act as the focal points of their territories. The very nature of Roman public life encouraged the wealthiest people to bypass the towns, participate in the life of the central élite at Rome, and lavish their resources on their great residential estate centres. More and more of the wealth of Hispania passed from public to private hands, weakening centralised control and encouraging regionalism to develop within individual provinces and individual regions. At the same time the 'Christianisation' of the peninsula ensured the emergence of local bishoprics and the gradual disappearance of the pagan aristocracy. By AD 408–9 the Hispania of the first two centuries was changed beyond recognition, and the rapid disintegration of Roman control in the peninsula had begun.

Further reading

The momentous internal changes at work in the Roman Empire of the third and fourth centuries AD are documented by A. Jones, *The Later Roman Empire, 284–602* (Oxford, 1964, repr. 1973), and discussed in Brown 1974. Developments in Iberia are synthesised and discussed in Arce 1982. Pharr (1969) provides an English translation of Imperial letters and edicts in the Theodosian Code, including those concerning Iberia. The late Roman walls of towns are discussed in Richmond 1931 and S. Johnson, *Late Roman Fortifications* (London, 1983), while Dimas Fernández (1984) and Arce (1983) look at two important late Imperial urban centres, and L. García Moreno, 'La Cristianización de las ciudades de la península ibérica durante la antigüedad tardía', *AEA* 50–1 (1977–8), 311–21, studies the development of ecclesiastical centres in towns. The attempts of municipal élites to gain exemption from local responsibilities in towns is discussed in F. Millar, 'Empire and city, Augustus to Julian: obligations, excuses and status', *JRS* LXXIII (1983), 76–96. The late Roman aristocracy in Iberia is discussed in L. García Moreno, 'Andalucía durante la antigüedad tardía (ss. v–vii). Aspectos Socioeconómicos', in *Fuentes y Metodología. Andalucía en la Antigüedad* (1978), P. Palol, 'Romanos en la Meseta: El Bajo Imperio y la Aristocracia Agrícola', in *Bimilenario de Segovia, Segovia y la Arqueología romana* (Barcelona, 1977), and P. Palol, 'La cristianización de la aristocracia romana', *Pyrenae* 13–14 (1977–8), while Matthews (1975) discusses the role of the Spanish-born Emperor Theodosius and his clan in the twilight of the Western Empire. The great estate centres of the late Roman aristocracy are well illustrated in Hauschild and Schlunk 1961, Palol and Cortes 1974 and J. Arce, 'El mosaico de "Las Metamorfosis" de Carranque (Toledo)', *MM* 27 (1986), 365–74. The Church in Iberia is discussed in M. Sotomayor, *Historia de la Iglesia en España I. La Iglesia en la España Romana y Visigoda* (Madrid, 1979), and ecclesiastical architecture in Palol 1967 and Schlunk and Hauschild 1978. Late Roman imports to Iberia are studied by Keay (1984), indigenous ceramic production by López Rodríguez (1985) and coinage by Pereira, Bost and Hiernard (1974).

THE
END OF
ROMAN
SPAIN

B y the early fifth century Rome's control of its Spanish provinces had weakened. By AD 476 the Visigoths had finally wrested control of Hispania from other barbarian peoples and a defunct Roman administration. The cause of this dramatic transfer of power is to be sought in the misguided policies, incompetence and poor leadership shown by the emperor Honorius and his successors. These precipitated the disintegration of the western Roman Empire and, with it, the loss of the Spanish provinces.[1]

There are two sides to the end of Roman Spain. On the one hand, perceptive contemporary writers like Bishop Flavius Hydatius of Aquae Flaviae (modern Chaves) and Orosius of Bracara (modern Braga) have left us compelling, and often moving, accounts of the tumultuous events happening around them between the years 409 and 469.[2] On the other hand, archaeological evidence gives us a different viewpoint. Research in recent years has shown that despite the rapid collapse of Roman control and the settlement of barbarian peoples in Iberia Roman life continued uninterrupted through the fifth and sixth centuries AD. The Visigoths, after all, were only a minority of the population and had long been influenced by contact with the Romans.

The historical narrative demonstrates how Rome actually lost control of the Spanish provinces, one after the other. In AD 407 Constantine was elected by the armies in Britain as a rival to the emperor Honorius at Ravenna. He marched across Gaul from Britain, establishing his capital at Arelate (modern Arles) in Gallia Narbonensis. Hispania, meanwhile, was held by the family of Honorius and therefore posed a threat to Constantine's west flank. He sent his Master of the Soldiers, Gerontius, supported by his son Constans, to wrest control of Hispania from Honorius' supporters. Dissatisfaction with Honorius' performance as emperor, however, had split

Votive gold crown studded with jewels, and bearing the name of the 7th-century Visigothic King Recceswinth.

their defence, and two of his relatives, Lagodius and Theodosiolus, declined to fight on his behalf. Didymus and Verenianus, however, remained loyal and quickly assembled a private army of slaves and peasants from their vast estates in southern Lusitania. Indeed, this was probably a larger version of the private militias that were attached to major estate centres like Olmeda (near Pedrosa de la Vega), in north-central Spain (see Chapter 8). In the final instance Didymus and Verenianus were defeated, and Hispania fell into the hands of Constans and Gerontius. Constans entrusted the defence of the Pyrenean mountain passes to his barbarian federates and then returned to Arelate. Gerontius was left as sole commander in Hispania.

A few years earlier, in AD 406, a group of barbarians crossed the Rhine into the Roman provinces of Germania and Gaul. By AD 409 they had reached the western Pyrenees. Hydatius records that between 28 September and 13 October the combined force of 200,000 Asding and Siling Vandals, Suebi and Alans crossed into northern Tarraconensis, and describes how they 'pillage and massacre without pity'.[3] Gerontius' barbarian federates offered precious little resistance, and the invaders roamed the provinces at will. This was only the third time that Hispania had ever been invaded by a foreign force and, as in AD 262, the Romans seemed incapable of countering with any consistent strategy. Rather than trying to defeat the barbarians in battle, Gerontius rebelled against Constantine at Arelate and set up a Hispano-Roman aristocrat called Maximus as emperor of the Dioceses of the Spains. This man was a client and dependent of Gerontius and established his court at Tarraco (modern Tarragona). Shortly afterwards he proclaimed his legitimacy by minting his own coinage at Barcino (modern Barcelona).[4] Assured of his authority in Hispania, Gerontius stripped Hispania of all the regular troops in AD 410 and crossed over to Narbonensis to eliminate Constantine and Constans. In the end Constans was killed, and both Gerontius and Constantine were defeated by an army sent out from Italy by Honorius. In Hispania Maximus fled from Tarraco and took refuge with some of the barbarians at large in the peninsula.

The bitter legacy of this episode was that some 50,000 Siling Vandals had settled in Baetica, 30,000 Alans in Lusitania and Carthaginensis, and 80,000 Suebi and 40,000 Asding Vandals in Gallaecia. The imperial government had therefore lost control of most of the Iberian peninsula and retained only Tarraconensis. The situation was never fully retrieved, and a wholly Roman Spain ceased to exist after AD 411.[5]

It was not long before the Roman government tried to claw back its lost provinces. In AD 410 another group of barbarians, the Visigoths, sacked the City of Rome after having traversed the eastern empire for nearly forty years. They then marched into Gaul under the leadership of King Athaulf and were enlisted by the Romans into helping them regain control of Gaul and Hispania. Thus in AD 415 between 70,000 and 300,000 Visigoths crossed the eastern Pyrenees and established their court at Barcino. Before Athaulf was able to achieve much in Hispania, he was murdered in a private feud. His successor, Wallia, waged a vigorous campaign against the other barbarian peoples in Hispania and effectively eliminated the Siling Vandals in Baetica and the Alans in Lusitania. Having used the Visigoths as mercenaries, the Master of the Soldiers Constantius then signed a treaty with Wallia. This neatly extracted the Visigoths from Hispania and granted them land for settlement in Gallia Aquitania. Their territory straddled the provinces of Aquitania I and II, Novempopulana and Narbonensis, and came to be known as Septimania.

In a sense this treaty had been concluded too hastily, leaving the Suebi and the Asding Vandals in control of Gallaecia, with no Roman or Visigothic forces to contain them. Indeed, it was not long before the Asding Vandals left Gallaecia and established themselves in Baetica and southern Lusitania. In AD 421 the Roman government responded by sending the Master of the Soldiers Castinus to oust them with a mixed force of Roman regular soldiers and barbarian mercenaries. However, Castinus was defeated, and Baetica remained in the hands of the Vandals under the leadership of King Gaiseric. As it turned out, the Vandals stayed only a short while. In AD 429 they crossed the Straits of Gibraltar to Africa and within ten years had taken possession of the provinces of Numidia, Zeugitana, Byzacena and Tripolitania.[6]

The next twenty-seven years were dominated by the expansion of the Suebic kingdom in Hispania, as successive kings broke out of the fastness of Gallaecia and tried to take over all the provinces. In 429 the Suebic king Hermigarius marched southwards from Bracara, crossed the lower Tagus, and ravaged southern Lusitania. By the time he reached Emerita (modern Mérida) the Vandal king Gaiseric was still sufficiently near to make a lightning strike against him. Hermigarius was defeated and then drowned in the river Guadiana. Gaiseric then withdrew definitively. The Suebic cause was then taken up by Hermeric (AD 429–36) and Rechila (AD 438–48); the latter campaigned widely in southern Lusitania, Baetica and western Carthaginensis and established his royal capital at Emerita. The impotence of Roman authority during these years was such that when Bishop Hydatius led a delegation to Aetius, the Master of the Soldiers, in Gaul he could only respond by sending Count Censorinus. This man acted as the Roman ambassador to the Suebi and also attempted to co-ordinate resistance to the barbarians amongst the Gallaecians. He achieved little of note and after being captured by the Suebi at Myrtilis (modern Mertola) in southern Lusitania was ignominiously strangled to death at Hispalis (modern Seville).

By AD 446 the military situation in Gaul had stabilised sufficiently for the Romans to make an attempt to seize back Baetica, Lusitania, Gallaecia and Carthaginensis from the Suebi. Vitus, the Master of the Soldiers, invaded Baetica and Carthaginensis with a large force of Visigothic mercenaries but was comprehensively defeated. Nevertheless, the Romans drew up a treaty with the Suebi, which may have engineered the return of Carthaginensis to Roman hands for a short while.

Early Visigothic colonnade and other buildings beneath the Plaça del Rei at Barcino (modern Barcelona).

During this period Tarraconensis was largely insulated from the depredations of the Suebi and was Rome's last foothold in the peninsula. Inscriptions discovered at the site of the great provincial forum in Tarraco record dedications to the emperors of the western and eastern empires until as late as 468–72.[7] The only recorded disturbances came during the 440s when there were major peasant uprisings along the Ebro valley. The rebels, or *bagaudae*, were probably disenchanted labourers or *coloni* from the great aristocratic estates around Pallantia, Segovia, Clunia and Termes.[8] This area was probably one of the last sources of recruits for Roman forces in the western empire and was also an area of great economic importance to Rome. Asturius, the Master of the Soldiers, thus rapidly suppressed the revolt in 441, but trouble erupted again shortly afterwards and was put down by Merobaudes, Asturius' successor. The *bagaudae* rebelled again in 449, under the leadership of a certain Basilus. This time the threat to Rome's interests in Tarraconensis was even greater, since Basilus joined forces with the Suebic king Rechiarius and pillaged as far west as Ilerda (modern Lleida).

In 455 the last member of the House of Theodosius, Valentinian III, was succeeded by the emperor Avitus (AD 455–7), who encouraged the Visigoths to intervene in Hispania and end the ravaging of Tarraconensis by Rechiarius and the *bagaudae*. The Visigothic king Theoderic I quickly quelled Suebic resistance and finally defeated Rechiarius near Asturica (modern Astorga) in Gallaecia. He then sacked the capital at Bracara (modern Braga). Hydatius records that although the sack was not bloody '... it was no less sad and lamentable. Numerous Romans are taken prisoner; the churches of the Saints are broken into, the altars overturned and burnt; the nuns consecrated to God are then rapidly led away, but without being raped; the priests are stripped to the limit of their modesty; everybody of both sexes and small children are ejected from [the] holy places where they had taken refuge; the horses, livestock and camels [then] profaned the holy place . . .'.[9] After executing Rechiarius, Theoderic pressed his advantage by marching south and capturing the Suebic royal capital at Emerita, and then left his generals to mop up remaining resistance by brutally massacring the inhabitants of towns like Asturica and Pallantia.

The Visigoths had thus advanced the Roman cause by shattering the Suebic kingdom which had so seriously imperilled the Roman province of Tarraconensis. Between AD 457 and 466 the Visigoths were the undisputed masters of Baetica, Lusitania and Carthaginensis, while the Romans still clung on to Tarraconensis and the Suebi were cut off in Gallaecia. In 468 the emperor Anthemius (AD 467–72) upset this balance by siding with the Suebi. They had tried again to break out of Gallaecia and began sacking towns in Lusitania: Hydatius records how 'Conimbriga, surprised in peace, is pillaged: the houses and part of the walls are razed, the inhabitants are captured and deported . . .'.[10] This treachery spurred the Visigoths to take aggressive action in Hispania. The new king of the Visigoths, Euric (AD 466–84), seized Emerita and expelled the Suebi altogether from Lusitania. He then fell upon the Roman province of Tarraconensis. Accounts by Saint Isidore of Hispalis and the *Gallic Chronicle* tell us that Euric organised a two-pronged attack upon the province, probably between 470 and 475. The first was led by one of his generals, Gauterit, and culminated in the capture of Pompaelo (modern Pamplona), Caesaraugusta (modern Zaragoza) and other towns in the Ebro valley. Hedlefredus and Vincentius, a renegade Duke of the Spains, led the other attack, advancing into Tarraconensis across the eastern Pyrenees and taking the coastal towns including Tarraco itself.[11] Apart from some resistance by Hispano-Roman nobles during the conquest, and again in AD 506 at Dertosa (modern Tortosa), the Visigoths now controlled the whole of Hispania except for Gallaecia, as well as Gallia Narbonensis and Septimania. By contrast Rome had lost her last western province and the following year, in AD 476, the emperor Romulus Augustulus (AD 475–6) was deposed and the western Roman Empire ceased to exist.

The Roman loss of Hispania was a complicated process which began in AD 411 and ended in 475. Unified Roman control of the peninsula was shattered by the invasions of 409, and the different barbarian peoples rapidly established themselves in the different provinces. Roman power in the western empire was rapidly fading and despite the efforts of various generals and ambassadors proved unequal to the task of regaining control.

The regionalism of Iberia, the lack of manpower and the absence of a coherent strategy doomed Rome's efforts to failure. In the end it was the Visigoths who erased the last formal traces of Roman authority in 470–5 and imposed a new order on Iberia. However, the story does not end here: by AD 508 the Visigoths had lost their possessions in Gaul and were confined to Hispania. Then, until AD 522, Visigothic Hispania became a protectorate of the Ostrogothic king of Italy, Theoderic, whose capital was at Ravenna. The Visigothic kings eventually asserted their independence from Ostrogothic Italy, although it was only under the strong and able King Leovigild (AD 573–86) that unity was imposed on Hispania. His greatest military achievement had been finally to annex the Suebic kingdom of Gallaecia, while he also established the definitive capital of the Visigothic kingdom at Toletum (modern Toledo). There is, however, a sting in the tail: the Byzantine emperor Justinian (AD 527–65) harboured great imperial ambitions, including the reconquest of all the lands which had belonged to the western Roman Empire from their Germanic masters. Thus, in AD 552 southern Carthaginensis and Baetica were annexed to form the Byzantine province of Spania, but this proved a temporary aberration and the Visigoths finally reconquered it by AD 621. This marked the very end of active Roman involvement in Iberia.

What effects did the sixty years of conflict between AD 409 and 475 and the eclipse of Roman control have upon the provinces of Hispania? The first point to remember is that Tarraconensis, Carthaginensis, Baetica, Lusitania and Gallaecia were no longer united under centralised Roman authority. Each province, or group of provinces, was responsible to a new, local, authority and acted independently. For most of this period Tarraconensis responded to Roman authority – whether directed from Ravenna, or Arelate (modern Arles) in Gaul. On the other hand, the capital of the province was frequently switched in response to political events. Tarraco was the natural choice for Maximus Tyrannus, while Constans chose Caesaraugusta, and Athaulf settled for Barcino. Gallaecia was the domain of the Suebi, although for a while Emerita was the capital of their enlarged kingdom. Baetica was initially Vandal, then passed into Suebic hands, and finally became a Visigothic possession with the capital at Hispalis. Later, during the Ostrogothic protectorate, the provinces were administered from Arelate, while prior to the establishment of the definitive capital at Toletum the Visigoths experimented with Barcino, Hispalis and Emerita.

The provinces therefore ceased to function together, and any semblance of administrative order was lost. Revenue collection by the Roman authorities had broken down in every province except Tarraconensis. Even here the task was complicated by the closure of major mints in the western empire in the first half of the fifth century. Of those closest to Tarraconensis, Lugudunum (modern Lyon) closed in AD 423 and Arelate in 425, which left only a regular supply from Rome until 472 and a trickle of issues from Mediolanum (modern Milan) and the imperial capital at Ravenna in northern

Visigothic gold *trientes* and *tremisses* of the 6th and 7th centuries AD.

Italy. However, finds of these late coins are rare, and it is probable that revenue in Tarraconensis was increasingly collected in kind. The disappearance of a regular supply increased the value of earlier coins in circulation, inducing people to hoard them as a hedge against an uncertain future. Thus a large number of coin hoards of late fourth- and early fifth-century date have been found throughout Baetica and southern Lusitania: that discovered at Quelpes (near Faro) consisted of 100 gold pieces (*solidi*), while another from Garciaz (Cáceres) comprised 1,642 coins. The greatest concentration of hoards, however, comes from Gallaecia at sites like Palmeira (Braga) and Bracara itself.[12] It may be no coincidence that this area was savagely laid waste by the Vandals, Suebi and Visigoths until the 450s, thereby adding to the people's sense of insecurity.

However, during the course of the fifth century regional identities started to develop as the Suebi and Visigoths tightened their hold on the peninsula. They too needed coinage as a convenient means of establishing their legitimacy and collecting revenue from their subject territories. The Suebi started issuing their own gold coins at mints in Gallaecia, in the name of the reigning emperor, from as early as the reign of Valentinian III (AD 425–55). By contrast Visigothic gold coins do not appear until after their conquest of Tarraconensis. They were first issued by Alaric II in AD 507, from mints at Narbo (modern Narbonne) and Arelate in Gallia Narbonensis, in the name of the Byzantine emperor Anastasius. Later finer issues (*tremisses*) were minted at Barcino and other mints in Tarraconensis, Baetica and Lusitania.[13] However, it was only with the unification of the Visigothic kingdom by Leovigild that Hispania again enjoyed frequent good-quality gold coins (*trientes*).[14]

One of the greatest consequences of the Visigothic conquest was an influx of Goths into the towns, where they lived side by side with Hispano-Roman officials and resident aristocrats. They were racially distinct, and advertised the fact by speaking their own language and wearing their own clothing. They also embraced Arianism – a Christian heresy not recognised by the Hispano-Roman establishment which professed the Catholic doctrine. It is difficult to estimate the proportion of Goths to Hispano-Romans on the basis of the archaeological evidence alone; literary evidence, however, suggests that towns throughout the provinces had twin populations until the earlier seventh century, even though the Gothic element was always in

Visigothic marble screen from Emerita (modern Mérida), depicting the Christian chi-rho symbol.

a minority.[15] The Visigothic kings recognised this and developed a suitable administrative framework. Two sets of laws were laid down: one, published by Euric (AD 466–84), catered for the Goths and was updated by Leovigild;[16] the other, published by Alaric II in AD 506, was based upon the great *Theodosian Code* and protected the interests of Hispano-Romans.[17] As a result there was one set of administrative posts for Hispano-Romans and another for Visigoths.

Throughout the fifth and sixth centuries AD Hispano-Roman land-owners still served as aediles and duumvirs on town councils but now assisted their Gothic masters in the collection of taxes. The highest local officials were now the *curator* and the *defensor,* the latter being a judicial post. The Visigothic king delegated the supervision of tax collection in each province and arbitration in civil cases between Hispano-Romans to a provincial governor (*iudex provinciae*) of Hispano-Roman origin. From the later sixth century onwards, however, the king appointed officials to each town and they started to take over all the tasks that had been carried out by the local council. Unlike the Hispano-Romans the Visigoths were taxed and were directly subject to regal authority by Gothic judicial officials like the *iudex territorii* and the *comes civitatis.* The Gothic counterpart to the Roman provincial governor was the *dux provinciae.*[18]

The great Visigothic law codes have always shown that the Visigoths were content to adapt Roman towns to fit their needs rather than consciously developing their own brand of urbanism. Indeed, archaeological evidence is beginning to reveal that many towns continued to be occupied, despite what the historical sources say about the sacking of such towns as Bracara, Conimbriga and Tarraco. Certain towns like Barcino, Toletum and Caesaraugusta gained especial importance with the rapidly changing political scenario. Other, hitherto obscure towns, like Egara (modern Terrassa) and Turiaso (modern Tarazona), achieved sufficient regional importance to become bishoprics during the fifth century. By the later sixth century there were at least nine bishoprics in Gallaecia, thirteen in Lusitania, fourteen in Baetica, twenty-seven in Carthaginensis and seventeen in Tarraconensis.[19] Some of them, like Emporiae (Empúries), heralded the return to prominence of old regional centres of the Republic and Roman Empire. However, all of them stood apart from the many other towns and settlements in the provinces as high-status centres. Indeed, some illustrious old Roman towns like Saguntum (modern Sagunto), Gades (modern Cádiz), Carteia (modern El Rocadillo) and Onuba (modern Huelva) were not bishoprics and did not regain the regional importance they had enjoyed during the Roman Empire.

In physical terms towns continued to develop along the same lines as during the later empire. Roman public buildings and monuments were abandoned and allowed to fall into ruins. Strategically important structures, however, were often maintained. At Emerita King Euric ordered the restoration of the great stone bridge over the Guadiana leading up to the town, while his Gothic assistant, Count Salla, collaborated with Bishop

Zeno of Emerita in restoring the town walls.[20] One hundred years later King Leovigild restored the walls of Italica.[21] By the side of decaying Roman buildings, churches and episcopal palaces proliferated in the centres of the bishoprics. They reflect the tremendous wealth and power of the Church, which had accumulated through property endowments from wealthy individuals, the rents from their many estates and the offerings of the faithful.

Recent work at Tarraco has begun to reveal the character of a major town during the late fifth and sixth centuries AD. The inhabitants now congregated exclusively within the Roman Republican walls of the upper town. By contrast the lower town, which for so many centuries had been the focus of residential and commercial life, was virtually abandoned. At the highest point of the town the great precinct wall of the upper terrace was partially demolished and large, functional, stone buildings were constructed against its outer face. Inside, the Visigothic cathedral was built in the shell of the great temple of Augustus.[22] The old provincial forum immediately to the south was used as a quarry and most of its paving slabs and marble decoration were removed. A short distance to its east a large building with a monumental colonnade was erected, some of whose columns still stand in the Plaça Rovellat.[23] Little is known about the fate of the forum itself at this time, although the two great corner towers – the *torre de pilatos* and the *torre de audiencia* – were converted into small cemeteries and living quarters.[24] The great circus to the south was probably used for public entertainment, since the town theatre had long been abandoned. Indeed, King Sisebut (AD 612–621) is known to have sent a strong reprimand to Bishop Eusebius of Tarraco for spending so much time enjoying shows.[25] In the later sixth century a small stone church was built within the ruins of the amphitheatre on the site of the martyrdom of the Saints Fructuosus, Eulogius and Augurius in AD 257.[26] However, by far the richest church at Tarraco was built on the south side of the early Christian cemetery on the right bank of the river Francolí, towards the middle fifth century. This large building (44 by 20 metres) consisted of a very wide central nave and two aisles divided from each other by a twin colonnade of eighteen columns. Two side-chambers flanked the semicircular apse, and several ancillary buildings and a mausoleum were built against its north and south sides.[27] Fragments of its immensely rich marble decoration can still be seen in the Museu Paleocristià.

Archaeological evidence is scarcer at other towns. However, written sources tell us that during the term of office of Bishop Fidelius the great church of Santa Eulalia at Emerita collapsed for reasons that are unknown and was rebuilt on a truly magnificent scale with soaring towers. Bishop Masona of Emerita (AD 571–606), one of the best-known personalities of Visigothic Hispania, was personally responsible for much building in the town, not least a large public hospital which was dedicated in AD 572.[28] San Leucadio and Santa María (built by King Reccared in AD 587) were the principal churches at Toletum. However, the town also boasted no fewer than four monasteries, the most important of which – Agalí – was situated in the suburbs. By the sixth century Barcino had assumed a new importance, as a temporary royal residence, a royal mint and as the centre of a special financial district, which comprised towns like Tarraco and Gerunda.[29] It comes as no surprise, therefore, to find a major ecclesiastical complex here. A church has been discovered in the north-eastern corner of the old Roman town, beneath the great Gothic cathedral of Santa Eulalia. It can still be seen, and the visitor can readily appreciate its fine coloured wall-paintings and its sumptuous marble chancel and altar screens. The church had its own baptistery and was part of a major complex, which includes a forbidding barrack-like building, built from Roman tombstones and freshly cut masonry.[30] This large building has been identified by some scholars as the Visigothic palace of Barcino. The substantial remains of churches have also been found at less important towns, like Segobriga (Cabeza del Griego), Saetabis (modern Játiva), Egara, Egitania (modern Idanha-a-Velha) and Emporiae.[31] Moreover, literary sources tell us about many others, at towns like Caesaraugusta, Iria Flavia and Valentia.

In addition to these there are towns like Clunia, Termes, Complutum and Conimbriga, which seem to have been virtually abandoned. However, the presence of small cemeteries of sixth- and seventh-century date and small medieval villages within the ambit of the old Roman towns suggests that they persisted as small, fortified nuclei clustering around churches. Thus modern Alcalá de Henares may be the successor of Roman Complutum, and Peñalba de Castro the successor of Roman Clunia.

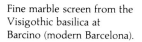

Fine marble screen from the Visigothic basilica at Barcino (modern Barcelona).

Sadly little is known about the development of towns in either the Suebic kingdom of Gallaecia or the Byzantine province of Spania. However, there is no reason to suppose any radical difference in either area. Ecclesiastical buildings played a prominent role, with Bishop Andreas of Iria Flavia, in Gallaecia, putting up an episcopal palace in AD 572, and a small church and related buildings dominating the centre of Silniana (modern San Pedro de Alcántara) in Spania.[32] Predictably enough, after the Byzantines had seized Carthago Nova, Commenciolus, the Byzantine governor of Spania, restored the town walls, adding towers and massive double gateways with vaulted porticoes.[33]

It is clear, therefore, that the Visigoths, unlike the Romans, never had an urban policy as such. Occasionally, however, circumstances dictated a need for new towns. Leovigild's first choice for his capital of Hispania, Reccopolis, may perhaps be identified with the wide plateau of the Cerro de la Oliva (near Zorito de los Canes), to the east of modern Madrid.[34] Excavations here in the 1940s show that he encircled it with substantial stone walls and built a large church and several long halls, which were influenced by contemporary Byzantine fashions. By contrast research at Begastri, in eastern Carthaginensis, has revealed a Visigothic settlement with an irregular plan, strongly reminiscent of Iberian hilltop settlements.[35] Nothing is known about the Visigothic foundations at either Victoriacum (modern Vitoria) or Ologicus (modern Olite) in northern Spain.

The Mediterranean towns of the late fifth and sixth centuries were just as reliant upon imported foodstuffs as they had been in the later Roman period. Rather than breaking commercial links with other parts of the Mediterranean the Visigothic conquest of Tarraconensis and Carthaginensis ushered in an era of even more intensive exchange. East Mediterranean and Jewish merchants frequented coastal towns, buying and selling goods in special premises called *cataplus*, and paying taxes (*portoria*) collected by special officials (*telonarii*). Archaeological research has shown that the most intensive exchange was carried on with Vandal Africa, and that Spanish coastal towns were importing large amounts of olive oil carried in large cylindrical amphorae (Keay types xxxv, xxxvi, lxi and lxii). This was accompanied by quantities of fine-quality orange-gloss tableware (African Red Slip), usually bowls and plates that were often decorated by an original range of religious (Christian and pagan) and secular motifs. Merchants also imported goods from further afield: wine, olive oil, perfumes and a different variety of fine tableware (Late Roman c), manufactured in the East Mediterranean provinces of Asia, Palestina and Syria. The foodstuffs were carried in globular Bi, Bii, Biv and Almagro 54 amphorae.[36]

These imports are not so much an index of urban prosperity as symptoms of the economic dislocation of towns from their surrounding territory. This was very much a feature of the late empire too (see Chapter 8). The coastal towns had lost much of their market role, while the villas continued as large and populous self-sufficient estate centres. This is graphically illustrated by a remarkable document discovered in the monastery of Asán (near Boltán, Huesca), in central Tarraconensis. It records the bequest to the monastery by a young aristocrat called Vincentius, upon taking holy orders, in AD 551.[37] He bequeathed all his earthly wealth, which consisted of great swathes of land scattered in the vicinity of Ilerda and Caesaraugusta. Many were replete with their own estate centres, like that of Trigarius which was populated with many slaves and tied peasants (coloni), as well as ample livestock, sheep, cows, vineyards, olive-groves, gardens, lawns and water-pools. Archaeology is now beginning to provide examples of these late Roman estate centres, continuing well into the Visigothic period. One of the most sumptuous has been discovered at Baños de Valdearados (Burgos), near Clunia (modern Coruña del Conde).[38] The villa was built in the later fourth century, and towards the middle of the fifth century five magnificent coloured mosaics were laid down in the central part of the residential area. Despite this late date the theme of two of them is still blatantly pagan – a reminder that there were flickers of paganism alive as late as the seventh century in some parts of Hispania. In one mosaic the central panel illustrates two very complex mythological themes associated with Bacchus in a charming 'primitive' style. The other mosaics display a mastery of complex, interwoven, geometric shapes. On a much more modest scale excavations at the villa of Vilauba (near Camós), in the hinterland of Gerunda (modern Gerona), have uncovered a series of rooms for the pressing of olive oil: these were added to the south-eastern side of the villa towards the beginning of the sixth century AD.[39] Some parts of the villa at Can Santromá (near Tiana), in the hilly hinterland of Baetulo (modern Badalona), were occupied as late as the fifth century AD. The residential area is covered by an imposing medieval farmhouse, suggesting that the site was occupied from late antiquity until the present day.

Such continuity suggests that Hispano-Roman aristocracy had not really been displaced by the Visigothic conquest and that many aristocrats were still enormously wealthy. Indeed, the Visigothic king Teudis (AD 531–48) married a Hispano-Roman noblewoman who was so wealthy that he was able to field a private militia of 2,000 men.[40] Other landholders were often reluctant to compromise their independence to the Visigothic kings. Aspidius, who held estates in the region of the Montes Aregenses (in the vicinity of the modern provinces of León/Orense) had to be forcibly subjugated by Leovigild in AD 575.[41] Nevertheless, there is no doubt that, as in the towns, the arrival of the Visigoths spelt a new chapter in rural life. The great law code of Leovigild reveals that the Visigothic nobles were often granted two-thirds of the more choice estates of Hispano-Romans, leaving their original owners with only one third. One Visigothic noble, Vagrila – a comes civitatis in later sixth-century Lusitania – had been granted property in this way, only to lose it after rebelling against King Reccared (AD 586–601). It is not known how widely this system of hospitalitas was used in Hispania.

Medieval farmhouse on top of a late Roman villa at Sentroma, near Badalona, reflecting the continuity of rural settlement in late antiquity.

By the sixth century it is clear that a new pattern of rural settlement was beginning to emerge. Alongside continuing villas like Valdearados and Vilauba other sites were clearly abandoned during the fifth and sixth centuries AD. This should be understood in relation to early medieval villages, which in many parts of Spain and Portugal represent a new pattern of settlement in the seventh and eighth centuries AD. Documentary evidence shows that many of these fortified settlements were born in the troubled years following the start of the Christian reconquest of Spain from the Arabs in the ninth and tenth centuries onwards. At the same time archaeological field-work shows that many were directly on top of Hispano-Roman or Hispano-Visigothic estate centres. Nowhere is this clearer than in modern Catalonia which formed the eastern seaboard of Tarraconensis.

From the sixth century onwards churches became the focal point for many estate centres, like the later, medieval villages. With the continued decline of the towns estate-owners came to provide for their dependents' spiritual as well as material needs. Fine examples of these estate churches have been discovered at the villas of Villafortunatus (near Fraga, Huesca), in Tarraconensis and Torre de Palma (near Monforte, Alto Alentejo), in southern Lusitania, etc. At Marialba (León) in Gallaecia, Bobala-Seròs (Lleida) in Tarraconensis, El Germo (Córdoba) in Baetica and at Casa Herrera (Badajoz) in Lusitania churches richly decorated with marble ornament were probably the centre-pieces of small, rural, ecclesiastical settlements.

By the later sixth century AD Iberia was finally reunited around a centralised authority. Leovigild eventually chose Toletum as the royal capital, and it remained the focus of religious, political and administrative life until the Arab invasions of the early eighth century AD. The provinces were, in cultural terms, very much heirs to the late Roman tradition, although influenced by the architectural and artistic fashions of the Byzantine east, and just beginning to show the first signs of Hispano-Visigothic originality. The later sixth century also marks Hispania embarking on a period of commercial isolation from other western Mediterranean countries. After over 1,000 years of close participation in the major commercial networks of the Mediterranean as a whole, Hispania faded into an era of comparative isolation. In face of the disintegration of the Roman town system the Visigoths ruled Hispania from a highly centralised patchwork of towns, dominated by churches and stark administrative buildings. Increasingly the work of government was carried out by royal appointees and the Church, whose national councils at Toletum were progressively used to promulgate secular issues put forward by the king. Thus, whereas the late fifth century signalled the end of Roman Spain in political terms, the late sixth century marks its end in cultural terms and represents the maturity of Visigothic Spain.

FURTHER READING

The works of contemporary writers like Orosius and Hydatius, who witnessed the disintegration of Roman authority in Hispania, are fully exploited by E. Thompson, *Romans and Barbarians. The Decline of the Western Empire* (1982), and compared with contemporary events in Italy and Gaul. A longer perspective, with more detail, dealing with the character of Visigothic Spain and Portugal is provided in Thompson 1969 and P. King, *Law and Society in Visigothic Spain* (1972), while C. Sánchez Albórnoz, *Ruina y Extinción del Municipio Romano en España e Instituciones que le Reemplazan* (1943), charts the gradual disappearance of Roman municipalities in the Visigothic period. M. Martínez Andreu, 'La Muralla Bizantina de Carthago-Nova', in *Antigüedad y Cristianismo. Monografías Históricas sobre la Antigüedad Tardía II. Del Conventus Carthaginensis a la Chora de Tudmir. Perspectivas de la Historia de Murcia entre los siglos III–VIII* (Murcia, 1985), 129–45, discusses late Roman Carthago Nova and its Byzantine walls, while a strip of sixth-century AD shops in Valentia are discussed in 'Valentia a l'època Visigoda', in *L'Almoina. Viatge a la Memòria Històrica de la Ciutat* (Valencia, 1987). J. Hillgarth, 'Popular religion in Visigothic Spain', in E. James (ed.), *Visigothic Spain: New Approaches* (1980), looks at religion in Visigothic Iberia, while A. Molinero, 'La Necrópolis Visigoda de Duraton (Segovia)', *Acta Arqueológica Hispánica* IV (Madrid, 1948), and W. Reinhart, 'Sobre el asentamiento de los Visigodos en la península', *AEA* 18 (1945), look at Visigothic settlement as reflected through cemeteries. Schlunk and Hauschild (1978) and P. Palol, *Arte Hispánico de la Época Visigoda* (1968), look at architectural and artistic achievements, while Keay (1984), and L. García Morena, 'Colonias de comerciantes en la península, siglos V–VII', *Habis* 3 (1980), study trade in the Visigothic period.

Gazetteer of sites to visit

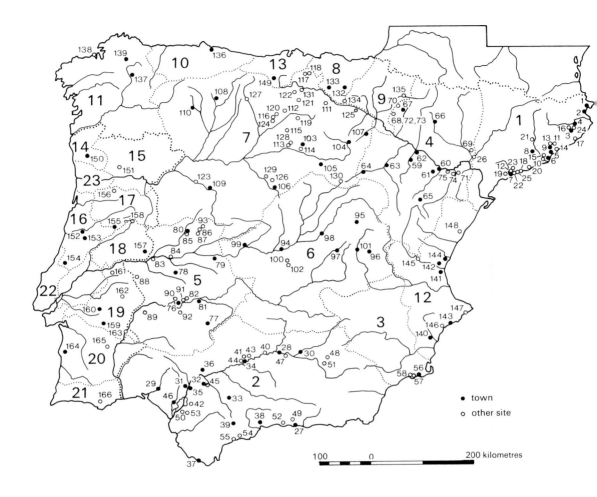

At present no comprehensive gazetteer exists for archaeological sites of any period in either Spain or Portugal. As far as the Roman period is concerned, the *Blue Guide* to Spain provides details about the larger sites. However, there are inaccuracies, and lesser sites are often omitted. This gazetteer is conceived as a complement to the text of *Roman Spain* and lists only the more notable sites in Spain and Portugal. Space allows only the briefest details about the location of the site and what is to be seen. Indeed, the gazetteer should be used in conjunction with more detailed maps. One of the most important is the *Atlas Nacional de España*, published in three volumes by the Instituto Geográfico y Catastral, Madrid, and which covers both Spain and Portugal at a scale of 1:500,000. The most practical coverage is provided by the Michelin 1:400,000 touring maps of different regions of Spain (New Series). More detailed coverage for Spain can be obtained from a series of 1:50,000 maps published by the Servicio

Geográfico del Ejército. Portugal is served by maps at a scale of 1:100,000 published by the Instituto Geográfico e Cadástral.

Sadly, few sites are adequately signposted, and access is often difficult. Thus, as far as possible the more easily accessible sites have been denoted by a star in the gazetteer, leaving the others for the more adventurous visitor. The opening hours of museums and sites (where appropriate) vary from region to region and are often subject to sudden change. They have therefore been omitted, and the visitor would be best advised to consult the Tourist Office in each provincial capital. It should also be remembered that nearly all sites and museums are closed on Mondays and feast-days.

For convenience the sites in the gazetteer have been grouped within the autonomous regions of Spain and the provinces of Portugal. In Catalonia (Catalunya) and El Pais Valenciano place names are currently identified by their

Catalan spellings. This will be followed in the gazetteer unless otherwise indicated. For example, Gerona is now spelt Girona. The modern name is followed by the Latin name, where this is known: the main sources are *CIL* II and II Supplement, and Tovar 1974, 1976.

SPAIN

1. Catalonia

(Modern provinces of Lleida, Girona, Barcelona and Tarragona)

TOWNS

1 La Ciutadella, Roses (*Rhode*): late Roman buildings, Greek colony
*2 Empúries (*Emporion/Emporiae*): Greek and Roman towns, with forum, houses, amphitheatre, gymnasium, walls, roads, baths, early Christian church and harbour mole
*3 Caldes de Malavella (*Aquae Calidae*): baths
*4 Girona (*Gerunda*): Republican and late Imperial walls
*5 Badalona (*Baetulo*): baths, *tabernae*
*6 Barcelona (*Barcino*): temple, late Roman walls, gate, early Imperial cemetery, early Christian baptistery and church, aqueduct
*7 Tarragona (*Tarraco*): Republican walls, provincial forum, amphitheatre, theatre, basilica of municipal forum, houses and street, early Christian cemetery, circus
*8 Terrassa (*Egara*): houses and early Christian church
*9 Caldes de Montbui (ancient name unknown): baths

BRIDGE

*10 Pont del Diable (Martorell, Barcelona)

AQUEDUCTS

11 Can Cua (Pineda, Barcelona)
*12 Els Ferreres (3 km to N. of Tarragona)

VILLAS

13 Can Tarrès (La Garriga, Barcelona)
*14 Can Llauder (Mataró, Barcelona)
15 Can Santromà (Tiana, Barcelona)
16 Vilauba (Camòs, Girona)
*17 Els Ametllers (Tossa de Mar, Girona)
*18 Els Munts (Altafulla, Tarragona)
*19 Centcelles (Constantí, Tarragona)

TRIUMPHAL ARCH

*20 Roda de Berà (Berà, Tarragona)

MAUSOLEA

21 Torre del Breny (Manresa, Barcelona)

*22 Torre dels Escipions (Tarragona)
*23 Vilarrodona (Alt Camp, Tarragona)
24 Vilarblareix (Girona)

QUARRY

25 El Médol (Tarragona)

ECCLESIASTICAL COMPLEX

26 Bobala-Seròs (Lleida)

MUSEUMS

Museu Arqueológic Provincial de Barcelona
Museu Arqueológic Nacional de Tarragona
Museu Arqueológic del Institut d'Estudis Ilerdencs (Lleida)
Museu Monográfic d'Empúries
Museu Arqueológic Provincial de Girona (Sant Pere de Galligans, Girona)
Museu Arqueológic Comarcal de Banyoles
Museu Municipal de Badalona
Museu d'Historia de la Ciutat de Barcelona
Museu d'Historia de Sabadell
Museu de Granollers
Museu de Vilanova i Geltru (Vilanova i Geltru)
Museu de Tossa (Tossa de Mar)
Museu Paleocristià de Tarragona
Museu d'Historia de la Ciutat (Barcelona)
Museu de Tortosa

2. Andalusia

(Modern provinces of Granada, Málaga, Cádiz, Seville, Huelva, Córdoba, Jaén)

TOWNS

*27 Almuñécar (*Sexi*): walls, vaulted platform, fish-vats
*28 Andújar (*Isturgi*): bridge
*29 Niebla (*Ilipula*): walls, bridge
*30 Cazlona (*Castulo*): late Roman walls, house
*31 Santiponce (*Italica*): amphitheatre, theatre, houses, walls, baths (site museum)
*32 Carmona (*Carmo*): walls, Republican/early Imperial cemetery, amphitheatre (site museum)
*33 Osuna (*Urso*): cisterns, theatre, late Roman cemetery (site museum)
*34 Córdoba (*Corduba*): bridge, temple
*35 Seville (*Hispalis*): columns, aqueduct (calle Luis Montoto)
36 Castillo de Mulva (*Munigua*): sanctuary, forum, houses, late Roman walls, mausoleum
*37 Bolonia (*Baelo*): forum, theatre, houses, baths, walls and gate, *macellum*, roads, fish-vats
*38 Málaga (*Malaca*): theatre
*39 Ronda la Vieja (*Acinipo*): theatre

BRIDGES

40 Villa del Río (Montoro, Córdoba)
*41 Pedroches (1 km to N. of Córdoba)
*42 Alcantarillas (on Salado de Porcuna stream, Seville)
*43 Hocho (on river Guadalmellato, Córdoba)
*44 Rabañales (3 km from Córdoba)
45 Carmona (immediately to E. of town, Seville)
46 Aznalcazar (river Guadimar, Seville)
47 Arroyo Molino (near Andújar, Jaén)
48 Las Herrerías (Cazorla, Jaén)

AQUEDUCT

49 Torrecuevas (Almuñécar, Granada)

VILLAS

50 Casa de Toruno del Casquete (Lebrija, Seville)
*51 Pago de Brunel Bajo (Quesada, Jaén)
52 Faro de Torrox (Torrox, Málaga)
53 El Cuervo (La Torre, Cádiz)
54 Río Verde (Marbella, Málaga)
*55 San Pedro de Alcántara (Málaga)

MUSEUMS

Museo Arqueológico Provincial de Granada
Museo de Huelva
Museo Provincial de Bellas Artes (Jaén)
Museo Arqueológico de Linares
Museo Arqueológico de Málaga
Museo Arqueológico Provincial de Sevilla
Museo Arqueológico de Cádiz
Museo Arqueológico Provincial de Córdoba
Museo Arqueológico Municipal de Almuñécar

3. Murcia

(Modern provinces of Murcia, Albacete, Almería)

TOWN

*56 Cartagena (*Carthago Nova*): colonnaded street (calle de la Morería Baja), street (Caja de Ahorros de Alicante y Murcia), early Christian cemetery

VILLAS

57 Playa (Puerto Mazarrón, Murcia)
58 Loma de las Herrerías (Puerto Mazarrón, Murcia)

MUSEUMS

Museo Arqueológico Provincial de Murcia
Museo de Jumilla
Museo de Orihuela
Museo Arqueológico Municipal de Cartagena
Museo Provincial de Albacete

4. Aragón

(Modern provinces of Huesca, Zaragoza and Teruel)

TOWNS

*59 Cabezo de las Minas, Botorrita (*Contrebia*): houses
*60 Velilla del Ebro (*Celsa*): houses, roads, shops
*61 Cabezo de Alcalá, Azaila (?*Beligiom*): houses, walls, temple, baths, roads
*62 Zaragoza (*Caesaraugusta*): late Roman walls
63 Cerro de la Bámbola, Calatayud (*Bilbilis*): *capitolium*, porticoes, theatre, baths
64 Cerro Vilar (*Arcobriga*): walls, cisterns, houses, baths, basilica
65 Hinojosa de Jarque (ancient name unknown): walls, floors
*66 Huesca (*Osca*): mosaics (in Ayuntamiento)
67 Los Bañales, Uncastillo (ancient name unknown): baths, aqueduct

AQUEDUCT

68 Sádaba (Zaragoza): Los Bañales

VILLA

*69 Villafortunatus (Fraga, Huesca)

MAUSOLEA

70 Sofuentes (Zaragoza); built into medieval tower at centre of town; tomb of Atilii family)
*71 Fabara (Teruel): tomb of L. Aemilius Lupus
*72 Sádaba (Zaragoza): tomb of Atilii family
73 Sádaba (Zaragoza): La Sinagoga
*74 Caspe (Zaragoza): originally located at Miralpeix
*75 Chiprana (Zaragoza): tomb of Fabia Severa

MUSEUMS

Museo Provincial de Zaragoza
Museo de Huesca

5. Extremadura

(Modern provinces of Badajoz and Cáceres)

TOWNS

*76 Mérida (*Emerita*): house and street, private mansions, theatre, aqueducts, amphitheatre, circus, gate, mausolea, temple, bridges
*77 Zalamea de la Serena (*Iulipa*): mausoleum
*78 Cáceres (*Norba*): gateway, walls
*79 Talavera la Vieja (*Augustobriga*): temple
80 Caparra (*Capera*): four-sided arch
*81 Medellín (*Metellinum*): theatre

BRIDGES
82 Arroyo Caganchez (Cáceres)
*83 Alcántara (on river Tagus, Cáceres)
*84 Alconétar (on river Tagus, Cáceres); recently rebuilt
85 Caparra (on river Ambroz, Cáceres)
86 Aldeanueva del Camino (Cáceres)
87 Segura (on river Eljas, Cáceres)

AQUEDUCT
88 Valencia de Alcántara (on Peje stream, Cáceres)

VILLA
89 La Dehesa de la Cocosa (Badajoz)

DAMS
*90 Lago de Proserpina (to N. of Mérida)
91 Embalse de Cornalvo (to N.E. of Mérida)

BATHS
*92 Alanje (Badajoz)

ROAD
93 Baños de Montemayor (Cáceres)

MUSEUMS
Museo Nacional de Arte Romano (Mérida)
Museo Provincial de Cáceres

6. Castille – La Mancha

(Modern provinces of Cuenca, Ciudad Real, Toledo, Madrid, Guadalajara)
TOWNS
*94 Toledo (*Toletum*): circus
95 Cañaveruelas, Cuenca (*Ercavica*): houses, baths, streets
96 Valera Vieja, Cuenca (*Valeria*): forum platform and *nymphaeum*
*97 Cabeza del Griego, Cuenca (*Segobriga*): theatre, amphitheatre, baths (site museum)
98 Cerro de la Oliva, Zorito de los Canes (*Reccopolis*): walls, church, other buildings
99 Talavera de la Reina (*Caesarobriga*): gate

BRIDGES
*100 Orgaz (Toledo)
*101 Puente de Castellar (Cuenca)

DAM
*102 La Alcantarilla (Los Yebenes, Guadalerzas, near Toledo)

MUSEUMS
Museo de Santa Cruz (Toledo)

Museo Arqueológico Nacional (Madrid)
Museo de la Real Academia de la Historia (Madrid)
Biblioteca Nacional de Madrid
Museo Provincial de Cuenca

7. Castille and León

(Modern provinces of Ávila, Segovia, Valladolid, Palencia, Santander, Burgos, Logroño, Soria, León, Zamora, Salamanca and Astorga)
TOWNS
*103 Peñalba de Castro, Coruña del Conde (*Clunia*): forum, baths, houses, theatre
*104 Numantia, Garray (*Numantia*): houses
105 Tiermes (*Termes*): houses, aqueduct, walls, public building (site museum)
*106 Segovia (*Segovia*): aqueduct
*107 Muro de Agreda (*Augustobriga*): walls
*108 León (*Legio*): late Roman walls
*109 Salamanca (*Salmantica*): bridge, walls
*110 Astorga (*Asturica*): walls, *cryptoporticus*

BRIDGES
111 Cihuri (river Tirón, Rioja)
112 Cañizar de los Ajos (river Hormazuelos, Burgos)
*113 Gumiel de Hizán (river Gromejón, Burgos)
114 Coruña de Conde (river Arandilla, Burgos)
115 Tordomar (river Arlanza, Burgos)
116 Itero de la Vega (river Bellarna, Burgos)
117 Burcena (river Ordunte, Burgos)
118 Burcena (Alisal stream, Burgos)
119 Olmosalbos (river Ausín, Burgos)
120 Puente de San Miguel (Sasamón, Burgos)
121 Lences (river Caderchano, Burgos)
122 Frías (river Ebro, Burgos)
123 Ledesma (Salamanca)

ROAD
124 Castrillo Matajudíos (near river Odra, Burgos)

AQUEDUCT
*125 Near Alcanadre (Logroño)

VILLAS
126 Las Tejeras (Pedraza, Segovia)
*127 La Olmeda (Pedrosa de la Vega, Palencia)
128 Baños de Valdearados (Burgos)
129 Aguilafuente (Segovia)

TRIUMPHAL ARCH
*130 Medinaceli (Soria)

BRIDGE
131 La Horadada, Ona

MUSEUMS
Museo Arqueológico Provincial de Burgos
Museo Numantino de Soria
Museo Arqueológico de Valladolid
Museo Provincial de Bellas Artes (Ávila)
Museo Diocesano (Astorga)
Museo de San Marcos de León
Museo Arqueológico Provincial de León

8. País Vasco

(Modern provinces of Vizcaya, Guipuzcoa and Alava)

TOWNS
132 Arcaya (*Suessatio*): baths
*133 Iruña (*Veleia*): late Roman walls, cisterns, house

BRIDGE
*134 Puente de Mantible (Assa, Alava)

MUSEUMS
Museo de Arqueología de Alava (Vitoria)
Museo Municipal de San Sebastián
Museo Histórico de Bilbao

9. Navarra

VILLA
135 Foz de Lumbier (Liedena)

MUSEUM
Museo de Navarra (Pamplona)

10. Asturias

TOWN
136 Gijón (?*Noega*): baths

MUSEUMS
Museo Arqueológico de Oviedo

11. Galicia

(Modern provinces of Orense, Pontevedra, La Coruña and Lugo)

TOWN
*137 Lugo (*Lucus Augusti*): late Roman walls

LIGHTHOUSE
138 Torre de Hércules (La Coruña)

SANCTUARY
139 Santa Eulalia de Bóveda (Lugo)

MUSEUM
Museo Arqueológico Provincial de Lugo

12. País Valenciano

(Modern provinces of Castellón, Valencia, Alicante)

TOWNS
*140 La Alcudia, Elche (*Illici*): walls, houses
141 Tossal de Manises (ancient name unknown): walls, houses
*142 Liria (*Edeta*): arch
*143 Villajoyosa (ancient name unknown): mausoleum
*144 Sagunto (*Saguntum*): walls, forum, theatre (site museum)

AQUEDUCT
145 Peña Cortada (Calles)

VILLAS
146 El Campello (Alicante)
147 Banyets de la Reina (Calpe): fish-vats

TRIUMPHAL ARCH
*148 Cabañes (Castellón)

MUSEUMS
Museo Arqueológico Municipal de Elche
Museo Monográfico de La Alcudia (2 km from Elche)
Museo Arqueológico Municipal Camilo Visedo Molto de Alcoy
Museo de Bellas Artes (Valencia)
Museo de la Patriarca (Valencia)
Museo del Ayuntamiento de Valencia
Museo Arqueológico Provincial de Alicante
Museo Municipal de Villajoyosa
Museo Municipal de Denia
Museo Municipal de Burriana
Museo de Prehistoria de Valencia
Museo Arqueológico Municipal de Elda

13. Cantabria

TOWNS
149 El Retortillo (*Iuliobriga*): houses

MUSEUM
Museo de Prehistoria (Santander)

PORTUGAL

14. Minho

TOWN

*150 Braga (*Bracara Augusta*): Roman spring (Fonte do
Idolo)

15. Tras os Montes

SANCTUARY

*151 Panoias (Vila Real)

16. Beira Litoral

TOWNS

152 Coimbra (*Aeminium*): *cryptoporticus*
*153 Condeixa a Velha (*Conimbriga*): late Roman walls,
forum, houses, baths, aqueduct (site museum)
154 São Sebastião do Freixo, Batalha (*Collipo*): ruins

MUSEUM

Museu Nacional de Machado do Castro (Coimbra)
Museu Municipal de Figueira da Foz

17. Beira Alta

TOWN

*155 Oliveira do Hospital (ancient name unknown):
triumphal arch

ROAD

*156 Estrada do Almargém (160 km on the Viseu-Lamego
road)

18. Beira Baixa

TOWN

*157 Idanha a Velha (*Igaeditani* and, in the late empire,
Egitania): gate and walls

VILLA

*158 Belmonte (?*Centum cellae*)

19. Alto Alentejo

TOWNS

*159 Ebora (*Evora*): walls and gate, temple
*160 Santana do Campo, Arraiolos (*Calantum*): temple

BRIDGE

161 Vila Formosa (river Seda)

VILLA

162 Torre de Palma (Monforte)

FORT

163 Castelo do Lousa (Mourão)

MUSEUMS

Museu de Ebora
Museu Municipal de Elvas

20. Baixo Alentejo

TOWNS

164 Santiago do Cacém (*Mirobriga*): road

VILLA

*165 Casarões Velhas Vila de Frades (São Cucufate)

21. Algarve

VILLA

166 Milreu, Estoi (Faro)

MUSEUM

Museu Municipal de Faro
Museu Arqueologico de Lagos

22. Estremadura

MUSEUM

Museu Nacional de Arqueologia e Etnologia (Lisboa)

23. Douro Litoral

MUSEUMS

Museu Nacional de Soares Dos Reis (Porto)
Museu do Servicio do Fomento Mineiro (Porto)

Notes

Chapter 1

1. English summaries in Coles and Harding 1979, 214–29; Arribas 1963; Savory 1968.
2. Ramírez 1982, 95 ff.; Schubart 1982, 74 ff.
3. Schubart 1982, 74 ff.
4. Summary in Maluquer 1985; Garrido and Orta 1974; Pellicer 1977; Arteaga 1977, 38–48.
5. Kukahn and Blanco 1959; Carriazo 1973.
6. Maluquer 1981.
7. Blanco and Luzón 1969, 1974.
8. Strabo, *Geography* 3, 2, 14.
9. Cuadrado 1974, 95 ff.
10. Savory 1968, 232–6.
11. Sanmartí and Padró 1977, 161–5; Arteaga *et al.* 1978.
12. Lamboglia 1974; Morel 1981, 334–9.
13. For example, Sanmartí 1973.
14. General review of evidence in Cuadrado 1974, 99 ff.
15. Almagro Gorbea M. 1977, 130 ff. and fig. 13.
16. For example, Pliny, *Nat. Hist.* 3, 3, 19–26.
17. Livy 21, 14.
18. Rouillard 1979.
19. Serra Ràfols 1941.
20. Martín 1980.
21. Respectively, Pericot 1952; Maluquer 1982; Beltrán 1976; Pallarès 1965, Fletcher *et al.* 1965, 1969.
22. García y Bellido 1957.
23. Serra Ràfols 1941; Nicolini 1974, 209 ff.
24. Pericot 1980.
25. Lucas 1981, 248 ff.
26. Simón 1977.
27. Maluquer 1985 and Bendala 1981, 34 ff., provide general discussions, while Pellicer 1977, 11 ff., presents archaeological evidence.
28. Strabo, *Geography* 3, 1, 6.
29. Schubart 1982, 91 ff.; Astruc 1951 (Villaricos); Blázquez 1980, 409 ff. (survey).
30. Livy 28, 13, 3 (Culchas); Strabo 3, 2, 1 (200 towns).
31. Respectively, Luzón and Ruiz 1973; Luzón 1973.
32. Corzo 1977, 7 ff. and fig. 1.
33. Nicolini 1974, 100 ff., on architecture.
34. Nicolini 1974, 188 ff., on jewellery.
35. Lucas 1981; Blázquez 1975 is a useful, if confusing, guide to sculptures of Turdetanian and Iberian deities.
36. Savory 1968, 221 ff. (Atlantic Bronze Age), 232 ff. (exchange with Tartessos).
37. Savory 1968, 242 ff., for instance.
38. Cabre 1929, 1932.
39. For example, Strabo, *Geography* 3, 3, 3–4 ff.
40. Martín Valls 1985, 123 ff.
41. Cabre *et al.* 1950; Maluquer 1958, 23 ff.
42. See, for example, Maya 1983, 23 ff.; more generally, Savory 1968, 254 ff.
43. Cardozo 1971.

Chapter 2

1. Livy, *The History of Rome from its Foundation*; Polybius, *Histories*; Appian, *Roman History*, I. *Fontes Hispaniae Antiquae*, vols II–V, for selections from these and other sources.
2. García y Bellido 1976 provides a useful summary. English summary of the Numantia and Castra Caecilia camps in Keppie 1984, 44–51, 71–5. Roldán 1974 and Le Roux 1982, on the organisation of the Roman army in Spain.
3. For this and the background to the Roman invasion see Scullard 1973, Montenegro 1982, 5–15, and Sutherland 1939, 22–31.
4. Hauschild 1983, 131–80.
5. Aquilue and Dupré 1986; 'Kese' is the name of the native

inhabitants of the pre-Roman settlement and hinterland, while Tarraco is the name used by the Romans for Scipio's bridgehead (Villaronga 1983, 12).
6. Appian 4, 18.
7. Polybius 10, 11–16.
8. Strabo 3, 4, 15.
9. Sandars 1913; Nicolini 1974, 214–16.
10. They also had to supply cloaks and six months' grain to the army (Livy 29, 3, 5).
11. Consisting of two new legions, troops from allied Latin towns, as well as the legions and other soldiers already in Iberia. Cato was supreme commander, with special jurisdiction in Citerior; Martínez Gázquez 1978 for commentary.
12. For the site of ancient Rhode see Martín *et al.* 1979, 270 ff.; also Maluquer *et al.* 1965.
13. Martín 1980; also Badía 1977, 435 ff.
14. Schulten 1931, 196–9; Taracena 1941, 36, fig. 5; Sanchez-Lafuente 1979 doubts the identification of Cerca as a Roman fort.
15. Tarradell 1978, 245–50.
16. Livy 34, 46. The identity of these coins is not certain and ultimately hinges upon the date of introduction of Iberian silver coins (denarii). Villaronga 1979 and Crawford 1985 hold two opposing opinions.
17. Livy 32, 28, 11; Knapp 1977, 61–5; Albertini 1923, 12–15. Sumner 1970, 85, doubts this date.
18. Aquilue *et al.* 1984, 36–44, and plan 3.
19. Their action concentrated around Toletum (modern Toledo) and its neighbours, since this was a key position for the control of the *meseta* and lands to the north, west and south (Salinas 1986, 11 ff.).
20. Appian 6, 43. For the tribes in the treaty Knapp 1977, 46 ff., and Salinas 1986, 13. Badian 1958, 122–3, and Knapp 1977, 37–57, on Rome's treaties and diplomacy in Iberia.
21. Knapp 1977, 29 ff., sees the Guadalquivir as a defensive line held by Rome until the early 130s BC, marked by 'defence-in-depth', with garrisons at forts like Castellum Ebora and in towns like Italica; for Iliturgis see Ch. 3, n. 11.
22. Strabo 3, 3, 6.
23. For instance, at the sites of Montealegre (in the Museo Etnologico, Lisbon), São Jorge de Vizela and São Ovidio Fafe (in the Guimarães museum, Braga).
24. Knapp 1977, 48.
25. Appian 6, 50: under leadership of Punicus and, later, Caucaenus.
26. Appian 6, 60.
27. Appian, 6, 63.
28. Appian 6, 69; Rome made such treaties only under duress (Knapp 1977, 42 ff.).
29. Appian 6, 74; Tautolus continued Lusitanian resistance to Rome for a short while.
30. Knapp 1977, 32, and García y Bellido 1959, on garrisons in the area.
31. Livy, *Periochae* 55: it is uncertain whether Valentia is correctly identified with modern Valencia, and whether Viriathus' soldiers were actually settled there. Knapp 1977, 125 ff., Ribera 1983 and Wiegels 1974, 153–76, present various arguments. Peña 1984, 63–6, suggests that Livy refers to a settlement of *Roman* veterans of the wars at Valentia.
32. Kalb and Hock 1983, 829–32.
33. Salinas 1986, 13–16.
34. Livy, *Periochae* 47: 1 January has remained the first day of the New Year ever since.
35. Schulten 1914, 1927, 1929, 1931.
36. Schulten 1929.
37. Appian calls the town Axinium (6, 47), which Salinas 1986, 15, and others have identified with Uxama.
38. This treaty was not sanctioned by the Roman Senate: Salinas 1986, 16.
39. Polybius 6, 19–42; also Fabricius 1932, 78–87, and Keppie 1984, 46–51.

40. Engel and Paris 1906; Fernández-Chicarro and Fernández 1980, 32; trumpeters and shield-bearing warriors with swords are depicted on reliefs from Osuna (now in the Museo Arqueológico Nacional, Madrid, and in the Louvre, Paris) and Estepa (Museo Arqueológico de Sevilla).
41. Livy, *Periochae* 47; Plutarch, *Marius* 14; see Villaronga 1979, 90 ff. Crawford 1985, 102, on coin hoards marking the path of invasion.
42. Appian 16, 99–100: up to 20,000 Arevaci perished in these revolts.
43. Principal sources for the Sertorian episode: Plutarch, *Sertorius*, and Livy, *Periochae* 90–6 (see also *Fontes Hispaniae Antiquae* IV, 100–250).
44. Schulten 1949; Sutherland 1939, 91–6, Roldán 1974, 113–39.
45. Sertorius' capital was set up as an alternative focus of Roman authority in Iberia. It had a senate composed of political refugees from Rome: Arco 1950, Gabba 1960.
46. Castra Caecilia: Schulten and Poulsen 1928, 1930, 1932; Ulbert 1985, for a re-analysis of the camp. Almazán: Gamer and Ortego 1969.
47. Beltrán, M. 1976 identifies this as Beligiom and proposes a chronology for the settlement; Villaronga 1977a for different opinions.
48. Excavations at the Plaza de San José and the Arcedianato, Pamplona, have revealed occupation of between 150 and 50 BC: Mezquíriz 1978.
49. Suetonius, *Julius Caesar*; Plutarch, *Julius Caesar*.
50. The ships were supplied by the immensely wealthy Lucius Cornelius Balbus of Gades.
51. Dio Cassius, *Histories* 39, 54.
52. They are, thus, not strictly part of the conquest and will not be discussed here. Detailed commentary in Harmand 1970, 181–203, and Roldán 1978, 155–73; principal sources in Caesar's *Civil War* 1, 37–87; 2, 17–21 and his *Spanish War*, and Dio Cassius 41–3, 45.
53. An immensely complicated episode, with a variety of Classical sources like Florus, Suetonius, Dio Cassius and Orosius: these are collected together in Schulten 1942, and commentaries provided by Forni 1970, Syme 1970, Rodríguez Colmenero 1979.
54. Absoló 1975.
55. This culminated in the siege of *Mons Medullius*, where the Romans encircled the Cantabri. Many committed suicide, while others were sold as slaves to owners in Gaul.
56. Assisted by the return of many Cantabri escaped from Gaul.
57. See Ch. 3, 62.

Chapter 3

1. Ch. 2, 31, n. 17.
2. Albertini 1923, 33 ff.; discussion in Mackie 1983, 16 ff.
3. Roldán 1971.
4. Sources usefully summarised in Roldán 1975.
5. For example, Casas and Sanmartí 1980.
6. Luzón 1973.
7. Knapp 1983, 9 ff.
8. Aquilue *et al.* 1984, 48 ff., 136 ff.
9. Livy, 43, 3.
10. *CIL* II, 5041.
11. Peña 1984, 54–6; Wiegels 1982 disputes Iliturgis as a Gracchan foundation.
12. See Ch. 2, n. 34.
13. Badian 1958, 118; Knapp 1977, 40 ff.
14. Cicero, *Pro Balbo* 19, 43 (Loeb edition, 684, n. a).
15. Ramírez 1982, 113 ff.
16. Pliny, *Nat. Hist.* 3, 1, 7; 3, 3, 18; 4, 22, 117.
17. Examples illustrated in Vives 1926; suggested by Crawford 1985, 84–102; Villaronga 1979, 137 ff., and Knapp 1987, for other interpretations.

18. Puertas 1982.
19. Beltrán, M. 1976.
20. Alarcão and Etienne 1977, 27–39.
21. Lostal 1980, 126 ff. and Beltrán, M. 1983, 25 ff. (archaeological evidence); Grant 1969, 217, and Beltrán, A. 1976 (historical evidence).
22. Granados 1984.
23. Alvárez 1977; Almagro 1983, fig. 2.
24. D'Ors 1953, 167–280 (no. 7); Chester Johnson *et al.* 1961, 97–104, for English trans.
25. Probably in AD 73–4: discussed by Mackie 1983, 215–17.
26. Richard *et al.* 1972, 576 ff. and fig. 9.
27. Mayet 1971, fold-out plan.
28. For example, Grünhagen and Hauschild 1979.
29. *CIL* II, 1423.
30. D'Ors 1953, 311–52 (no. 9) Malaca; 281–309 (no. 8) Salpensa; 345–6 (no. 11) Italica; D'Ors 1967, Emporiae; Palol and Arias Bonet 1969, Clunia; González 1986, Irni.
31. Strabo, *Geography* 3, 2, 15.
32. Livy 43, 2.
33. Richardson 1983.
34. Short summary in Mackie 1983, 8–11; Alföldy 1969 lists imperial officials.
35. Albertini 1923, 83–104.
36. Le Roux 1982, 103 ff.
37. Mann 1983, 21 ff.
38. Do Paco and Bacao 1966; it is possible that this was a customs post controlling traffic between Baetica and Lusitania.
39. Pliny, *Nat. Hist.* 37, 203.
40. Polybius 34, 9, 8.
41. Hopkins 1980, 106–12; Crawford 1974, 696–707.
42. Gosse 1942, 52 ff. (La Fortuna).
43. Domergue 1965, 1966.
44. Domergue and Tamain 1971; Tamain 1966.
45. Duncan-Jones 1974.
46. Bird 1984.
47. Jones 1980.
48. Domergue 1983, 48 ff.
49. Dupré 1986.
50. Hyginus (*De Limitibus* 135, 15 and 136), Frontinus (*De Controversiis* 9): in Blume *et al.* 1848, 170 ff. Discussion by Corzo 1977a, 220 ff.
51. Corzo 1982.
52. Rossello *et al.* 1974; Corzo 1977a; Columella, *De Re Rustica* 5, 1, 5 (Acnua).
53. For Spanish villas generally, Gorges 1979; specifically, Casas 1980; Guitart 1970; Hauschild and Schlunk 1961; Diez Coronel 1968; Castells Peig 1961.
54. Jordá Cerdá 1957; Fortes 1905 (repr. 1969); Wattemberg 1962.
55. For example, Cuadrado Diaz 1952 (Cabo de Palos).
56. Caesar, *Civil War* 2, 18 (120,000 *modii*); Ch. 5 on agricultural products of Spanish provinces.

Chapter 4

1. Brunt 1971, 204–64, especially 231 ff; Wilson 1966, 22–7, 29–42, on Roman emigration to Spain.
2. Mann 1983, 21 ff., and Brunt 1971, 255 ff., differ on the number of veteran colonies.
3. For example, Hasta, Acci and Asido.
4. For example, Illici, Barcino and Caesaraugusta.
5. For example, Emerita.
6. The *turma salluitana*: *CIL* I, 2, 709; discussed by Roldán 1974, 32 ff., n. 2.
7. Fatás 1980: English trans. and discussion in Richardson 1983, 33–41.
8. Rodríguez Neila 1973.
9. *CIL* II, 1728.
10. *CIL* II, 1585.

11. *CIL* II, 1343; *IRPC* 503; D'Ors 1953, 370 (no. 18).
12. Mackie 1983, 139 ff.
13. See Ch. 3, 62.
14. Generally, Caro Baroja 1970, 13–62; Albertos Firmat 1975; Tranoy 1981, 369 ff.
15. *CIL* II, 2633; commentary in Tranoy 1981, 379 ff.
16. Tranoy 1981, 362 ff.
17. Macro, son of Alluquius, for example (*CIL* II, 2465).
18. Mangas 1971, for slavery in Roman Spain.
19. *CIL* II, 3434.
20. *CIL* II, 2011.
21. *CIL* II, 1480 (Graecinus).
22. *RIT* 394.
23. *CIL* II, Suppl. 5812.
24. *CIL* II, 1552; Columella 11, 1, 21–2.
25. *IRPC* 521.
26. *CIL* II, 5181; full discussion in Domergue 1983.
27. *CIL* II, 5272.
28. *CIL* II, 2598.
29. *CIL* II, 3235.
30. *CIL* II, 984.
31. *IRB* nos 82–100; Rodà 1970 discusses this man.
32. Generally, Santero 1978, Waltzing 1900.
33. This *tabula patronatus* was in the form of a bronze tablet: *CIL* II, 2211 (Córdoba), Santero 1978, no. 95 (= *RIT* no. 43) and 112 ff.
34. *CIL* II, 1167.
35. *Piscatores et propolae*: *CIL* II, Suppl. 5929.
36. *Collegium sutorum*: *CIL* II, 2818.
37. *Collegium illychiniariorum*: Santero 1978, no. 94.
38. *Confectores aeris*: *CIL* II, 1179.
39. Suggested by Koppel 1985, 63–6.
40. *CIL* II, 1064.
41. *CIL* II, 128*; Santero 1978, no. 132, n. 446, on its authenticity.
42. Rodríguez Neila 1981, 51 ff.
43. Etienne and Fabre 1979, 108 ff.
44. Rodríguez Neila 1981, 54 ff.
45. Alföldy 1977a.
46. *CIL* II, 4509.
47. Pallarès 1970; Granados and Manera 1977.
48. *CIL* II, 1174.
49. *CIL* II, 4514.
50. Discussed in Ch. 7, 157 ff.
51. *CIL* II, 2126.
52. *RIT*, 262.
53. *CIL* II, 1936.
54. Canto 1981, 143 ff.
55. L. Fabius Hispaniensis: Wiseman 1971, 230, no. 168.
56. For example, Italica, Gades, Corduba, Obulco and Hispalis.
57. For example, Tarraco, Saguntum, Caesaraugusta, Castulo and Iuliobriga.
58. Pflaum 1965, 103.
59. Pflaum 1965, 88.
60. Pliny, *Letters* 2, 13.
61. Wiseman 1971, 248, no. 300.
62. Rodríguez Neila 1973; Wiseman 1971, 194.
63. Castillo 1965, 103, no. 192.
64. Italica, Gades, Illiberis, Corduba, Ucubi, Salpensa (Baetica); Barcino, Tarraco, Saguntum, Valentia (Tarraconensis): Etienne 1965.
65. García y Bellido 1960, 47, and Rodríguez Neila 1981, 129 ff., for links between the families of Hadrian and Trajan.
66. Strabo, *Geography* 3, 4, 3.
67. *CIL* II, 2892.
68. Respectively, *IRPC*, 134, *CIL* II, 354, and *FHA* VIII, 290 ff.
69. *ILER* 5683.
70. García y Bellido 1960b, no. 5.
71. García y Bellido 1960b, no. 14.
72. *CIL* II, 13.
73. *CIL* II, 1360, 1479, 1663.

74. *RIT*, 53.
75. For example, Pliny, *Nat. Hist.* 31, 80, 86, 100.
76. Floriano 1941, 417 ff.; Zaragoza Rubira 1971.
77. *CIL* II, 3118; *CIL* II, 3593.
78. Respectively, *CIL* II, 377, and *ILER* 3420.
79. Discussion in Santero 1978, 60–81.
80. Santero 1978, no. 49.
81. Bendala 1976, lam. XXII.
82. Respectively, Santero 1978, no. 87; *CIL* II, 4064; García y Bellido 1960b, no. 5.
83. *CIL* II, 203.
84. *RIT*, 441.
85. Almagro 1955.
86. Bonneville 1981.
87. Bendala 1972, 223–53.
88. Lostal 1980, 66, fig. 1; 175, figs 15–18.

Chapter 5

1. Previous important studies: Van Nostrand 1937, 199 ff.; Balil 1972; Blázquez 1982a.
2. Livy 34, 9.
3. Ulbert 1985, taf. 51, 52, 53; Gamer and Ortego 1969, abb. 7n; Schulten 1929, taf. 73, 1–22.
4. Comas i Sola 1985, 65 ff.
5. Comas i Sola 1985, 140 ff.
6. Gianfrotta 1982.
7. Serra Ràfols 1939.
8. Corsi-Sciallano and Liou 1985, 172, n. 217.
9. Pliny, *Nat. Hist.* 14, 71.
10. Martial 13, 118.
11. Pascual 1977.
12. Nieto and Nolla 1985, 267 ff.
13. Corsi-Sciallano and Liou 1985, 130 ff.
14. *RIT*, 449.
15. Ponsich 1974, 1979.
16. Remesal 1982, 69 ff., abb. 32, 34.
17. Remesal 1981.
18. Liou 1981, 164, no. 1.
19. *CIL* II, 1182.
20. *CIL* II, 1085.
21. Abad Casal 1975, 82 ff.
22. For example, Héron de Villefosse 1914.
23. *Satyricon* 76.
24. *CIL* II, 1180.
25. Colls *et al.* 1977.
26. Rodríguez Almeida 1981(a) site and 1981(b) finds; amphorae from Africa and Tripolitania are also present.
27. Tchernia 1981.
28. González 1983, no. 1.
29. Ponsich and Tarradell 1965.
30. Beltrán, M. 1977, 100 ff.
31. Grénier 1934, 616 ff.; Etienne 1970.
32. Pliny, *Nat. Hist.* 31, 94; Beltrán, M. 1970, 415 ff.
33. Beltrán, M. 1970, 244 ff.
34. Mayet 1975.
35. Mezquíriz 1961; Mayet 1984; Mezquíriz Irujo *et al.* 1983.
36. Mezquíriz Irujo 1982; Garabito Gómez 1978.
37. Roca Roumens 1976.
38. Boubé 1965.
39. Columella, *De Re Rustica* 7, 2–4.
40. For example, Caballero 1974, fig. 32.6, lam. IX.
41. Alfaro Giner 1984, fig. 25.
42. Pliny, *Nat. Hist.* 19, 3, 18.
43. Columella, *De Re Rustica* 12, 3, 7–10.
44. *RIT*, 9; González 1981, 52.
45. *CIL* II, 1743, 2235 (*purpurarii*); *CIL* II, 5519 (*infector*).
46. Martial, *Epigrams* 6, 93.

47. *CIL* II, 5812 (AD 239); *CIL* II, 2405.
48. *CIL* II, 2240.
49. Sanmartí *et al.* (forthcoming).
50. Canto 1977–8.
51. *CIL* II, 1043.
52. Del Amo 1981a.
53. *RIT,* 352, 923.
54. *CIL* II, 133 (Hermes), 2772 (Quartius).
55. Canto 1977–8.
56. Alföldy 1977.
57. Nolla *et al.* 1982.
58. *ILER* 5878, 5879.
59. García y Bellido 1970, figs 25, 42, 44, etc.
60. Pereira Menaut 1979, no. 79.
61. Etienne and Mayet 1971.

Chapter 6

1. Vitruvius, Ch. II: fundamental principles of architecture, 13 ff.
2. Aquilue *et al.* 1984, 48 ff.
3. Serra Vilarò 1932, 40–67; Mar and Ruiz de Arbulo 1986.
4. Beltrán, F. 1980, 78, no. 64; Alföldy 1977a, 7 ff., no. 3.
5. Hauschild 1972–4, 1977; Dupré *et al.* 1987 (forthcoming).
6. Alvárez 1977, 43 ff.
7. Dio Cassius 69, 10, 1.
8. León 1982, 99 ff; similar *agorai* in eastern Asia Minor: Akurgal 1985, 336, fig. 165 (Side), 234, fig. 87 (Nysa).
9. García y Bellido 1960, 102–7.
10. Respectively, Jiménez 1982; Almagro 1983, 43 ff.; Berges 1982; Almagro Gorbea, A. 1979; Thouvenot 1940, 431 ff.
11. García y Bellido 1960, 110 ff.
12. Fernández 1972.
13. Alvárez 1983; stretches have been restored since antiquity.
14. For example, Roldán 1971, figs 52 (bridge at Caparra) and 82 (bridge on the river Tormes at Salamanca). Absoló 1975a is a useful work. Fernández 1980 should be used with caution.
15. Hauschild 1976.
16. Nieto 1979–80, 313 ff.
17. García y Bellido 1960, 94 ff.
18. Blanco 1978.
19. Vitruvius I, Ch. II, 9.
20. Beltrán *et al.* 1984.
21. Vitruvius VI, Introduction, 6.
22. Lostal 1980, 205, fig. 21 (Arcobriga); Hauschild 1969, abb. 1 (Munigua).
23. Bonneville *et al.* 1981, 420 ff., figs 15, 19.
24. Bonneville *et al.* 1984, 470 ff.
25. Alarcão and Etienne 1977, 87 ff.
26. For example, Martín Bueno *et al.* 1985, 258 ff.
27. *CIL* II, 2559.
28. Beltrán, M. 1976, fig. 41.
29. Guitart 1976, 61–78.
30. Alarcão and Etienne 1977, 113 ff.
31. Alvárez 1972.
32. Beltrán, M. 1976, fig. 38.
33. Guitart 1976, 81–8 (calle Lladó).
34. Argente *et al.* 1985, 42 ff.
35. Balil 1974, 53 ff.
36. Oleiro 1965.
37. García y Bellido 1953; illustrated on p. 193.
38. Ribas 1966.
39. Balil 1980 (El Puaig); Blázquez 1981, lám. 62–6 (Marbella).

Chapter 7

1. Useful introductions: Ferguson 1970, Mangas 1982, 579–612, 613–48.
2. Bendala 1982, fig. 21.
3. Hauschild 1976–7, fig. 4, lam. II.
4. Generally, Ogilvie 1969, 10 ff.; Scullard 1981, 19 ff.

5. Ch. 6, 117.
6. Lucas 1981, 237 ff.
7. Generally, Chaves and Cruz 1981; specifically, Gaudán 1980, 36, no. 127; 224, no. 875; 218, no. 846.
8. Gaudán 1980, 219, no. 852; 82, no. 291; 245, no. 945; 35, no. 122.
9. García y Bellido 1964, 70 ff.; Strabo, *Geography* 3, 5, 5, 5; also Almagro 1981.
10. Guadán 1980, 32, no. 109.
11. Guadán 1980, 216, no. 842 (Carbula) for portrait.
12. Villaronga 1977, series 17, pl. IX. 69a–c.
13. García y Bellido 1956.
14. *RIT,* 32.
15. Santero 1978, no. 25.
16. Santero 1978, no. 82.
17. *RIT,* 36.
18. *IRB,* 15.
19. *CIL* II, 3337.
20. *CIL* II, 2816.
21. For example, *CIL* II, 5277; *ILER* 321.
22. *CIL* II, 4490.
23. *ILER* 188.
24. *CIL* II, 3725.
25. *CIL* II, 799.
26. García y Bellido 1949, nos 82 and 106.
27. García y Bellido 1949, nos 111, 140; *CIL* II, 470.
28. Palol and Vilella 1986.
29. Peña 1981, 47 ff.
30. *ILER* 611.
31. *CIL* II, 3871.
32. *CIL* II, 145.
33. Grünhagen 1977.
34. Peña 1981, no. 7; Aquilue *et al.* 1984, 109, 132–3 for example.
35. *CIL* II, 2991, 2413, 1060.
36. *Epigrams* 3, 38.
37. Liebescheutz 1979, 197 ff.
38. *CIL* II, 1346.
39. Snyder 1940.
40. *CIL* II, 1343; Snyder 1940, 265 ff., suggests that this is more than a coincidence.
41. Santero 1978, 43 ff.; respectively, *CIL* II, 2008 and *RIT,* 39.
42. Etienne 1958.
43. *CIL* II, 182.
44. Fishwick 1982, 230 ff.
45. *RIT,* 294: Cnaeus Numisius Modestus was elected to take charge of the gold statues of the emperors in the upper town.
46. García y Bellido 1967, 82–95.
47. *CIL* II 4310.
48. *IRC,* 48.
49. *CIL* II, 462; trans. from Ogilvie 1969.
50. Albertos 1975, 56 ff.
51. *ILER* 689.
52. Tovar 1981, 280.
53. García y Bellido 1967, 132–5, fig. 16.
54. Brown 1974, 51.
55. Liebescheutz 1979, 110 ff.
56. Ferguson 1970, 26 ff.
57. *ILER* 379.
58. Bendala 1976, 49–72.
59. *The Golden Ass,* 199.
60. *CIL* II, 5260.
61. Ferguson 1970, 104 ff.
62. *ILER* 6784.
63. *CIL* II, 5521.
64. Ferguson 1970, 23 ff., 106 ff.; García y Bellido 1967, 106–24.
65. *The Golden Ass,* 286.
66. *CIL* II, 3386.
67. Blanco *et al.* 1972.
68. Respectively, García y Bellido 1949, nos 66, 88, 116, 118–22, 145, 147, 184, 191; *IRC,* 85; Santero 1978, no. 9.

69. García y Bellido 1960a.
70. Almagro 1955, 126 ff., fig. 109.
71. Cumont 1924, 342 ff.
72. Blázquez 1982b, 418 ff.
73. *FHA* VIII, 46–7.

Chapter 8

1. Le Roux 1982, 373–7.
2. *CIL* II, 1120 (Italica); *CIL* II, 6183 (Emporiae).
3. Corbier 1978.
4. For example, Keay 1981, 461 ff.
5. *CIL* II, 2661.
6. Aquilue *et al.* 1984, 80 ff., figs 44, 45.
7. Shops on the east side of the forum were abandoned during the first century AD, while the municipal *curia* and parts of the *macellum* were out of use during the third century AD.
8. Remesal 1986 examines military markets on the Rhine.
9. Drinkwater 1983, 86 ff., for conditions leading to the emergence of the Gallic Empire.
10. Principal sources for the invasions: Orosius (7, 22, 7) and Aurelius Victor (*Liber de Caesaribus* 33, 3).
11. Panegyric dedicated to Constantius I (AD 293–306): Mynors 1964, no. 8 (5), 18, 5. Panegyric dedicated to Constantine I (AD 321): Mynors 1964, no. 4 (10).
12. Pereira *et al.* 1974, 232 ff.
13. Albertini 1923; Arce 1982, 31 ff.
14. Nolla and Nieto 1979; Nolla 1978, 23–7.
15. Balil 1961 is the fundamental work; see also Granados 1984, 1976.
16. Richmond 1931; Arias Vilas 1972.
17. Argente *et al.* 1985, 56 ff.
18. Sanmartín Moro 1985, 348 ff.
19. Arce 1982, 41–52.
20. *Theodosian Code* 11, 9, 2 (Pharr 1969).
21. *Theodosian Code* 11, 9, 1 (Pharr 1969).
22. Richmond 1931; García y Bellido 1970.
23. Amongst others Saint Felix (Prudentius, *Crowns of Martyrdom* 4, 29), Saint Cucufatus (Prudentius, *Crowns of Martyrdom* 4, 33) and Saints Justa and Rufina (Cumont 1927). Generally, see Blázquez 1982b.
24. *RIT*, 91.
25. *RIT*, 155.
26. *RIT*, 94–7.
27. *CIL* II, Suppl. 6340.
28. Commemorated on an inscription discussed by Chastagnol 1976, Arce 1982, 213.
29. *CIL* II, 481 (Emerita), 5239 (Aeminium), 2203–6 (Corduba), 1171 (Hispalis) and 2202 (Astigi).
30. Serra Vilaró 1932.
31. Valentia: Reynolds 1984, 478 ff.; Termes: Argente *et al.* 1985, 34 ff.; Italica: Luzón 1982, 88 ff.
32. Balil 1974; Abad Casal 1982 (vol. II), 16 ff., figs 21–7 (wall-paintings).
33. Blázquez 1981, 36 ff., lám. 84 (La Compañía); 35, lám. 83 (Generalísimo); Blázquez 1982, 25 ff., láms 7–9 (Astigi).
34. Dimas Fernández 1984.
35. Blázquez 1979, 109–257.
36. Barral i Altet 1978, nos 6 and 8.
37. Gisbert 1983 (Dianium); Mezquíriz 1978, fig. 6 (Pompaelo).
38. Prudentius, *Crowns of Martyrdom* 3, 190–200.
39. Canto 1982, 227 ff.
40. Recently reassessed by Del Amo 1979, 1981.
41. Keay 1984, 1987.
42. Nolla and Nieto 1981 (Roses *villa*); Ausonius, *Epistulae* 25.
43. López Rodríguez 1985.
44. Keay 1987; more generally, Whittaker 1983.
45. *PLRE* I, 834 (Acilius Severus); *PLRE* I, 683–4 (Paulus Catena).
46. *Theodosian Code* 12, 19, 1.

47. Palol and Cortés 1974; Palol 1986.
48. Taracena 1956; Mezquíriz 1956.
49. Los Villares: Ortego 1954–5; Quintanares: Ortego 1976; Dehesa de Soria: Taracena 1941, 59–60.
50. Caballero 1974; generally, Arce 1982, 76–80.
51. Serra Ràfols 1943.
52. Hauschild and Schlunk 1961, 111 ff.
53. Castillo 1939.
54. Schlunk and Hauschild 1978.
55. *PLRE* I, 251 (Nummius Aemilianus Dexter), 681–3 (S. Paulinus), 593 (Melania); Hunt 1982, 163 ff. (Egeria).
56. Prudentius, *Crowns of Martyrdom* 1, 68–70.
57. Matthews 1975, 110 ff., 142–4.
58. Chadwick 1976; Matthews 1975, 160 ff.
59. *Theodosian Code* 16, 10, 15.
60. Matthews 1975, 93 ff.
61. Arce 1976.

Chapter 9

1. Summaries of historical narrative: D'Abadal 1974, 27–56; Collins 1983, 11–41; Thompson 1976 and 1977; Arce 1982, 151–62.
2. Hydatius, *Chronicon*; Orosius, *Seven Books of History against the Pagans*; Gallic Chronicle (Mommsen 1892).
3. Hydatius, *Chronicon*, 46 (trans. by author).
4. Nuix 1976.
5. It is at this point that most scholars conclude their studies of late Roman Spain.
6. Koenig 1981, 346 ff., reviews archaeological evidence for Vandal settlement in Hispania.
7. *RIT*, 100, for example.
8. Thompson 1952.
9. Hydatius, *Chronicon*, 174 (trans. by author).
10. Hydatius, *Chronicon*, 241 (trans. by author).
11. Gallic Chronicle, 664, 651, 652.
12. Pereira *et al.* 1974, 306 ff.
13. Tomasini 1964.
14. Miles 1952.
15. Archaeological evidence for Visigothic settlement: Zeiss 1934; Palol 1966.
16. *Codex Euricianus* in Zeumer 1902.
17. *Breviarum of Alaric* in Pharr 1969.
18. Thompson 1969, Chs 5 and 6.
19. Lists of bishops attending Church Councils in Vives 1963.
20. *ICERV*, 363.
21. John of Biclar, chronicle for the year AD 583; see Alvárez 1942.
22. Serra Vilaró 1960; rebuilt by Bishop Sergius before AD 554; *RIT*, 939.
23. Berges 1974; Keay 1984, 15 ff., fig. 6.
24. Keay 1984, 17 ff., fig. 7.
25. Gundlach 1892, 'Epistolae Wisigoticae', 7.
26. Schlunk and Hauschild 1978, 160 ff., abb. 92.
27. Schlunk and Hauschild 1978, 131 ff.
28. *ICERV*, 348, probably refers to this.
29. Recorded on a document called the *De Fisco Barcinonensi*: Vives 1963, 53.
30. Schlunk and Hauschild 1978, abb. 19.
31. Listed in Schlunk and Hauschild 1978.
32. Palol 1967, 71 ff.
33. *ICERV*, 362.
34. Schlunk and Hauschild 1978, 169–71; Olmo Enciso 1986.
35. González *et al.* 1983.
36. Keay 1984, 399 ff.
37. Lara Peinado 1974.
38. Argente 1979.
39. Jones, Keay *et al.* 1983.
40. García Moreno 1974.
41. García Moreno 1974.

Select bibliography

Care has been taken to cite most books and articles on Roman Spain published in English. The vast majority of relevant works, however, are in Spanish and Portuguese, with fewer in Catalan, French and German. Nevertheless, it is hoped that all the titles cited will provide a starting-point for further reading and research.

Sadly, there are few standard archaeological source books on Roman Spain in English or, indeed, any other language. One exception is the *Princeton Encyclopedia of Classical Sites* (ed. R. Stillwell 1987), even though much new material has been published subsequently. Also useful are *Essai sur le province romaine de Bétique* (Thouvenot 1940), *La Galice romaine* (Tranoy 1981) and *Portugal Romano* (Alarcão 1973), which treat different regions of the Iberian peninsula. The ancient sources are not listed, although English translations of most texts can be found in the Loeb Classical Library and in the Penguin Classics. Lesser known texts, especially those of later antiquity, are fully cited.

ABBREVIATIONS
AEA   *Archivo Español de Arqueología*
BAR   British Archaeological Reports
BIDR   *Bollettino dell'Istituto di Diritto Romano*
BRAH   *Boletín de la Real Academia de Historia*
BSEAA   *Boletín del Seminario de Estudios de Arte y Arqueología*
CIL   *Corpus Inscriptionum Latinarum*
CIL Suppl. *Corpus Inscriptionum Latinarum Supplementum*
CNA   *Congreso Nacional de Arqueología*
EAE   *Excavaciones Arqueológicas en España*
JRS   *Journal of Roman Studies*
ICERV   *Inscripciones Cristianas de la España Romana y Visigoda*, J. Vives, 1969
ILER   *Inscripciones Latinas de la España Romana*, J. Vives, 1971
IRB   *Inscripciones Romanas de Barcelona*, S. Mariner, 1973
IRC   *Inscriptions Romaines de Catalogne I: Barcelone Sauf Barcino*, G. Fabre, M. Mayer and I. Roda, 1984
IRPC   *Inscripciones Romanas de la Provincia de Cádiz*, J. González, 1982
MCV   *Mélanges de la Casa de Velázquez*
MEFR   *Mélanges de l'Ecole Française à Rome*
MJSEA   *Memorias de la Junta Superior de Excavaciones y Antigüedades*
MM   *Madrider Mitteilungen*
NAH   *Noticiario Arqueológico Hispánico*
NAH Arq.   *Noticiario Arqueológico Hispánico, Arqueología*
PLRE I   *Prosopography of the Late Roman Empire*, vol I, A. Jones, J. Martindale and J. Morris, 1971
RIT   *Römische Inschriften von Tarraco*, G. Alföldy, 1975
RSL   *Rivista di Studi Liguri*
ZPE   *Zeitschrift für Papyrologie und Epigraphik*

ABAD CASAL, L. 1975. *El Guadalquivir, vía fluvial romana* (Seville).
ABAD CASAL, L. 1982. *Pintura Romana en España* (Alicante-Seville).
ABSOLÓ, J. A. 1975. 'Notas sobre el campanento romano de Sasamón', *Pyrenae* 11, 127–32.
ABSOLÓ, J. A. 1975a. *Comunicaciones de la época romana en la provincia de Burgos* (Burgos).
AKURGAL, E. 1985. *Ancient civilizations and ruins of Turkey* (Ankara).
ALARCÃO, J. 1973. *Portugal Romano* (Lisbon).
ALARCÃO, J. and R. ETIENNE, 1977. *Fouilles de Conimbriga volume I: L'Architecture*, 2 vols (Paris).
ALBERTINI, E. 1923. *Les Divisions administratives de l'Espagne romaine* (Paris).
ALBERTOS FIRMAT, M. L. 1975. 'Organizaciones suprafamiliares en la Hispania Antigua', *Studia Archaeologica* 37.
ALFARO GINER, C. 1984. *Tejido y Cestería en la Península Ibérica*, Bibliotheca Praehistorica Hispana (Madrid).
ALFÖLDY, G. 1969. *Fasti Hispanienses: senatorische Reichsbeamte und Offiziere in den spanischen Provinzen des römischen Reiches von Augustus bis Diokletian* (Wiesbaden).
ALFÖLDY, G. 1975. *Römische Inschriften von Tarraco*, 2 vols (Berlin).
ALFÖLDY, G. 1977. 'Ein Ziegelstempel mit dem Namen eines Senators aus Villajoyosa in der Hispania Citerior', *ZPE* 27, 217–21.
ALFÖLDY, G. 1977a. *Los Baebii de Saguntum*, Servicio de Investigaciones Prehistóricas, Trabajos Varios 56.
ALMAGRO, M. 1955. *Las Necrópolis de Ampurias*, II (Barcelona).
ALMAGRO, M. 1981. 'Sobre la dedicación de los altares del templo de Hercules Gaditanus', *La Religión Romana en Hispania*, 301–38.
ALMAGRO, M. 1983. *Guía de Mérida* (Madrid).
ALMAGRO GORBEA, A. 1979. 'Estudio fotogramétrico del teatro de Sagunto', *Saguntum* 14, 165–79.
ALMAGRO GORBEA, M. 1977. 'La iberización de las zonas orientales de la Meseta', *Simposi Internacional: Els Origens del Mon Iberic*, *Ampurias* 38–40, 93–156.
ALVÁREZ, J. 1972. 'Las termas romanas de Alanje', *Habis* 3, 267–90.
ALVÁREZ, J. 1977. 'El templo de Diana', *Augusta Emerita. Actas del bimilenario de Mérida*, 43–53.
ALVÁREZ, J. 1983. *El Puente Romano de Mérida* (Badajoz).
ALVÁREZ, P. 1942. 'La crónica de Juan Biclarense', *Analecta Sacra Tarraconense* 16, 7–44.
AQUILUE, J., R. MAR, J. M. NOLLA, J. RUIZ and E. SANMARTÍ 1984. *El forum Romà d'Empúries*, Monografies Emporitanes IV (Barcelona).
AQUILUE, J. and J. DUPRÉ 1986. 'Reflexions entorn de Tarraco en època tardo-Republicana', *Forum* 1.
ARCE, J. 1976. 'El Missorium de Teodosio I: precisiones y observaciones', *AEA* 49, 119–40.
ARCE, J. 1982. *El último siglo de la España romana: 284–409* (Madrid).
ARCE, J. 1983. 'Mérida Tardorromana (284–409 d.c.)', *Homenaje a Saenz Buruaga* (Badajoz), 209–36.
ARGENTE, J. L. 1979. *La villa tardorromana de Baños de Valdearados (Burgos)*, EAE 100.
ARGENTE, J. L. *et al.* 1985. *Tiermes. Guía del yacimiento arqueólogico* (Madrid).
ARCO, R. 1950. 'Sertorio en Huesca', *Argensola* I.
ARIAS VILAS, F. 1972. 'Las murallas romanas de Lugo', *Studia Archeologica* 14.
ARRIBAS, A. 1963. *The Iberians* (London).
ARTEAGA, O. 1977. 'Problemática general de la iberización en Andalucía oriental y en el sudeste de la península', *Simposi Internacional: Els origens del mon Iberic*, *Ampurias*, 38–40, 23–60.
ARTEAGA, O., J. PADRO and E. SANMARTÍ 1978. 'El factor fenici a les costes catalanes i del Golf de Lio. Els pobles pre-Romans del Pirineu', *2 Col. loqui Internacional d'Arqueologia de Puigcerdà*, 129–35.
ASTIN, A. 1967. *Scipio Aemilianus* (Oxford).
ASTIN, A. 1978. *Cato the Censor* (Oxford).
ASTRUC, M. 1951. 'Le necrópolis de Villaricos', *Informes y Memorias de la Comisaría General de Excavaciones Arqueológicas* 25.
BADÍA, J. 1977. *L'Arquitectura Medieval de l'Empordà. I: Baix Emporda* (Girona).
BADIAN, E. 1958. *Foreign Clientelae (264–70 BC)* (Oxford).
BALIL, A. 1961. 'Las murallas romanas de Barcelona', *Anejos del Archivo Español de Arqueología* II (Madrid).
BALIL, A. 1972. 'Economía de la Hispania romana (s.I–III d.c.)', *Studia Archaeologica* 15.

BALIL, A. 1974. 'Casa y urbanismo en la España antigua IV', *Studia Archaeologica* 28.

BALIL, A. 1980. 'Mosaico con representación de las nueve Musas hallado en Moncada (Valencia)', *Studia Archaeologica* 37.

BARRAL I ALTET, X. 1978. *Les Mosaiques romaines et médiévales de la Regio Laietania* (Barcelona).

BELTRÁN, A. 1976. 'Caesaraugusta', *Symposion de Ciudades Augusteas* I (Zaragoza), 224–30.

BELTRÁN, F. 1980. *Epigrafía latina de Saguntum y su territorium*, Servicio de Investigaciones Prehistóricas, Trabajos Varios 67.

BELTRÁN, M. 1970. *Las Ánforas Romanas en España* (Zaragoza).

BELTRÁN, M. 1976. *Arqueología e Historia de las ciudades antiguas del cabezo de Alcalá de Azaila (Teruel)*, Monografías Arqueológicas 19 (Zaragoza).

BELTRÁN, M. 1977. 'Problemas de la morfología y del concepto histórico-geográfico que recubre la noción tipo', *Méthodes classiques et méthodes formelles dans l'étude des amphores*, Collections de l'Ecole Française à Rome 32, 97–131.

BELTRÁN, M. 1983. *Los orígenes de Zaragoza y la época de Augusto*, Institución Fernando el Católico (CSIC) (Zaragoza).

BELTRÁN, M., A. MOSTALAC and J. LASHERAS 1984. *Colonia Victrix Iulia Lepida-Celsa (Velilla del Ebro): I. La arquitectura de la Casa de los Delfines* (Zaragoza).

BENDALA, M. 1972. 'Los llamados "columbarios" de Mérida', *Habis* 3, 223–93.

BENDALA, M. 1976. *La Necrópolis Romana de Carmona*, 2 vols (Seville).

BENDALA, M. 1981. 'La etapa final de la cultura ibero turdetana y el impacto romanizador', *La baja época de la cultura ibérica* (Madrid), 33–48.

BENDALA, M. 1982. 'Excavaciones en el cerro de los palacios', *Italica. Actas de las primeras jornadas sobre excavaciones arqueológicas en Italica*, EAE 121, 29–74.

BERGES, M. 1974. 'Columnas romanas y cruces visigóticas en la Plaza del Rovellat de Tarragona', *Miscelanea Arqueológica I, XXV Aniversario de los cursos de Ampurias (1947–71)*, 153–67.

BERGES, M. 1982. 'El teatro romano de Tarragona', *El Teatro Romano en Hispania* (Badajoz), 115–21.

BIRD, D. G. 1972. 'The Roman Gold Mines of North-West Spain', *Bonner Jahrbucher* 172, 36–64.

BIRD, D. G. 1984. 'Pliny and the gold mines of north-west Iberia', *Papers in Iberian Archaeology*, ed. T. Blagg, R. Jones and S. Keay, BAR International Series 193, I, 341–63.

BLANCO, A. 1978. *Mosaicos Romanos de Mérida*, Corpus de Mosaicos Romanos de España, Fascículo I.

BLANCO, A. and J. M. LUZÓN 1969. 'Pre-Roman silver miners at Rio-Tinto', *Antiquity* 43, 124–32.

BLANCO, A., J. GARCÍA and M. BENDALA. 1972. 'Excavaciones en Cabra (Córdoba). La Casa de Mitra', *Habis* 3, 297–320.

BLANCO, A., and J. M. LUZÓN 1974. 'Resultados de las excavaciones del poblado primitivo de Rio-Tinto', *Huelva: Prehistoria y Antigüedad*, ed. M. Almagro *et al.* (Madrid), 235–48 and lám. 221.

BLÁZQUEZ, J. M. 1964. *Estructura Económica y Social de Hispania durante la Anarquía Militar y el Bajo Imperio. Cuadernos de la Catedra de Historia Antigua de España I* (Madrid).

BLÁZQUEZ, J. M. 1975. *Diccionario de las religiones prerromanas de Hispania* (Madrid).

BLÁZQUEZ, J. M. 1975a. 'Hispania desde el año 138 al 235', *Hispania* XXXV, 5–87.

BLÁZQUEZ, J. M. 1979. *Castulo II*, EAE 105.

BLÁZQUEZ, J. M. 1980. 'Colonización cartaginesa en la península

ibérica', *Historia de España Antigua Tomo I: Protohistoria*, ed. Blázquez *et al.*, 409–38.

BLÁZQUEZ, J. M. 1981. *Mosaicos Romanos de Córdoba, Jaén y Málaga*, Corpus de Mosaicos Romanos de España, Fascículo III.

BLÁZQUEZ, J. M. 1982. *Mosaicos Romanos de Sevilla, Granada, Cádiz y Murcia*, Corpus de Mosaicos Romanos de España, Fascículo IV.

BLÁZQUEZ, J. M. 1982a. 'La economía de la Hispania Romana', 295–607, *Historia de España. España Romana (218 a de JC-414 de JC), Volumen I: La conquista y la explotación económica*, ed. A. Montenegro *et al.* (Madrid).

BLÁZQUEZ, J. M. 1982b. 'Origen del cristianismo Hispano', 415–47, *Historia de España. España Romana (218 a de JC-414 de JC), Volumen II: La sociedad, el derecho, la cultura*, ed. J. Mangas *et al.* (Madrid).

BLÁZQUEZ, J. M. 1982c. *Mosaicos Romanos de la Real Academia de la Historia, Ciudad Real, Madrid y Cuenca*, Corpus de Mosaicos Romanos de España, Fascículo V.

BLÁZQUEZ, J. M., and T. ORTEGO 1983. *Mosaicos Romanos de Soria*, Corpus de Mosaicos Romanas de España, Fascículo VI.

BLUME, F. *et al.* 1848. *Die Schriften der römischen Feldmesser* (Berlin).

BONNEVILLE, J. N. 1981. 'Les cupae de Barcelone', *MCV* 17, 7–36.

BONNEVILLE, J. N., S. DARDAINE, F. DIDIERJEAN, P. LE ROUX and P. SILLIÈRES 1981. 'La quinzième campagne de fouilles de la casa de Velazquez à Belo en 1980 (Bolonia, Province de Cadix)', *MCV* 17, 393–456.

BONNEVILLE, J. N., F. DIDIERJEAN, N. DUPRÉ, P. JACOB and J. LANCHA 1984. 'La dix-huitième campagne de fouilles de la casa de Velazquez à Belo en 1983 (Bolonia, Province de Cadix)', *MCV* 20, 439–86.

BOUBÉ, J. 1965. *La terra sigillata hispanique en Maurétanie Tingitanie I. Les Marques* (Rabat).

BOUCHIER, E. 1914. *Spain under the Roman Empire* (Oxford).

BROWN, P. 1974. *The World of Late Antiquity* (London).

BRUNT, P. 1971. *Italian Manpower 225 BC–AD 14* (Oxford).

CABALLERO, L. 1974. 'La necrópolis tardorromana de Fuentespreadas (Zamora)', EAE 80.

CABRÉ, J. 1929. 'Excavaciones de las Cogotas (Cardeñosa, Ávila) I: El Castro', *MJSEA* 110.

CABRÉ, J. 1932. 'Excavaciones de las Cogotas (Cardeñsa, Ávila) II: La Necrópolis', *MJSEA* 120.

CABRÉ, J., E. CABRÉ DE MORÁN and E. MOLINERO 1950. 'El castro y la necrópolis del hierro céltico de Chamartín de la Sierra (Ávila)', *Acta Arqueológica Hispánica* V.

CANTO, A. 1977–8. 'Avances sobre la explotación del mármol en la España romana', *AEA* 50–1, 165–87.

CANTO, A. 1981. 'Notas sobre los pontífices coloniales y el origen del culto imperial en la Bética', *La Religión Romana en Hispania*, 143–53.

CANTO, A. 1982. 'Excavaciones en "el Pradillo" (Italica 1974): un barrio tardío', *Italica. Actas de las primeras jornadas sobre excavaciones arqueológicas en Italica*, EAE 121, 225–42.

CARDOZO, M. 1971. *Citania de Britieros e castro de Sabroso* (Guimarães).

CARO BAROJA, J. 1970. 'Organización social de los pueblos del norte de la península ibérica en la antigüedad', *Legio VII Gemina*, 13–62.

CARRIAZO, J. 1973. *Tartessos y el Carambolo* (Madrid).

CASAS, J. 1980. 'L'Estació Romana del camp del Bosquet, Camallera (Alt Empordà): L'Aljub', *Revista de Girona* 91, 77–81.

CASAS, J., and E. SANMARTÍ 1980. 'El Cami d'Empúries: approximacio a la xarca viaria del Baix Emporda', *Informació Arqueologica* 33–4, 59–63.

CASTELLS PEIG, A. 1961. *L'Art Sabadellenc* (Sabadell).

CASTILLO, A. 1939. 'La Costa Brava en la antigüedad, en particular la zona entre Blanes y Sant Feliu de Guixols', *Ampurias* I, 186–267.

CASTILLO, C. 1965. *Prosopographía Baetica II* (Pamplona).

CHADWICK, H. 1976. *Priscillian of Avila* (Oxford).

CHASTAGNOL, A. 1976. 'Les inscriptions Constantiniennes du cirque de Merida', *MEFR* 88, 259–76.

CHAVES, F., and M. CRUZ 1981. 'Numismática y religión romana en Hispania', *La Religión Romana en Hispania*, 25–46.

CHESTER JOHNSON, A., *et al.* 1961. *Ancient Roman Statutes*, University of Texas Press.

COLES, J., and A. HARDING 1979. *The Bronze Age in Europe* (London).

COLLINS, R. 1983. *Early Medieval Spain: Unity in Diversity, 400–1000* (London).

COLLS, D., R. ETIENNE, R. LEQUEMENT, B. LIOU and F. MAYET 1977. 'L'Epave Port-Vendres II et le commerce de la Bétique a l'époque de Claude', *Archaeonautica I* (Paris).

COMAS I SOLA, M. 1985. *Baetulo. Les ámfores* (Badalona).

CORBIER, M. 1978. 'Dévaluations et fiscalité (161–235)', *Les dévaluations' à Rome. Epoque Républicaine et Imperiale*, Collection de l'Ecole Française à Rome 37, 273–309.

CORSI-SCIALLANO, M., and B. LIOU 1985. 'Les Epaves de Tarraconaise à chargement d'amphores Dressel 2–4', *Archaeonautica 5* (Paris).

CORZO, R. 1977. *Osuna de Pompeyo à César. Excavaciones en la muralla republicana*, University of Seville.

CORZO, R. 1977a. 'In finibus Emeritensium', *Augusta Emerita: Actas del Bimilenario de Mérida*, 217–33.

CORZO, R. 1982. 'Organización del territorio y la evolución urbana en Italica', *Italica. Actas de las primeras jornadas sobre excavaciones arqueológicas en Italica*, EAE 121.

CRAWFORD, M. 1974. *Roman Republican Coinage*, 2 vols (Cambridge).

CRAWFORD, M. 1985. *Coinage and money under the Roman Republic* (London).

CUADRADO DIAZ, E. 1952. 'Villa romana de Cabo de Palos', *NAH* I, 134–56.

CUADRADO, E. 1974. 'Pénetración de las influencias colonizadoras greco-fenicias en el interior peninsular', *Symposio de Colonizaciones*, 93–104.

CUMONT, F. 1924. 'Une dédicace à des dieux Syriens trouvés à Cordoue', *Syria* 5, 342–5.

CUMONT, F. 1927. 'Les Syriens en Espagne et les Adonies à Seville', *Syria* 8, 330–41.

D'ABADAL, R. 1974. *Dels Visigots als Catalans. La Hispània Visigòtica i la Catalunya Carolíngia* (Barcelona).

DAVIES, O. 1935. *Roman Mines in Europe* (Oxford).

DEL AMO, M. D. 1979. *Estudio Crítico de la Necrópolis Paleocristiana de Tarragona* (Tarragona).

DEL AMO, M. D. 1981. *Estudio Crítico de la Necrópolis Paleocristiana de Tarragona, Ilustraciones* (Tarragona).

DEL AMO, M. D. 1981a. 'Aportación al estudio de las canteras romanas de la zona arqueológica de "Els Munts"', *Estudis Altafullencs* 5, 5–26.

DIEZ CORONEL, L. 1968. 'Una bodega romana en Balaguer', *CNA*, 774–83.

DIMAS FERNÁNDEZ 1984. *Complutum I (excavaciones)*, EAE 137.

DIMAS FERNÁNDEZ 1984. *Complutum II (mosaicos)*, EAE 138.

DIXON, P. 1940. *The Iberians of Spain* (Oxford).

DOMERGUE, C. 1965. 'Les Planii et leur activité industrielle en Espagne sous la République', *MCV* I, 9–28.

DOMERGUE, C. 1966. 'Les lingots de plomb romains du musée archéologique de Carthagène et du musée naval de Madrid', *AEA* 39, 41–72.

DOMERGUE, C. 1983. *La mine antique d'Aljustrel (Portugal) et les tables de bronze de Vipasca* (Paris).

DOMERGUE, C., and G. TAMAIN 1971. 'El cerro del plomo, mina el Centenillo (Jaén)', *NAH* 16, 265–382.

D'ORS, A. 1953. *Epigrafía jurídica de la España romana* (Madrid).

D'ORS, A. 1967. 'Una nueva inscripción ampuritana, *Ampurias* 29, 293–5.

DO PACO, A., and J. BACAO 1966. 'Castelo de Lousa, Mourão (Portugal). Una fortificación romana de la margen izquierda del Guadiana', *AEA* 39, 167–83.

DRINKWATER, J. 1983. *Roman Gaul. The three provinces, 58 BC–AD 260* (London).

DUNCAN-JONES, R. 1974. ' The procurator as civic benefactor', *JRS* LXIV, 79–85.

DUPRÉ, X. 1986. 'Els capitells corintis de l'Arc de Berà', *Forum 6*.

DUPRÉ, X., J. MASSÒ, L. PALANQUES and M.-L. VERDUCHI 1987. *El Circ Romà de Tarragona*.

DYSON, S. 1980–1. 'The distribution of Roman Republican family names in the Iberian peninsula', *Ancient Society* 11/12, 258–99.

ENGEL, A., and P. PARIS 1906. 'Une fortresse ibérique à Osuna (fouilles de 1903)', *Nouvelles Archives des Missions Scientifiques* 13.

ETIENNE, R. 1958. *La Culte Impérial dans la Péninsule Ibérique d'Auguste à Dioclétien* (Paris).

ETIENNE, R. 1965. 'Les sénateurs espagnols sous Trajan et Hadrien', *Les Empereurs romains d'Espagne*, 55–85.

ETIENNE, R. 1970. 'A propos du "garum sociorum" ', *Latomus* 29, 297–313.

ETIENNE, R. and F. MAYET 1971. 'Briques de Belo: relations entre la Mauretanie Tingitane et la Bétique au bas-Empire', *MCV* 7, 59–75.

ETIENNE, R. and G. FABRE 1979. 'L'Immigration à Tarragone, capitale d'une province romaine d'Occident', *Homenaje a García y Bellido IV: Revista de la Universidad Complutense* XVIII, 95–116, 118.

FABRICIUS, E. 1932. 'Some notes on Polybius' discussion on Roman camps', *JRS* 22, 78–87.

FATÀS, G. 1980. *Contrebia Belaisaca II: Tabula Contrebiensis* (Zaragoza).

FERGUSON, J. 1970. *The religions of the Roman Empire* (London).

FERNÁNDEZ, C. 1972. *Acueductos romanos en España* (Madrid).

FERNÁNDEZ, C. 1980. *Historia del puente en España. Puentes romanos*.

FERNÁNDEZ CASTRO, M. C. 1982. *Las Villas Romanas en España* (Madrid).

FERNÁNDEZ-CHICARRO, C., and F. FERNÁNDEZ 1980, *Catálogo del Museo Arqueológico de Sevilla. II. Salas de Arqueología Romana y Medieval*.

FISHWICK, D. 1982. ' The altar of Augustus and the municipal cult of Tarraco', *MM* 23, 222–33.

FLETCHER, D., E. PLÀ and J. ALCACER 1965. *La Bastida de les Alcuses (Mogente-Valencia)* Servicio de Investigaciones Prehistóricas, Trabajos Varios 14.

FLETCHER, D., E. PLÀ and J. ALCACER 1969. *La Bastida de les Alcuses (Mogente-Valencia)*, Servicio de Investigaciones Prehistóricas, Trabajos Varios 25.

FLORIANO, A. 1941. 'Aportaciones arqueológicas a la historia de la medicina romana', *AEA* 14.

Fontes Hispaniae Antiquae: Vol. II *500 a de JC hasta Cesar*; Vol. III *Las Guerras de 237–154 a de JC*; Vol. IV *Las Guerras de 154–72 a de JC*; Vol. V *Las Guerras del 72–19 a de JC*.

FORNI, G. 1970. 'L'occupazione militare romana della Spagna nord-occidentale: analogie e paralleli', *Legio VII Gemina*, 207–25.

FORTES, J. 1905 (1969). 'Restos de uma villa Lusitano-Romana na Povoa de Varzim', *Boletim Cultural de Povoa de Varzim, 8 (2)*, 313–41.

GABBA, E. 1960. 'Senati in esilio', *BIDR* LXIII, 22–232.

GALSTERER, H. 1971. *Untersuchungen zum römischen Städtewesen auf der iberischen Halbinsel* (Berlin).

GAMER, G. and T. ORTEGO 1969. 'Neue Beobachtungen am römischen Lager bei Almazán (prov. Soria)', *MM* 10, 172–84.

GARABITO GÓMEZ, T. 1978. *Los alfares Romanos Riojanos. Producción y comercialización*, Bibliotheca Praehistorica Hispana XVI.

GARCÍA MORENO, L. 1974. *Prosopografía del Reino Visigodo de Toledo* (Salamanca).

GARCÍA Y BELLIDO, A. 1949. *Esculturas romanas de España y Portugal* (Madrid).

GARCÍA Y BELLIDO, A. 1953. 'Dos villae rusticae recientemente excavadas, *AEA* 26, 207–13.

GARCÍA Y BELLIDO, A. 1956. 'El culto a Serapis en la península ibérica', *BRAH* 139, 313 ff.

GARCÍA Y BELLIDO, A. 1957. 'Estado actual del problema referente a la expansión de la cerámica ibérica por la cuenca occidental del Mediterráneo', *AEA* 30, 90–106.

GARCÍA Y BELLIDO, A. 1959. 'Del carácter militar actual de las colonias romanas de Lusitania y regiones inmediatas', *Trabalhos de Antropologia e Etnologia* 17.

GARCÍA Y BELLIDO, A. 1960. 'Colonia Aelia Augusta Italica', *Bibliotheca Archaeologica* II (Madrid).

GARCÍA Y BELLIDO, A. 1960a. 'Iupiter Dolichenus y la lápida de Villadecanos', *Zephyrus* 11, 199–204.

GARCÍA Y BELLIDO, A. 1960b. 'Lápidas funerarias de Gladiadores en Hispania', *AEA* 33, 124–44.

GARCÍA Y BELLIDO, A. 1964. 'Hercules Gaditanus', *AEA* 36, 70–153.

GARCÍA Y BELLIDO, A. 1967. *Les religions orientales dans l'Espagne romaine* (Leiden).

GARCÍA Y BELLIDO, A. 1970. 'Estudios sobre la Legio VII Gemina y su campamento en León', *Legio VII Gemina*, 571–99.

GARCÍA Y BELLIDO, A. 1976. 'El ejército romano en Hispania', *AEA* 49, 59–101.

GARRIDO, J., and E. M. ORTA 1974. 'El problema de Tartessos: una interpretación arqueológica', *Huelva: Prehistoria y Antigüedad*, ed. M. Almagro *et al.*, 249–63.

GIANFROTTA, P. 1982. 'Lentulo Augure e le anfore Laietane. Epigrafia e ordine senatorio', *Tituli* 4, 475–9.

GISBERT, J. 1983. 'Excavaciones arqueológicas en el "Hort de Morand" (Denia, Alicante)', *Primeras Jornadas de Arqueología en las ciudades actuales* (Zaragoza), 133–42.

GONZÁLEZ, A., P. LILLO, S. RAMALLO and A. YELO 1983. 'La Ciudad Hispano-Visigoda de Begastri (Cabezo de Roenas, Cehegín-Murcia)', *CNA* XVI, 1011–22.

GONZÁLEZ, J. 1981, 'Inscripciones inéditas de Córdoba y su provincia', *MCV* 17, 38–54.

GONZÁLEZ, J. 1983. 'Nueva inscripción de un diffusor olearius en la Bética', *Producción y comercio del aceite en la antigüedad. Segundo Congreso Internacional* (Madrid), 183–91.

GONZÁLEZ, J. 1986, 'The Lex Irnitana: a New Copy of the Flavian Municipal law', *JRS* 76, 147–243.

GORGES, J. G. 1979, *Les Villas Hispano-Romaines. Inventaire et Problématique Archéologiques* (Paris).

GOSSE, G. 1942. 'Las minas y el arte minero de España en la antigüedad', *Ampurias* IV, 42–68.

GRANADOS, O. 1976. 'Estudios de la arqueología romana barcelonesa: la puerta decumana o del noroeste', *Pyrenae* XII, 157–71.

GRANADOS, O. 1984. 'La primera fortificación de la colonia Barcino', *Papers in Iberian Archaeology*, ed. T. Blagg, R. Jones and S. Keay, BAR International Series 193 (i), 267–319.

GRANADOS, O. and E. MANERA 1977. 'Notas sobre Barcelona: Sector B de la Plaza de San Miguel', *CNA* XIV, 1105–12.

GRANT, M. 1969. *From Imperium to Auctoritas* (Cambridge).

GRENIER, A. 1934. *Manuel d'Archéologie Gallo-Romaine. Vol. VI. 2: Navigation-Occupation du sol* (Paris).

GRÜNHAGEN, W. 1977. 'El monumento a Dis-Pater, de Munigua', *Segovia y la Arqueología Romana* (Barcelona), 201–8.

GRÜNHAGEN, W., and T. HAUSCHILD 1979. 'Sucinto informe sobre las investigaciones arqueológicas en Munigua en 1976', *NAH* 6, 301–6.

GUADÁN, A. 1980. *La Moneda Ibérica* (Madrid).

GUITART, J. 1970. 'Excavación de la zona sudeste de la villa romana de Sentroma (Tiana)', *Pyrenae* 6, 111–65.

GUITART, J. 1976. *Baetulo. Topografía arqueológica, urbanismo e historia* (Badalona).

GUNDLACH, W. (ed.) 1892. 'Epistolae Wisigoticae', *Epistulae Merowingici et Karolini Aevi* I. *Monumenta Germaniae Historica* (Berlin).

HARMAND, J. 1970. 'César et l'Espagne durant le second "bellum civile"', *Legio VII Gemina*, 181–203.

HAUSCHILD, T. 1969, 'Untersuchungen in Stadtgebiet Östlich von Forum', *MM* 10, 185–97.

HAUSCHILD, T. 1972–4. 'Römische Konstruktionen auf der oberen Stadtterrasse des antiken Tarraco', *AEA* 45–7, 3–44.

HAUSCHILD, T. 1976. 'Der Römische Leuchtturm von la Coruña (Torre de Hercules). Probleme seiner Rekonstruktion', *MM* 17, 238–57.

HAUSCHILD, T. 1976–7. 'Torre de Minerva (Sant Magi). Una torre de la muralla romana de Tarragona', *Butlletí Arqueològic* 133–40, 49–73.

HAUSCHILD, T. 1977. 'La terraza superior de Tarragona, una planificación axial del siglo I', *Bimilenario de Segovia: Segovia y la arqueología romana*, 209–14.

HAUSCHILD, T. 1983. 'La muralla romana de la ciutat de Tarragona. Excavacions a la torre de Minerva i al baluard de Santa Barbara', *Arquitectura Romana de Tarragona*, 131–80 (Tarragona).

HAUSCHILD, T. and H. SCHLUNK 1961. 'Vorbericht über die Arbeiten in Centcelles', *MM* 2, 119–82.

HENDERSON, M. 1942. 'Julius Caesar and *Latium* in Spain', *JRS* 32, 1–13.

HÉRON DE VILLEFOSSE, A. 1914. 'Deux armateurs Narbonnais. Sextus Fadius Secundus Musa et P. Olitius Apollonius', *Memoires de la Société Nationale des Antiquités de la France* CXXIV, 153 ff.

HOPKINS, K. 1980. 'Taxes and trade in the Roman Empire', *JRS* 70, 101–25.

HUNT, E. 1982. *Holy Land pilgrimage in the later Roman Empire AD 312–460* (Oxford).

HYDATIUS, *Chronicon see* Tranoy, A. 1974.

JIMÉNEZ, A. 1982. ' Teatro de Italica: primera campaña de obras', *Italica. Actas de las primeras jornadas sobre excavaciones arqueológicas en Italica*, EAE 121, 279–89.

JONES, B. 1980. ' The Roman mines at Río Tinto', *JRS* LXX, 146–65.

JONES, R. 1976. 'The Roman military occupation of north-west Spain', *JRS* 66, 45–66.

JONES, R., and BIRD, D. G. 1972. 'Roman gold-mining in north-west Spain II: workings on the Río Duerna', *JRS* 62, 59–74.

JONES, R., S. KEAY *et al.* 1983. 'The late Roman villa of Vilauba and its context. A first report on fieldwork and excavation in Catalunya, north-east Spain 1979–1981', *Antiquaries Journal* 62.2, 245–82.

JORDÁ CERDÁ, F. 1957. *Las murias de Beloño. Una villa romana en Asturias* (Oviedo).

KALB, P., and M. HOCK 1983. 'El alto do Castello, Alpiarça (Distrito de Santarém, Portugal)', *CNA* XVI, 829–32.

KEAY, S. 1981. 'The Conventus Tarraconensis in the third century AD: Crisis or Change?' *The Roman west in the third century. Contributions from Archaeology and History,* ed. A. King and M. Henig, BAR International Series 109 (2 vols), 451–86.

KEAY, S. 1984. *Late Roman amphorae in the Western Mediterranean: a typology and economic study. The Catalan evidence,* BAR International Series 196 (2 vols).

KEAY, S. 1987. 'La importación del vino y aceite a la Tarraconense en la antigüedad', *El ví a l'antiguitat. Economía, producció i comerç al Mediterrani occidental* (Badalona).

KEPPIE, L. 1984. *The making of the Roman army, from Republic to Empire* (London).

KNAPP, R. 1977. *Aspects of the Roman experience in Iberia, 206–100 BC,* Anejos de Hispania Antiqua IX (Valladolid and Alava).

KNAPP, R. 1983. *Roman Córdoba,* University of California, Classical Studies, vol. 30.

KNAPP, R. 1987. 'Spain', *The Coinage of the Roman World in the Late Republic,* ed. A. Burnett and M. Crawford, BAR International Series 326, 19–41.

KOENIG, G. 1981. 'Wandalische Grabfunde des 5 und 6 Jhs', *MM* 22, 299–360.

KOPPEL, E. 1985. *Die Römische skulpturen von Tarraco. Madrider Forschungen* 15 (Berlin).

KUKAHN, E., and A. BLANCO 1959. 'El tesoro de "el Carámbolo"', *AEA* 32, 38–49.

LAMBOGLIA, N. 1974. 'Encore sur la fondation d'Ampurias', *Simposio de Colonizaciones,* 105–8.

LARA PEINADO, F. 1974. 'En torno a los toponimios "terra hilardensi" de la donación del diácono Vincente de Huesca', *Ilerda* XXXV, 33–43.

LEÓN, P. 1982. 'La zona monumental de la nova urbs', *Italica. Actas de las primeras jornadas sobre excavaciones arqueológicas en Italica,* EAE 121, 97–132.

LE ROUX, P. 1975. 'Aux origines de Braga (Bracara Augusta)', *Bracara Augusta* XXIX, 155–9.

LE ROUX, P. 1977. 'Lucus Augusti, Capitale administrative au Haut-Empire', *Actas del Coloquio Internacional Sobre el Bimilenario de Lugo* (Lugo), 83–101.

LE ROUX, P. 1982. *L'Armée Romaine et l'organisation des provinces ibériques d'Auguste à l'invasion de 409* (Paris).

LE ROUX, P., and A. TRANOY 1973. 'Rome et les indigènes dans le nord-ouest de la peninsule ibérique. Problèmes d'epigraphie et d'histoire, *MCV* IX, 177–231.

LEWIS, P., and G. D. B. JONES, 1970. 'Roman gold-mining in north-west Spain', *JRS* 60, 169–85.

LIEBESCHEUTZ, J. 1979. *Continuity and change in Roman religion* (Oxford).

LIOU, B. 1981. 'Les amphores à huile de l'épave Saint Gervais 3 à Fos-sur-mer: premières observations sur les inscriptions peintes', *Producción del aceite en la antigüedad. Primer Congreso Internacional y comercio,* 161–76.

LÓPEZ, G. 1982. 'Las esculturas zoomorfas "célticas" de la península ibérica y sus paralelos polacos', *AEA* 55, 3–30.

LÓPEZ RODRÍGUEZ, J. 1985. *Terra Sigillata Hispanica Tardía decorada a molde de la península ibérica* (Salamanca).

LOSTAL, J. 1980. *Arqueología del Aragón romano* (Zaragoza).

LUCAS, M.-R. 1981. 'Santuarias y dioses en la baja época ibérica', *La baja época de la cultura ibérica,* 233–93 (Madrid).

LUZÓN, J. 1973. 'Excavaciones en Italica: estratigrafía en el Pajar de Artillo, EAE 78.

LUZÓN, J. 1982. 'Consideraciones sobre la urbanística de la ciudad nueva de Italica', *Italica. Actas de las primeras jornadas sobre excavaciones arqueológicas en Italica,* EAE 121, 75–96.

LUZÓN, J. M., and D. RUIZ 1973. *Los raíces de Córdoba. Estratigrafía de la colina de los quemados,* Real Academia de Córdoba.

McELDERRY, K 1918. 'Vespasian's Reconstruction of Spain', *JRS* 8, 53–102.

MacKENDRICK, P. 1967. *The Iberian Stones Speak* (New York).

MACKIE, N. 1983. *Local administration in Roman Spain AD 14–212,* BAR International Series 172.

MALUQUER, J. 1958. *El castro de los Castillejos en Sanchorreja* (Ávila-Salamanca).

MALUQUER, J. 1981. *El santuario protohistórico de Zalamea de la Serena 1978–1981,* University of Barcelona.

MALUQUER, J. 1982. 'Moli de l'Espigol, Tornabous', *Les excavacions arqueologiques a Catalunya en els darrers anys.* 272–7 (Barcelona).

MALUQUER, J. 1985. *La civilización de Tartessos* (Seville).

MALUQUER, J., P. PALOL and M. TARRADELL 1965. Various articles in *Revista de Gerona* 31.

MANGAS, J. 1971. *Esclavos y libertos en la España romana* (Salamanca).

MANGAS, J. 1971. 'Servidumbre en la Bética prerromana', *MHA* I.

MANGAS, J. 1982. 'Religiones indígenas en Hispania' and 'Religiones romanas y orientales', 579–612, 613–48, *Historia de España. España Romana (218 a de JC-414 de JC), Volumen II: La sociedad, el derecho, la cultura,* ed. J. Mangas *et al.* (Madrid).

MANN, J. 1983. *Legionary recruitment and veteran settlement during the principate,* Institute of Archaeology Occasional Publication no. 7 (London).

MAR, R., and J. RUIZ 1986. 'La basilica de la colonia Tarraco', *Forum* 3.

MARTÍN, A. 1980. *Ullastret. Guide to the excavations and its museum* (Girona).

MARTÍN, A., J. NIETO and J.-M. NOLLA 1979. *Excavaciones en la Ciudadela de Roses* (Girona).

MARTÍN BUENO, M., M. L. CANCELA RAMÍREZ and J. JIMÉNEZ 1985. 'Municipium Augusta Bilbilis', *Arqueología de las Ciudades Modernas Superpuestas a las Antiguas* (Madrid), 255–70.

MARTÍN VALLS, R. 1985. 'Segunda edad de hierro', *Historia de Castilla y León I: La prehistoria del valle del Duero,* 104–31.

MARTÍNEZ GÁZQUEZ, J. 1974. *La Campaña de Catón en Hispania* (Barcelona).

MATTHEWS, J. 1975. *Western Aristocracies and Imperial Court AD 364–425* (Oxford).

MAYA, J. 1983. 'La cultura Castreña Asturiana: de los origenes a la romanización', *Indigenismo y romanización en el Conventus Asturum,* 13–44.

MAYET, F. 1971. 'La cinquième campagne de fouilles à Belo-Bolonia (province de Cadix) en 1970', *MCV* 7, 405–9.

Mayet, F. 1975. *Les céramiques à parois fines dans la Péninsule Ibérique* (Paris).

Mayet, F. 1984. *Les céramiques sigillées hispaniques: contribution à l'histoire économique de la péninsule ibérique sous l'Empire romain,* 2 vols (Paris).

MÉLIDA, J. 1925. *Monumentos Romanos en España* (Madrid).

MÉLIDA, J. 1929. *Arqueología Española* (Barcelona–Buenos Aires).

MEZQUÍRIZ, M. 1956. 'Los mosaicos de la villa romana de Liédena', *Excavaciones en Navarra II: 1947–1951*, 189–215.

MEZQUÍRIZ, M. 1961. *Terra Sigillata Hispánica*, 2 vols (Valencia).

MEZQUÍRIZ, M. 1978. *Pompaelo II*.

MEZQUÍRIZ IRUJO, M. 1982. 'Un taller de Terra Sigillata Hispánica en Bezares', *Rei Cretariae Romanae Fautorum Acta XXI/XXII*, 25–40.

MEZQUÍRIZ IRUJO, M. et al. 1983. *Terra Sigillata Hispánica*, Monografías del Museo Arqueológico Nacional 2 (Madrid).

MILES, G. 1952. *The coinage of the Visigoths of Spain. Leovigild to Achila II* (New York).

MOMMSEN, T. 1892. *Monumenta Germaniae Historica. Auctorum Antiquissimorum* IX.I (Berlin).

MONTENEGRO, A. 1982. 'La conquista de Hispania por Roma (218–19 antes de Jesucristo)', 5–192, *Historia de España. España Romana (218 a de JC-414 de JC), Volumen I: La Conquista y la explotación económica*, ed. A. Montenegro et al. (Madrid).

MOREL, J.-P. 1981. 'Emporion en el març de la colonització Focea', *L'Avenc* 38, 334–9.

MYNORS, R. (ed.) 1964. *XII Panegyrici Latini* (Oxford).

NICOLINI, G. 1974. *The Ancient Spaniards* (Farnborough).

NIETO, J. 1979–80. 'Repertorio de la pintura mural romana de Ampurias', *Ampurias* 41–2, 279–342.

NIETO, J., and J.-M. NOLLA. 1985. 'El yacimiento arqueológico submarino de Riells-La Clota y su relación con Ampurias', *VI Congreso Internacional de Arqueología Submarina, Cartagena 1982*, 265–83.

NOLLA, J.-M. 1978. *La Ciudad Romana de Gerunda*, Universidad autónoma de Barcelona.

NOLLA, J.-M., and J. NIETO 1979. 'Acerca de la cronología de la muralla romana tardía de Gerunda: La terra sigillata clara de "Casa Pastors"', *Faventia* 1/2, 263–83.

NOLLA, J.-M., and J. NIETO 1981. 'Una factoria de salao de peix a Roses', *Fonaments* 3, 187–200.

NOLLA, J.-M., J.M. CANES and X. ROCAS 1982. 'Un forn romà de terrissa a Llafranc (Palafrugell, Baix Empordà). Excavacions de 1980–1981', *Ampurias* 44, 147–84.

NUIX, J. 1976. 'Un bronce inédito de Máximo Tirano acuñado en Barcelona, hallado en Terrassa (Barcelona)', *Numisma* XXVI, 138–43, 165–9.

OGILVIE, R. 1969. *The Romans and their Gods* (London).

OLEIRO, J. M. 1965. 'Mosaïques romaines du Portugal', *La mosaique gréco-romaine*, Colloques Internationaux du Centre Nationale de la Recherche Scientifique, 257–64 (Paris).

OLMO ENCISO, L. 1986. 'Recopolis. La ville du roi Leovigild. Dossiers d'Histoire et archéologie', *Les Visigothes*, no. 108, 67–71.

ORTEGO, T. 1954–5. 'Excavaciones en la villa romana de Santervás del Burgo', *NAH* III–IV, 169–94.

ORTEGO, T. 1976. 'Excavaciones arqueológicas realizidas en la villa romana de "Los Quintanares", en el término de Rioseco de Soria, *NAH Arq.* 4, 359–76.

PALLARÈS, F. 1965. 'El poblado ibérico de San Antonio de Calaceite', *Institución Internacional de Estudios Ligures, Colección de Monografías Prehistóricas y Arqueológicas* 5 (Bordighera-Barcelona).

PALLARÈS, F. 1970. 'La topografia e le origini di Barcellona Romana', *RSL* 36, 63–102.

PALOL, P. DE 1966. *Demografía y arqueología hispánica de los siglos IV al VIII. Ensayo de Cartografía* (Valladolid).

PALOL, P. DE 1967. *Arqueología Cristiana de la España Romana* (Madrid).

PALOL, P. DE 1986. *La Villa Romana de la Olmeda de Pedrosa de la Vega (Palencia). Guía de las excavaciones*, 3rd edn (Palencia).

PALOL, P. DE, and J. ARIAS BONET 1969. 'Tres fragmentos de bronces con textos jurídicos hallados en Clunia', *BSAA* 34–5, 313 ff.

PALOL, P. DE, and J. CORTES 1974. 'La Villa Romana de la Olmeda, Pedrosa de la Vega (Palencia). Excavaciones de 1969 y 1970', *Acta Arqueológica Hispánica* 7.

PALOL, P. DE, and J. VILELLA 1986. '¿Un santuario priápico en Clunia?' *Koiné* 2, 15–25.

PASCUAL, R. 1977. 'Las ánforas de la Layetania', *Méthodes classiques et méthodes formelles dans l'étude des amphores*, Collection de l'Ecole Française à Rome 32, 47–96.

PELLICER, M. 1977. 'Problemática general de los inicios de la iberización en Andalucía occidental', *Simposi Internacional: Els Origens del Mon Iberic*, Ampurias 38–40, 3–21.

PFLAUM, H. 1965. 'La part prise par les chevaliers romains originaires d'Espagne à l'administration Impériale', *Les Empereurs romains d'Espagne* (Paris), 87–121.

PEÑA, M.-J. 1981. 'Contribución al estudio del culto de Diana en Hispania', *La Religión Romana en Hispania*, 47–59.

PEÑA, M.-J. 1984. 'Apuntes y observaciones sobre las primeras fundaciones romanas en Hispania', *Estudios de la Antigüedad* 1 (Barcelona), 47–85.

PEREIRA, I., J.-P. BOST and J. HIERNARD 1974. *Fouilles de Conimbriga III. Les Monnaies* (Paris).

PEREIRA MENAUT, G. 1979. *Inscripciones romanas de Valentia*, Servicio de Investigaciones Prehistóricas, Trabajos Varios 64.

PERICOT, L. 1952. *La labor de la comisaría provincial de excavaciones arqueológicas de Gerona durante los años 1942 a 1943*, Informes y Memorias de la Comisaría General de Excavaciones Arqueológicas 27, 110–29.

PERICOT, L. 1980. *La Céramique Ibérique* (Paris).

PHARR, C. 1969. *The Theodosian Code* (New York).

PONSICH, M. 1974. *Implantation rurale antique sur le Bas-Guadalquivir*, I (Paris).

PONSICH, M. 1979. *Implantation rurale antique sur le Bas-Guadalquivir*, II (Paris).

PONSICH, M., and M. TARRADELL 1965. *Garum et industries antiques de salaison dans la Méditerranée Occidentale* (Paris).

PUERTAS, R. 1982. *Lacipo (Casares, Málaga)*, EAE 120.

RAMALLO, S. 1985. *Mosaicos Romanos de Carthago-Nova (Hispania Citerior)* (Murcia).

RAMÍREZ, J. 1982. *Los primitivos núcleos de asentamiento en la ciudad de Cádiz* (Cadiz).

REMESAL, J. 1981. 'Reflejos económicos y sociales en la producción de ánforas olearias béticas (Dressel 20)', *Producción y comercio del aceite en la antigüedad. Primer Congreso Internacional*, 131–53.

REMESAL, J. 1982. 'Die Olwirtschaft in der Provinz Baetica: neue Formen der Analyse', *Saalburg Jahrbuch* 38, 30–71.

REMESAL, J. 1986. *La annona militaris y la exportación de aceite Bético a Germania* (Madrid).

REYNOLDS, P. 1984. 'African Red Slip and Late Roman imports in Valencia', *Papers in Iberian Archaeology*, ed. T. Blagg, R. Jones and S. Keay, BAR International Series 193 (ii), 474–539.

RIBAS, M. 1966. *La villa romana de Torre Llauder de Mataró*, EAE 47.

RIBERA, A. 1983. *La arqueología romana de la ciudad de Valentia (informe preliminar)* (Valentia).

RICHARD, J., P. LE ROUX and M. PONSICH 1972. 'La sixième campagne de fouilles à Belo-Bolonia (Province de Cadix) en 1971', *MCV* 8, 571–8.

RICHARDSON, J. 1976. 'The Spanish mines and the development of provincial taxation in the second century BC', *JRS* LXVI, 139–52.

RICHARDSON, J. 1983. 'The tabula contrebiensis: Roman law in Spain in the early first century BC', *JRS* LXXIII, 33–41.

RICHARDSON, J. 1986. *Hispaniae. Spain and the development of Roman imperialism, 218–82 BC* (Cambridge).

RICHMOND, I. 1931. 'Five town walls in Hispania Citerior', *JRS* 21, 86–100.

RICKARD, R. 1928. 'The mining of the Romans in Spain', *JRS* 18, 129–43.

ROCA ROUMENS, M. 1976. *Sigillata Hispánica producida en Andújar* (Jaén).

RODA, I. 1970. 'Lucius Licinius Secundus, liberto de Lucius Licinius Sura', *Pyrenae* VI, 167–83.

RODRÍGUEZ ALMEIDA, E. 1981. 'Alcuni aspetti della topografia e dell' archeologia attorno al Monte Testaccio', 103–30; 'El Monte Testaccio, hoy; nuevos testimonios epigráficos', 57–100, *Producción y comercio del aceite en la antigüedad. Primer Congreso Internacional*.

RODRÍGUEZ COLMENERO, A. 1979. *Augusto e Hispania. Conquista y reorganización del norte peninsular* (Bilbao).

RODRÍGUEZ NEILA, J. 1973. *Los Balbos de Cádiz. Dos Españoles en la Roma de César y Augusto* (Seville).

RODRÍGUEZ NEILA, J. 1981. *Sociedad y administración local en la Bética Romana* (Córdoba).

ROLDÁN, J. 1971. *Iter ab Emerita Asturicam. El camino de la plata* (Salamanca).

ROLDÁN, J. 1974. *Hispania y el ejército romano. Contribución a la historia social de la España antigua* (Salamanca).

ROLDÁN, J. 1975. *Itineraria hispana. Fuentes antiguas para el estudio de las vías romanas en la península Ibérica* (Valladolid-Granada).

ROLDÁN, J. 1978. 'La guerra civil entre Sertorio, Metelo y Pompeyo (82-72 ac)', 113–20. *Historia de España Antigua. II. Hispania Romana*, ed. J. M. Blázquez *et al.* (Madrid).

ROSSELLO, V. *et al.* 1974. *Estudios sobre centuraciones romanas en España* (Madrid).

ROUILLARD, P. 1979. *Investigaciones sobre la muralla ibérica de Sagunto*, Servicio de Investigaciones Prehistóricas. Trabajos Varios 67.

SALINAS, M. 1986. *Conquista y Romanización de Celtiberia* (Salamanca).

SANDARS, H. 1913. 'The weapons of the Iberians', *Archaeologia* 64, 205–94.

SANCHEZ LAFUENTE, J. 1979. 'Aportaciones al estudio del campamento romano de la "Cerca" (Anguilar de Anguita, Guadalajara)', *Wad-Al-Hayara* 6, 77–82.

SANMARTÍ, E. 1973. 'Materiales cerámicos griegos y etruscos de época arcaica en las comarcas meridionales de Catalunya', *Ampurias* 35, 221–34.

SANMARTÍ, E., and J. PADRÓ 1977. 'Ensayo de aproximación al fenómeno de la iberización en las comarcas meridionales de Catalunya', *Simposi International: Els Origens del Mon Iberic, Ampurias* 38–40, 157–75.

SANMARTÍ, E. *et al.* (forthcoming). 'Excavaciones en el Parking de Empúries' *Empúries* (*Ampurias*) 45.

SANMARTÍN MORO, P. 1985. 'Cartagena: conservación de yacimientos arqueológicos en el casco urbano', *Arqueología de las ciudades superpuestas a las antiguas*, 335–56.

SANTERO SANTURINO, J. M. 1978. *Asociaciones populares en Hispania romana* (Seville).

SAVORY, H. 1968. *Spain and Portugal. The prehistory of the Iberian peninsula* (New York).

SCHUBART, H. 1982. 'Asentamientos fenicios en la costa meridional de la península ibérica, *Huelva Arqueológica* VI, 71–99.

SCHLUNK, H., and T. HAUSCHILD 1978. *Hispania Antiqua. Die Denkmäler der Frühchristlichen und westgotischen Zeit* (Mainz).

SCHULTEN, A. 1914. *Numantia. Die Ergebnisse der Ausgrabungen 1905–1912. Band I. Die Keltiberer und ihre Kriege mit Rom* (Munich).

SCHULTEN, A. 1927. *Numantia. Die Ergebnisse der Ausgrabungen 1905–1912. Band III: die Lager des Scipio* (Munich).

SCHULTEN, A. 1929. *Numantia. Die Ergebnisse der Ausgrabungen 1905–1912. Band IV: die Lager bei Renieblas* (Munich).

SCHULTEN, A. 1931. *Numantia. Die Ergebnisse der Ausgrabungen 1905–1912. Band II: die Stadt Numantia* (Munich).

SCHULTEN, A. 1933. 'Segeda', *Homenaje a Martins Sarmiento* (Guimarães), 373–5.

SCHULTEN, A. 1942. *Los Cantabros y Astures y su guerra con Roma* (Madrid).

SCHULTEN, A. 1949. *Sertorio* (Barcelona).

SCHULTEN, A., and R. POULSEN 1928, 1930, 1932. 'Castra Caecilia', *Archäologische Anzeiger* XLIII, XLV, XLVII, 1–30, 37–87, 334–87.

SUTHERLAND, C. 1939. *The Romans in Spain, 217 BC–AD 117* (London).

SCULLARD, H. 1970. *Scipio Africanus: Soldier and Politician* (London).

SCULLARD, H. 1973. *Roman Politics, 220–150 BC* (Oxford).

SCULLARD, H. 1981. *Festivals and ceremonies of the Roman Republic* (London).

SERRA RÀFOLS, J. 1939. 'Excavaciones en Baetulo (Badalona) y descubrimiento de la puerta NE de la ciudad', *Ampurias* I, 268–89.

SERRA RÀFOLS, J. 1941. 'El poblado ibérico del Castellet de Banyoles', *Ampurias* III, 15–34.

SERRA RÀFOLS, J. 1943. 'La villa Fortunatus de Fraga', *Ampurias* V, 5–35.

SERRA VILARÒ, J. 1932. 'Excavaciones en Tarragona', *MJSEA* 116 (Madrid).

SERRA VILARÒ, J. 1960. *Santa Tecla la Vieja* (Tarragona).

SILLIÈRES, P. 1982. 'Documents modernes et précisions sur la via Augusta de Castulo à Cordoue', *104e Congrès National des Sociétés Savantes*, Bordeaux 1979 (Paris).

SIMÓN, F. 1977. 'Dos esculturas ibéricas zoomorfas de El Palao (Alcañiz, Teruel)', *Simposi Internacional: Els Origens del Mon Iberic, Ampurias* 38–40, 407–14.

SIMON, H. 1962. *Roms Kriege in Spanien 154–133 v.chr* (Frankfurt).

SNYDER, W. 1940. 'Public anniversaries in the Roman Empire', *Yale Classical Studies* 7, 223–317.

SUMNER, G. 1970. 'Proconsuls and provinciae in Spain', *Arethusa* 3, 85–102.

SYME, SIR R. 1970. 'The conquest of north-west Spain', *Legio VII Gemina*, 83–107.

TAMAIN, G. 1966. 'Las minas antiguas de el Centenillo (Jaén)', *Oretania* 16–18, 148 ff.

TARACENA, B. 1941. *Carta arqueológica de España: Soria* (Madrid).

TARACENA, B. 1956. *La villa romana de Liédena. Excavaciones en Navarra II, 1947–1951* (Pamplona), 45–106.

TARRADELL, M. 1978. 'Un fortí Romà a Tentellatge (Navès, Solsona)', *Els pobles Pre-Romans del Pirineu. 2 Col.loqui Internacional d'Arqueologia de Puigcerdà*, 245–50.

TCHERNIA, A. 1971. 'Les amphores vinaires de Tarraconaise et leur exportation au début de L'Empire', *AEA* 44, 38–85.

TCHERNIA, A. 1981. 'D. Caecilius Hospitalis et M. Iulius Hermesianus', *Producción y comercio del aceite en la antigüedad. Primer Congreso Internacional*, 155–60.

Photographic acknowledgements

THOMPSON, E, 1952. 'Peasant revolts in Late Roman Gaul and Spain', *Past and Present 2*, 11–23.

THOMPSON, E. 1969. *The Goths in Spain* (Oxford).

THOMPSON, E. 1976. 'The end of Roman Spain, Part 1', *Nottingham Mediaeval Studies* xx, 3–28.

THOMPSON, E. 1977. 'The end of Roman Spain, Part 2', *Nottingham Mediaeval Studies* xxi, 3–31.

THOUVENOT, R. 1940 (REV. EDN 1973). *Essai sur la province romaine de Bétique* (Paris).

TOMASINI, W. 1964. *The Barbaric tremisses in Spain and southern France: Anastasius to Leovigild* (New York).

TOVAR, A. 1974. *Iberische Landeskunde. Band 1. Baetica* (Baden-Baden).

TOVAR, A. 1976. *Iberische Landeskunde. Zweiter teil. Band 2. Lusitanien* (Baden-Baden).

TOVAR, A. 1981. 'El Dios Céltico Lugu en España', *La Religión Romana en España*, 277–83.

TRANOY, A. (trans.) 1974. *Chronique, Tome I* (trans. of Hydatius' *Chronicon*), Sources Chrétiennes 218 (Paris).

TRANOY, A. 1981. *La Galice Romaine* (Paris).

TRANOY, A. 1981a. 'Romanisation et monde indigène dans la Galice Romaine: Problèmes et Perspectives', *Primera Reunión Gallega de Estudios Clásicos* (Santiago de Compostela), 105–21.

ULBERT, G. 1985. *Cáceres el Viejo. Madrider Beiträge* 11.

VAN NOSTRAND, J. 1937. 'Roman Spain', ed. T. Frank, *An economic study of Ancient Rome Volume III* (Baltimore), 119–224.

VILLARONGA, L. 1983. *Les monedes ibèriques de Tàrraco* (Barcelona).

VILLARONGA, L. 1977. *The aes coinage of Emporion*, BAR Supplementary Series 23.

VILLARONGA, L. 1977a. *Los tesoros de Azaila y la circulación monetaria en el valle del Ebro*, Asociación Numismática Española (Barcelona).

VILLARONGA, L. 1979. *Numismática Antigua de Hispania* (Barcelona).

VITRUVIUS. *The ten books on architecture*, trans. M. Hicky Morgan (New York).

VIVES, J. 1926. *La Moneda Hispánica* (Madrid).

VIVES, J. 1963. *Concilios Visigóticos e Hispano-Romanos* (Barcelona–Madrid).

WALTZING, J. 1900. *Etude historique sur les corporations professionelles chez les romains depuis les origines jusqu'à la chute de l'Empire de l'Occident*, vols I–IV (Brussels).

WATTEMBERG, F. 1962. 'El mosaico de Diana de la villa de Prado (Valladolid)', *BSEAA* xxxVIII, 35–48.

WEST, L. 1929. *Imperial Roman Spain, the Objects of Trade* (Oxford).

WHITTAKER, C. 1983. 'Late Roman trade and traders', ed. P. Garnsey, K. Hopkins and C. Whittaker, *Trade in the Ancient Economy* (Cambridge), 163–80.

WIEGELS, R. 1974. 'Liv. Per. und die Gründung von Valentia', *Chiron* 4, 153–76.

WIEGELS, R. 1982. 'Iliturgi und der "deductor" Ti. Sempronius Gracchus', *MM* 23, 152–221.

WILSON, A. J. N. 1966. *Emigration from Italy in the Republican Age of Rome* (Manchester).

WISEMAN, F. 1956. *Roman Spain* (London).

WISEMAN, T. 1971. *New men in the Roman Senate, 139 BC–AD 14* (Oxford).

ZARAGOZA RUBIRA, J. 1971. *Medicina y sociedad en la España romana*.

ZEISS, H. 1970. *Die gräbfunde aus dem Spanischen Westgotenreich* (Berlin).

ZEUMER, K. 1902. 'Codex Euricianus', *Monumenta Germaniae Historica. Leges I* (Hanover and Leipzig).

The author and publishers gratefully acknowledge the following for providing illustrations:

José María Blázquez p. 185
British Museum half-title page, pp. 30 (left), 39, 54, 76
Miguel Casanelles I Rahola p. 196
Deutsches Archäologisches Institut pp. 152–3
Dirección General de Bellas Artes del Ministerio de Cultura p. 187
Xavier Dupre I Raventos data for line-drawing on p. 121
John Edmonson p. 80
Espasa Calpe p. 34
Generalitat de Catalunya, Institut Cartogràfic p. 121
Kaiseraugst Museum, Switzerland p. 105
Museo Arqueológico Nacional, Madrid pp. 20, 30 (right), 57, 74, 203, 209
Museu Arqueologic Nacional de Tarragona pp. 73, 81, 82, 85, 127, 146, 151, 158, 160, 169
Museu Arqueologic Provincial de Barcelona p. 183
Museu d'Historia de la Ciutat de Barcelona p. 206
David Peacock p. 117
Estanis Pedrola p. 163
José Remesal Rodríguez p. 100

All other photographs are the copyright of the author. The maps and line-drawings are by Chris Unwin.

Index